CW00825481

Plato

Ancient Philosophies

Created especially for students, this series of introductory books on the schools of ancient philosophy offers a clear yet rigorous presentation of core ideas. Designed to lay the foundation for a thorough understanding of their subjects, these fresh and engaging books are compact and reasonably priced, with illustrative texts in translation.

Published in the series:

1. *Stoicism*, by John Sellars

2. *Presocratics*, by James Warren

3. *Cynics*, by William Desmond

4. *Neoplatonism*, by Pauliina Remes

5. *Ancient Scepticism*, by Harald Thorsrud

6. *The Ancient Commentators on Plato and Aristotle*, by Miira Tuominen

7. *Epicureanism*, by Tim O'Keefe

8. *Plato*, by Andrew S. Mason

Forthcoming in the series:

Classical Islamic Philosophy, by Deborah Black

Confucianism, by Paul R. Goldin

Indian Buddhist Philosophy, by Amber Carpenter

Socrates, by Mark McPherran

Plato

Andrew S. Mason

University of California Press
Berkeley   Los Angeles

University of California Press, one of the most distinguished university presses in the United States, enriches lives around the world by advancing scholarship in the humanities, social sciences, and natural sciences. Its activities are supported by the UC Press Foundation and by philanthropic contributions from individuals and institutions. For more information, visit www.ucpress.edu.

University of California Press
Berkeley and Los Angeles, California

© 2010 Andrew S. Mason

Published outside North America by Acumen Publishing Limited.

Library of Congress Cataloging-in-Publication Data

Mason, Andrew S.
  Plato / Andrew Mason.
      p.   cm. — (Ancient philosophies ; 8)
  Includes bibliographical references and index.
  ISBN 978-0-520-26540-0 (cloth : alk. paper)
  ISBN 978-0-520-26541-7 (pbk. : alk. paper)
  1. Plato.   I. Title.

B395.M3875   2010
184—dc22   2009031136

Manufactured in the United Kingdom

19   18   17   16   15   14   13   12   11   10
10   9   8   7   6   5   4   3   2   1

The paper used in this publication meets the minimum requirements of ANSI/NISO Z39.48-1992 (R 1997) (*Permanence of Paper*).

Contents

Preface

This book aims to present Plato's thought to readers with no previous knowledge of it. In line with the general aims of the *Ancient Philosophies* series, it is written with senior undergraduates and first-year graduate students particularly in mind, but I have tried to make it accessible to a wider readership as well. No knowledge of philosophy is assumed, but I have sometimes referred to contemporary philosophical issues, so that readers who are familiar with them can see how Plato's thought relates to them.

No introduction can be a substitute for reading Plato's own works. This is true of every philosopher worth studying, but it is particularly true of Plato, since his dialogues are not only expositions of philosophical ideas, but also displays of philosophy in action; they aim to draw the reader into a philosophical discussion. This book concentrates on presenting major ideas that Plato puts forward in his works. (That these ideas can reasonably be seen as Plato's own is argued in Chapter 1.) In doing so, however, it reveals only one aspect of Plato; only by actually studying the dialogues can we appreciate Plato's thought as a whole.

Because of this focus on Plato's central ideas, I have not said much about those dialogues that seem not to reach definite conclusions, but, rather, aim to depict the process of enquiry. The classic example of such a dialogue, among those works that reflect Plato's mature thought, is the *Theaetetus*, and therefore it is only discussed briefly here. This work very much repays reading, but it is not easy to extract from it philosophical morals that can be presented in isolation.

Likewise, I have said little about the interaction between literary and philosophical elements in Plato's dialogues, although this is certainly an important aspect of his work. For this reason what is perhaps Plato's greatest work from a literary point of view, the *Symposium*, is not covered at length; only a small part of that work is actually devoted to the exposition of philosophical ideas, although the whole of it certainly illuminates Plato's philosophical thought in complex ways.

Another book in this series will deal with Socrates, and therefore I have not focused on Plato's so-called "Socratic" dialogues: those that are often seen as presenting the thought of Plato's teacher rather than his own. (That they are plausibly seen as Socratic is argued in Chapter 2.) I discuss these dialogues, for the most part, only when they can be used to illuminate Plato's mature thought, either by similarity or by contrast.

Of course, many aspects of the interpretation of Plato remain controversial. My readings are certainly not the only ones possible, and within the limits of this work I have not always been able to set out alternative views and to defend my positions at length. The Further Reading section should guide readers to other possible interpretations.

While working on this book, I have benefited from discussing Plato with colleagues and students at the University of Edinburgh and at King's College, London and members of the Archelogos group at Edinburgh. Earlier versions of some of the ideas used in this book have been presented to seminars at the universities of Edinburgh and Glasgow, at Trinity College Dublin, and at the APA Pacific Division meeting in Pasadena, 2004; I am grateful to all who took part in those discussions. Thanks are due to three anonymous referees for Acumen for their extremely helpful and challenging comments, and to Steven Gerrard for being a supportive and patient editor. Finally, I thank my parents, Kenneth and Barbara Mason, for all their support over the years. This book is dedicated to them.

ONE

Introduction

The figure of Plato

Plato is one of the most significant figures in the history of philosophy. His work has inspired and fascinated philosophers in all ages. Platonism was the dominant school of philosophy in the Mediterranean region in late antiquity, and has had many revivals since then; much philosophy has also been produced in reaction against his thought. Plato had an additional impact on the development of philosophy through his pupil Aristotle, who was both an admirer and a critic, and who has an equal claim to be the most influential philosopher of antiquity.

Plato stands at the beginning of many debates that have continued throughout the history of philosophy. Nevertheless he seems alien to us in many ways. His central metaphysical position, the "theory of Forms", involves the claim that things in the world that we see are images of eternal patterns; although this position has some affinities with more recent views, it is presented in his works in a way that makes it seem very unfamiliar. His dualist conception of the mind, according to which it can exist independently of the body, is unpopular in recent thought, and his conception of God is at least alien to mainstream philosophy. His political views are also now generally rejected; and while his scientific theories are in one way strikingly modern, as he sees the physical world as having a mathematical basis, they are, of course, in detail wholly out of date. However, his moral philosophy is certainly relevant to issues that are still being discussed and, with its emphasis on virtue and its relation to happiness, is perhaps becoming more so as these topics become more central in ethics. Some aspects of his philosophy of mind, in which he reflects on such topics as the conditions for responsibility and the connection between freedom and rationality, are also relevant to ongoing debates.

The study of Plato faces two dangers. One is to make him too much "one of us". By applying a principle of charity one can make him sound more like modern philosophers than he really was; alternatively, one may recognize the alien elements in his thought, but engage in a process of "rational reconstruction" to present an updated version of Platonism from which outlandish elements are excluded. The other danger is to assume that, because Plato's way of thinking is so different from ours, he has nothing to say to us as a philosopher, but is of purely historical interest.

I hope to show that it is possible to trace a path between these two extremes, and to see Plato as a philosopher who writes from a very different perspective from ours, and yet has things to say that are relevant to us. Sometimes his ideas may actually be seen as making a contribution to current debates; at other times they may draw our attention to issues that are unfairly neglected.

The emphasis that Plato places on argument is important here; he was committed to following an argument wherever it might lead. It may be that he did not always live up to that commitment, but nevertheless his works are full of arguments; he is not just the spokesman of a worldview, but presents reasons for his beliefs, which we can still follow and either accept or argue against.

Plato's thought has two dominating features, which may at first sight seem to conflict with one another. On the one hand, he is often seen as an "otherworldly" philosopher; this is certainly true by contrast with Aristotle, and even more so by contrast with the materialist philosophers who were influential both before and after Plato's time. Indeed, he did not believe in a literal other world, wholly detached from this one. But he did believe that there is more in the world than we can be aware of through the senses, and that the part that is not perceptible is the most significant.

One of his most distinctive beliefs was in what he calls "Forms"; put very briefly Forms are universal essences, for instance the essence of goodness, of beauty, of justice, and also of human being, of fire and so on. They are grasped by reason, not by perception; they are eternal and unchanging; and they do not depend for their existence on particular instances of goodness, beauty, humanity or whatever it might be. They may also be thought of as patterns, of which the things we perceive in the world are imitations.

Plato believed in an immortal soul that is able to exist in separation from the body. He also believed in a God who designed and made the world; although, like most Greeks of his time, he probably believed in many gods, this single supreme God played a central part in his thought. It seems likely that while in the earlier part of his career the Forms and the immortal soul were central to his view of the world, later the figure of God became more important to him.[1]

The other major feature of Plato's thought is that he is an intensely practical philosopher. By this I mean not that he is down to earth and realistic – on the contrary he is extremely idealistic – but that his philosophy is always directed towards action. Philosophy for him is a way of life, and philosophical reasoning is important in guiding the way we should live. While for Aristotle the practical life and the life of philosophical contemplation are distinct, each with their own virtues and their own kinds of happiness, Plato makes no such distinction; for him philosophical knowledge helps us make practical decisions, and to live a good life one should either be a philosopher oneself or be guided by someone who is. Only through philosophy can we gain knowledge or understanding of the good, and we need this knowledge if we are reliably to do what is good. This is relevant both at the personal, ethical level – people need knowledge of the good if they are to guide their own lives effectively – and at the public, political level – rulers need knowledge of the good to guide the states they rule effectively. While Plato's writings deal with a wide range of subjects – metaphysics, theory of knowledge, theories about the soul, God, nature and so on – these are always related to practical concerns.

Equally, though, this practical orientation is always guided by Plato's metaphysical vision. Forms are ideals that we should strive to be like, and knowledge of them will help us govern our lives; central to the system of Forms is the Form of the good. The immortality of the soul is important because we must take care of our souls and prepare them for the afterlife. God is significant because he gives purpose to things in the world, and in his later works Plato puts forward an ideal of "becoming like God" (*Tht.* 176b; *Ti.* 90c).

Plato's life

Plato was born in 427 BCE to a wealthy upper-class family in Athens. Athens was a city state, and at that time was, in the Ancient Greek sense, a democracy; indeed, it was seen as the prime example of democracy in Greece. This is not a democracy in the modern sense – women were excluded from politics, and slavery was practised – but all adult male citizens were allowed, and to some extent expected, to take part in politics. All were allowed to take part in the assembly that made major state decisions; many office-holders were selected by lot. This, together with the small size of the state, meant that politics played an important part in many people's lives.

During his youth Plato became a friend and companion of the philosopher Socrates. At that time Socrates was a public figure in Athens; he was eccentric, and not universally popular (the comedian Aristophanes wrote a play, the *Clouds*, largely devoted to satirizing him); but was on good terms with some influential people. He did not write, and did not teach formally, but hung out in public places, markets, gymnasia and so on, meeting people, asking questions and starting discussions. Socrates was immensely influential; people came from all over the Greek world to see him. Not only Plato but also many other philosophers were influenced by him; later, most of the great schools of Greek philosophy would trace back their lineage to him.

During much of Plato's youth Athens was at war with Sparta, a rival state with a contrasting, oligarchic political system. In 404, when Plato was twenty-three, the war came to an end with a Spartan victory. A commission of thirty members was set up, with Spartan support, to reform the constitution on oligarchic lines; this included two relations of Plato, Charmides and Critias, both of whom also had links with Socrates. In practice the thirty took over the government of the city. They rapidly alienated the people, behaving in an unscrupulous manner, and carrying out unlawful arrests and executions in order to seize people's wealth, and swiftly came to be known as the thirty tyrants. Soon there was a popular uprising in which they were overthrown, and Charmides and Critias were killed.

It seems likely that these events would have led to Plato becoming disillusioned with the oligarchic politics to which his upbringing might have attracted him; that he was so disillusioned is suggested by a letter, ascribed to Plato (*Seventh Letter* 325a), although it is uncertain whether it is really by him. If so, he was soon to become disillusioned with democracy as well (325b–c). In 399, four years after the fall of the thirty, Socrates was accused of "corrupting the youth, and not recognising the gods whom the city recognises" (*Ap.* 24b), tried by a democratic court, found guilty and put to death. Socrates was seventy years old, and had been practising philosophy for thirty years or more, and had been at least tolerated up to that point, so it is surprising that the Athenian people turned against him; perhaps his links with Charmides and Critias, and the thought that he had influenced them, contributed to this change in public attitudes.

In any case, after Socrates' death Plato, with other companions of Socrates, left Athens. It is not known where he went. A tradition has him spending some time in Egypt – this may have been inspired by references to Egypt in his writings. A rather more secure tradition, supported by his letters, if they are genuine, suggests that he went to Syracuse in Sicily, at that time a Greek city, where he came into conflict with Dionysius, the dictatorial ruler of Syracuse. About the mid 380s he returned to Athens, and made it his base for the rest of his life, but did not take part in the political life of the city.

Plato founded a school at Athens; it was in the precincts of a shrine dedicated to the hero Academus, and so became known as the Academy: the precursor of all the schools, colleges and learned societies that have since been given that name. It was a school not only of philosophy but also of mathematics; Plato himself does not seem to have been an active mathematician, but his colleagues Eudoxus and Theaetetus were, and Eudoxus was also an astronomer. Plato thought mathematics was valuable because it encouraged the practice of abstract thought and turned us away from reliance on the senses. Aristotle, the most important philosopher of the next generation, was a student, and perhaps later a teacher, in the Academy.

Teaching in the Academy seems to have been informal, and based on discussion, rather in the manner of Socrates. Plato gave only one public lecture, which was not very successful (Aristox. *Elem. Harm.* II.30–31); most of his teaching was carried out in private.

Plato's aim in founding the Academy was practical; he hoped that the teaching would enable people to govern states more effectively; young members of ruling families were encouraged to come there to make them into better rulers. Having been disillusioned both with elites based on wealth or military ability and with democracy, Plato wanted a government formed by people who had understanding of the aims of government: philosophers. His most famous work, the *Republic*, is, among other things, a manifesto for philosophical government and an explanation of what it might look like. It is also possible that Plato remained involved in politics at Syracuse throughout his life – although once again the evidence for this depends on his letters – and that there, in particular, he tried to establish a philosophical government by educating Dionysius the Younger, son of the tyrant Dionysius, as a philosopher. If so, the plan was unsuccessful.

Plato died in 347 BCE. He had never married and had no children; his nephew, Speusippus, succeeded him as head of the Academy.

Plato's writings

We have handed down to us from antiquity thirty-five dialogues and a number of letters under the name of Plato. It is disputed whether the letters and a few of the dialogues are really Plato's; but we know that most of the dialogues are his from the testimony of his pupil Aristotle, who often refers to them. So far as we can tell, nothing that Plato wrote for publication has been lost; this is very unusual among ancient writers.

It is not clear when Plato began writing dialogues. Possibly, as some stories from antiquity suggest, it was during Socrates' life; if not, as is now more widely believed, it was shortly after his death.

The dialogue – what purports to be a record of a philosophical discussion – was a new literary form in Plato's time. In the *Poetics* Aristotle refers to it specifically as the Socratic dialogue (*Poet.* 1447b10), suggesting that it developed among the followers of Socrates, and was inspired by his method of philosophical discussion, as if his style of philosophy could not be captured in a treatise. Many disciples of Socrates wrote dialogues, although most survive only in fragments; apart from Plato's, only Xenophon's still exist as complete works.

Socrates is the chief speaker in most of Plato's dialogues. In a few late dialogues – the *Timaeus*, *Critias*, *Sophist*, *Statesman* and *Laws* – he is replaced as chief speaker by someone else, although he appears in all these dialogues except the *Laws*; while in the *Parmenides* he shares the honours with Parmenides, a leading philosopher of the previous generation. Most of the dialogues are called after a character who appears in them, but there are a few exceptions. The *Apology* (defence speech) has a name that expresses its form; the *Symposium* is called after its setting (a drinking party); and the *Republic*, *Sophist*, *Statesman* and *Laws* are called after their themes.

In general, each of Plato's dialogues is an apparent record of a philosophical conversation, although again there are a few exceptions: the *Apology*, a reconstruction of Socrates' defence speech at his trial, is a continuous speech; the *Menexenus* and *Timaeus* are introduced by passages of dialogue, but the main portion of each of them is a single speech; and it seems that the *Critias*, an unfinished sequel to the *Timaeus*, would have been similar.

Plato's dialogues cover an immensely wide range of themes. They include material that we would now class as moral and political philosophy, aesthetics, metaphysics, theory of knowledge, logic, and philosophy of mind, of science and of religion, and also material that we would find hard to classify under any of these standard headings, perhaps most notably his discussion of love. What is more, his philosophy is a seamless web; discussion of one of these topics is always bound up with discussion of the others, and while there is generally in each dialogue a single theme that dominates the discussion, simply stating that theme often does not indicate the complexity of the work.

The topic that receives the most discussion in Plato's work is ethics. There is a large group of dialogues that are widely thought to have come early in Plato's career and to reflect the philosophy of his teacher, Socrates, whose own interests were exclusively ethical. (Questions about Plato's development and his portrait of Socrates will be discussed in Chapter 2.) These include two dialogues devoted to the defence of Socrates, the *Apology* and the *Crito*, and many dialogues in which he is shown pursuing his enquiry into the virtues, including the *Protagoras*, *Euthyphro*, *Charmides*, *Laches*, *Lysis*, *Euthydemus* and *Gorgias*. The *Meno* also includes an enquiry into the nature of virtue in Socratic style, but adds to this a discussion of knowledge and of philosophical method, and ventures into metaphysics when it puts forward a hypothesis about the previous life of the soul.

Plato's best-known work, the *Republic*, is generally thought to have been written about the middle of his career. It is a good illustration of the way in which Plato interweaves many themes in one work. One of its central claims is that there is a parallel between justice in the individual soul and justice in the state; it is, therefore, a contribution both to ethics and to politics, describing an ideal state and asking how it might be brought about, while also discussing justice in the individual and whether it is beneficial. Because Plato's vision of the ideal state involves rule by philosophers, it also includes a discussion of metaphysics and the theory of knowledge, as well as an extended contribution to aesthetics in a discussion of the place of poetry in the state.

Other works often seen as belonging to the central period of Plato's career are the *Phaedo* – which, in the context of an account of Socrates' death, argues for the immortality of the soul – and the *Symposium* and *Phaedrus*, both of which are discussions of love; they approach it from rather different perspectives, but both see it as something that stimulates us to philosophy. The *Cratylus* is a discussion of language, the *Theaetetus* an enquiry into the nature of knowledge, and in the *Parmenides* Plato subjects his best-known metaphysical theory, that of Forms, to criticism.

Plato did not abandon his ethical and political interests in the last phase of his life. Among works commonly thought to have been written then, the *Philebus* is an account of pleasure from an ethical perspective, while both the *Statesman* and the *Laws* have a political theme; the *Laws* is another plan for an ideal state, less utopian and so perhaps more realizable than that of the *Republic*. The *Sophist* discusses a logical problem concerning the possibility of negative statements and of falsehood, while the *Timaeus* deals with the origin and nature of the world, including both theology and physical science.

The dialogue form

One of the most striking features of Plato's works is that they are dialogues, not treatises. This both raises the question why he wrote in this form and presents us with a puzzle as to whether the dialogues can really be used as evidence for Plato's own views.

We have seen that the dialogue form was a new one in Plato's time, and was created by the followers of Socrates. To them it must have seemed a suitable way of capturing their master's approach to philosophy. Since he was concerned more with enquiring and questioning than with stating positive views, it was not possible simply to expound his philosophy; it had to be demonstrated, by recording the kind of conversation in which he engaged. Yet Plato continued to use the dialogue form in works where he seems clearly to be developing his own ideas, and where the chief speaker expresses positive claims. It is true that whereas in some dialogues a real enquiry or debate seems to be taking place, others are more like treatises, with the chief speaker dominating discussion and others mostly agreeing with him. Yet Plato never wrote a book simply setting out his positions, but always used the dialogue form. Why is this?

In the *Phaedrus*, Plato's Socrates expresses the view that speech is preferable to writing as a medium for philosophy (*Phd.* 275d ff.); writings can be read without understanding, and if their meaning is unclear they cannot be asked to explain it. The best way of learning philosophy is through a face-to-face discussion. There is, of course, a paradox here; it is through his *writings* that we learn that Plato defended this position. But the paradox is not insurmountable; Socrates is not saying that a philosopher never commits his own views to writing, only that if they are so committed they cannot be a source of knowledge. It seems likely that Plato did indeed believe something like this, and that he did not intend his writings, by themselves, to give his readers the kind of knowledge that a philosopher aims at; this, for him, could only be achieved by actual discussion. "Philosophy" for him is the name of a way of life or of a motive, love of wisdom; the actual activity of philosophers he calls "dialectic", the art of discussion (although by a fruitful ambiguity it can also mean the art of making distinctions). The point of his writings, in this case, will be to give a demonstration of what philosophy is like, attracting people to philosophy and stimulating philosophical thought.

This may make us uncertain whether we can actually see any teachings of Plato in the dialogues; the views expressed are always, strictly speaking, those of a character, not of the author, and we may wonder why we should believe what that character says, if the work is not meant to be a source of philosophical knowledge. Certainly, we should be cautious in ascribing views to Plato on the basis of what his characters say. He need not be committed to every point that they make; the dialogue form allows him to put ideas forward while standing at a remove from them. But it is generally clear which character has most of Plato's sympathy; Socrates, and the chief speakers of the later dialogues, seem to be seen as philosophers with real insight, and so it seems probable that the views they put forward are ones Plato agrees with, at least provisionally. When the same ideas turn up in the mouth of the chief speaker in several dialogues, it is likely that they are fairly settled features of Plato's thought.

One specific reason why we should be careful about attributing the views of a chief speaker to Plato is that, if a dialogue depicts a genuine ongoing enquiry, the views of the chief speaker may not be stable throughout it. For instance, it is controversial whether Plato sees the ideal state that he describes in the *Republic* as a real possibility. When Socrates is asked this question he says that it is possible, *if* philosophers should ever become rulers (*Resp.* 473c–e), and in a couple of later passages he explicitly says that this is a real possibility, although hard to achieve (502c, 540d); he even explains how philosophers should put his proposal into action by sending away from the city everyone over the age of ten, so that those who remain can be trained in the kind of life that he proposes as an ideal (541a).

On the other hand, he gives a lengthy description of the training a philosopher needs to reach the insight required for government, in a way that suggests it could only happen within the ideal state (536d ff.),[2] leaving it unclear how philosophers could bring that state into being in the first place; and at the end of the main discussion of the *Republic*, he accepts that this city does not exist on earth, but says that "perhaps it is a pattern laid up in heaven, which he who wishes can look upon, and looking upon it establish himself" (592b). This echoes an earlier passage (472b ff.), which says that the description of an ideal is valuable even if it is not achievable; it can be read, in the light of the claim that justice in the soul and in the state are parallel, as meaning that a person can take the ideal state not as a political proposal, but as a pattern for ordering his own life.

If we look for a consistent position for Socrates it is hard to find, but it is possible to see his view as evolving within the dialogue: at first he is trying to see the ideal state as a practical possibility, but later he accepts that it is a pattern, not practicable but still useful as an inspiration.

There is another reason why it might be thought dangerous to look in the dialogues for Plato's thought; it is not simply that the views put forward in them are put forward by characters rather than by Plato himself, but that each dialogue is rooted in a particular situation, and its arguments are directed to a particular interlocutor. It is reasonable to think that the chief speaker in each dialogue will tailor his arguments to the person with whom he is debating, arguing in a way that is likely to appeal to that person, and perhaps appealing to his convictions (as Socrates does explicitly in some dialogues).

It is certainly true that the situation and characters are important in each dialogue – although they are emphasized more in some dialogues than in others, where they tend to fade into the background – and that for this reason we cannot simply identify what Socrates says, or the assumptions he seems to make, with what Plato thinks. Yet we should remember that although in the first instance Plato's arguments are addressed to the characters in the dialogues, Plato created those characters (even if they are based on real people, as most of them seem to be); he gave them the specific commitments they are shown in the dialogues as having. His reason for creating them in the form in which he did is presumably to enable him to make philosophical points that will be relevant to his ultimate audience, the readers of his work.

I have suggested that Plato's aim is not simply to show a philosopher in action but also to stimulate philosophical thought in his audience: not just to report debate, but to start a debate in which we, the audience, can become participants. If we are to do this, we must to some extent be able to abstract the positions and arguments put forward in his works from the particular context in which he shows them arising, although this will obviously affect the way they are presented; it must be possible to consider those arguments from our own point of view, and ask whether they are philosophically convincing.

Certainly the fact that a dialogue deals with a specific situation does not always prevent it having relevance beyond that situation. Of Plato's works, one of the most clearly rooted in a particular context is the *Crito*, in which Socrates, facing the prospect of death, defends his decision not to escape from prison. Yet the arguments of the *Crito* are among the most "live" of Plato's arguments even today, and are still discussed in debates about the source and extent of our duty to obey the law. Those who face these issues now are not in exactly the same situation as Socrates, and this has to be taken into account in considering whether his arguments are relevant; but this does not stop us seeing those arguments as a contribution to the debate.

If we consider both that Plato's chief speakers are, in general, figures whom he intends us to see sympathetically and that he wants us to see his arguments as having relevance beyond the specific context in which they are put forward, it is reasonable to think that we can see Plato's own thought lying behind what his characters say – as indeed his readers have done since antiquity – although care must always be taken in ascribing particular views to him.

The plan of this book

My aim in this work is to introduce some of Plato's central ideas. To gain a full appreciation of his thought, one needs to see it in the context in which he presented it, within the specific dialogues; this introduction cannot be a substitute for that. But there are continuing themes in his work, which develop from one dialogue to another, and it is useful, in understanding Plato, to get an overview of these themes; hence, I have adopted a thematic structure.

After a short chapter on Plato's development and his relation to Socrates, I deal first with Plato's principal contribution to metaphysics, the "theory of Forms", which, although rarely Plato's central theme, forms a necessary background to his thought in many areas, and next with his theory of knowledge, which is intimately linked with the Forms. I consider his view of the soul, which is both an important theme in itself and a significant background to his thought on practical issues, and then move on to his practical philosophy, considering first his politics and then his ethics. Finally I deal with two areas of Plato's thought that have had an especially important historical impact, not confined to academic philosophy: his theory of God and nature, and his aesthetics.

Many aspects of Plato are missing from this account. His view of love, an intriguing topic in itself, will be mentioned here only in so far as it illuminates other aspects of his thought; and his contributions to the theory of logic and language will also not receive much attention. I hope I can nevertheless present enough of Plato's thought to give a picture of this fascinating philosopher, and inspire readers to study his work further.

TWO

Plato's development and Plato's Socrates

Two puzzles

Two major problems confront anyone who wants to study Plato's philosophy. First, Plato's writing career lasted at least fifty years, and it is reasonable to think that there were some changes in his views during that time. But how radical were the changes, and to what extent can we trace the development of his thought? Can we use positions expressed in one dialogue in interpreting another?

This problem is particularly acute because we have no direct evidence on when each of his works was written. Occasionally it may be possible to date a work by a reference to a real world event, or to find in one dialogue a reference to another, which enables us to determine the order in which they were written. Many scholars have believed that they can trace, by scientific means, the development of Plato's style, which allows them to work out the order of his works (see Brandwood 1992), but it is highly controversial how much this method can show. Often, therefore, hypotheses about the order of the works depend on theories about how his thought might plausibly have developed; but this obviously produces a danger of circularity.

Some interpreters stress the unity of Plato's thought. Others focus more on differences between the dialogues.[1] One influential theory sees his thought as falling into three periods. In the first, the theory claims, he was exclusively concerned with ethical issues, and his work was exploratory in nature; in the second, the "middle period", he became more dogmatic, and, while still concerned with ethics, also developed the metaphysical views for which he is famous, the immortality of the soul and the theory of Forms. It is to this period that what are probably his most famous works, the *Phaedo*, *Symposium*, *Republic* and *Phaedrus*, belong. In the last period, which includes the *Parmenides*, *Theaetetus*, *Sophist* and *Laws*, he was more interested in questions to do with logic and knowledge, together with practical issues. Some have even argued that during this period he abandoned his most distinctive metaphysical theory, that of Forms; others suggest that, at least, it became less important to him.[2]

The second problem is this: in most of Plato's dialogues, the chief speaker is his teacher, Socrates. Should we suppose that this is a portrait of Socrates as he really was? Or is the Socrates who appears in the dialogues a spokesman for Plato, expressing either his own views, or at least views he wants his audience to consider? Since antiquity, people have looked to Plato's dialogues for the expression of his own philosophy, but also for evidence about Socrates. But is it really possible to find both of these in the dialogues at once?

The view that Plato's Socrates represents the real Socrates in *every* place where he appears is now generally rejected; in the dialogues with the strongest metaphysical content, such as the *Phaedo* and the *Republic*, he is expressing views that are distinctive of Plato. But one group of dialogues is often seen as giving us evidence of the historical Socrates, and for this reason they are often called "Socratic dialogues". This group includes two works, the *Apology* and the *Crito*, that deal with Socrates' trial and the events leading up to his death, and a number of works in which he appears engaged in an investigation of virtue and the virtues, such as the *Protagoras* (virtue as a whole), *Euthyphro* (holiness), *Charmides* (temperance) and *Laches* (courage).

If this is right, the question of Plato's Socrates becomes closely linked with that of his development, for the "Socratic" dialogues are precisely those that are often seen as coming at the beginning of Plato's career. It is widely thought that, at the beginning of Plato's development, he would have been very much under the influence of his master, and would have written works that closely reflected Socrates' thought, while later he may have found his own voice and begun to express distinctive views of his own.

In what follows I shall consider to what extent we should follow this view of Plato. I shall begin with the Socratic question, in the hope that this will illuminate Plato's development.

Plato's picture of Socrates

The dialogues commonly called "Socratic" paint a distinctive picture of Socrates. His primary concern is with ethics, and he does not obviously hold distinctive metaphysical views about Forms or the soul. He denies that he has knowledge of moral subjects (*Ap.* 21b), and his investigations rarely reach a definite conclusion. He is committed to the testing and, where necessary, refutation of views: often these are the views of others with whom he is engaged in debate, although sometimes they are proposed for discussion by him. He is often concerned with definition of ethical terms; as well as the *Euthyphro*, *Charmides* and *Laches*, mentioned above, there is the *Lysis* (friendship) and the *Hippias Major* (the fine or beautiful). He often uses inductive methods of argument, in a broad sense of the term; that is, he defends a general claim by looking at particular instances where it is true. Finally, despite his profession of ignorance, he maintains certain moral convictions. These include an "intellectualist" conception of virtue, involving the claims that virtue is knowledge[3] and that no one knowingly does wrong (*Prt.* 352b ff.); a belief that virtue is sufficient for happiness (361b; *Meno* 89a); and a conviction that one should not return evil for evil (*Cri.* 49b ff.).

This picture of Socrates seems to contrast in many respects – although not all – with that found in the classic works commonly assigned to Plato's "middle" period. The Socrates of those works has a much wider range of interests, holds metaphysical views about Forms and the soul, does not emphasize his ignorance (although occasionally he still professes it) and argues for definite conclusions.

We should be careful in just how we draw the contrast between these two groups of dialogues. Some of the contrasts that are perceived simply relate to an element that is present in one group but not in the other. Thus, in one group of dialogues there is a breadth of interests that is absent in the other, and specific metaphysical views that the other does not contain; but it is not clear that this means that they represent either two different thinkers or two different phases in Plato's thought; it might be explained simply by Plato's different purposes in writing them. We should not suppose that he was obliged to mention in every dialogue every topic he was interested in or every doctrine he held at the moment of writing it. Likewise, the fact that some dialogues lack definite conclusions, and seem more concerned with the testing and refutation of claims, while others argue for definite positions, can be explained in terms of a difference of purpose.

Nevertheless, there are at least two respects in which there seems to be a real opposition – not just a difference of focus and approach – between the two groups of dialogues. First, in the "Socratic" dialogues, perhaps most clearly in the *Protagoras*, Socrates defends the famously paradoxical view that everyone desires what is good and no one desires what is bad (*Prt.* 458d; *Meno* 77c ff.); hence if people pursue what is actually bad, this must be explained by ignorance of the good. This allows him to argue that virtue is knowledge, and that *akrasia* or weakness of will, the phenomenon by which good intentions, although we have them, are overcome by unruly desires, is not in fact possible. By contrast, in the *Republic* Plato's Socrates argues that there are different sources of motivation, not only the rational desire for the good but also desires for pleasure and for reputation, which can oppose our rational desires (*Resp.* 439c ff.). If this is so, it seems that *akrasia* is possible, that there are other sources of wrongdoing besides ignorance, and that knowledge is not sufficient for virtue, which also requires mastery of desire.

Secondly, in the "Socratic" dialogues Socrates is ready to discuss philosophy with everyone, and wants to encourage everyone to examine their views in a philosophical way; this is his vocation, as set out in the *Apology*, and we see him actually doing it in other works. By contrast, in the *Republic* he is shown taking the view that only a few are capable of philosophy, and that others should ideally be subject to their care and government. One might think that there is no direct opposition here, for the Socrates of the *Apology* could be seen as thinking not that all are actually capable of philosophy, but only that all should at least be given the chance to do it. But two points of contrast stand out. First, in the *Apology* Socrates claims that "the unexamined life is not worth living" (*Ap.* 38a), while in the *Republic* he seems to be encouraging many people to live unexamined lives. Secondly, in the *Republic* (539a ff.), encouraging the young to do philosophy, when they are not adequately prepared for it, is condemned as damaging, not just as unnecessary, thus seemingly condemning what Socrates is shown doing in many dialogues (for instance the *Charmides*, the *Lysis* and the *Euthydemus*).

It seems, then, that there is a real contrast in Plato's works between two points of view. It also seems that the first of these points of view – the intellectualist and egalitarian one – is found mainly in works that have the other features commonly seen as Socratic: an exclusively ethical concern, an exploratory rather than dogmatic outlook and the absence of metaphysical theories about Forms and the soul. This suggests that these features are not just explained by a difference of purpose, but reflect a different outlook from that found in classic Platonic works such as the *Republic*. It is reasonable, therefore, to divide Plato's works into two groups, reflecting different ways of thinking. (This is not to say that the distinction is an absolutely rigid one; two works in particular, the *Gorgias* and *Meno*, seem to have elements that link them with both groups). What is not yet clear is whether these just represent two stages in Plato's development, or whether one of them expresses the thought of the real Socrates.

Is this the real Socrates?

To answer this question we must look at what other authors have to say. Aristotle, Plato's pupil, frequently refers to Socrates; it is often not clear whether he is talking about the historical figure or the character in Plato's works. However, in two places in the *Metaphysics* (A 987a9–b10; M 1078b9–32) he contrasts Socrates with Plato.[4] In both he claims that Plato originated the idea of separated Forms, although in doing so he was trying to cope with a problem raised by Socrates' thought; Socrates was concerned only with ethics, and not with the nature of things as a whole. However, he did introduce into philosophy the search for definitions and the use of an inductive method. It seems that Aristotle is using some works of Plato as evidence for Socrates, since his picture of Socrates fits what we find in works such as the *Charmides*, *Laches* and *Euthyphro*, while he takes other works, such as the *Phaedo* and *Republic*, to reveal the thought of Plato.

Another work, the *Magna Moralia* (traditionally ascribed to Aristotle, but perhaps actually by a pupil of his) contrasts the ethical views of Socrates and Plato (*Mag. mor.* I 1182a15–30); it says that for Socrates the virtues are forms of knowledge, while Plato recognized an irrational element in the soul that meant that virtue could not simply be identified with knowledge. Once again, the views ascribed to Socrates seem to be those that are found in the *Protagoras* and related dialogues, while those ascribed to Plato can be found in the *Republic*, as well as the *Phaedrus* and *Timaeus*.

How might Aristotle (and his pupils) have known which elements in the dialogues reflected the thought of the real Socrates? We cannot say with certainty, but nor can we rule out the possibility of their knowing. Perhaps Plato was actually open about this, explaining to his students that some elements in his works represented his own thought while others came directly from Socrates. Or perhaps Aristotle was relying on the testimony of other pupils of Socrates who were still active in Athens when he first came there; if there was a consensus between them about some aspects of Socrates' thought, it would have been reasonable to ascribe at least these aspects to Socrates himself.

In any case Aristotle must have had some reason for drawing the distinction between Socrates and Plato in the way he did. If he had nothing to go on but the dialogues themselves it is not clear how he could have drawn that distinction; he might have thought either that everything ascribed to Socrates in the dialogues represents his real position, or that, as they are literary productions, nothing in them can be seen as historical. That he did neither, but distinguished between some elements that represent Socrates and some that do not, suggests that he did have independent evidence to support that distinction.

Some later authors seem to divide the dialogues in the same way. Cicero, writing in the first century BCE, contrasts Socrates with Plato (Cic. *Acad.* I.4.16–17), claiming that Socrates was concerned exclusively with ethics, denied that he knew anything and focused on refuting others, while Plato began to work out a definite philosophical system. He clearly is using some of Plato's dialogues as a source for Socrates, but he says that the writings of other followers of Socrates confirm this way of seeing him.

The Stoics, a philosophical school that began to flourish two generations after Plato, saw Socrates as a forerunner of their way of thinking; their picture of him seems, once again, to have been similar to that found in the "Socratic" dialogues. In particular the Stoic teacher Epictetus, who worked in the late first and early second century CE, describes the different tasks that God gives to philosophers (Epict. *Discourses* III.21.18–19), and says that he gave Socrates the task of elenchus – refutation or examination – as opposed to the task of positive teaching, which he reserves for Zeno, the founder of Stoicism.

All in all, it seems that these dialogues were widely seen as giving a portrait of Socrates, and as distinct from those that introduced Plato's own philosophy, and that it is reasonable to see them as genuinely Socratic.

Plato's Socratic dialogues

This need not mean that Plato's Socratic dialogues are actual reports of conversations in which Socrates engaged; they can be seen as fictions, but ones that seek to present Socrates as he was, with his real attitudes and views, trying to show how he would have confronted a particular issue or situation. One work that raises particular puzzles is the *Apology*, a reconstruction of Socrates' defence speech at his trial (in Greek *apologia* means a defence, not an apology in the modern sense). We need not see this as accurately representing what Socrates actually said at his trial – many of Socrates' pupils wrote defences for him, not all of which can be accurate reports of what was said – but as it is a defence *of Socrates*, it must reflect his life as Plato saw it.

Why should Plato write Socratic dialogues? One reason would be to honour his master and to defend him. This would obviously apply to the *Apology*; and in some other dialogues we see him following out the vocation, which he describes in the *Apology*, of testing the views of others and their claims to wisdom. The *Crito* is another dialogue that has the aim of defending Socrates; set in prison after his condemnation, it seeks to justify his action in refusing to escape (as he could easily have done) and remaining to face death. Another reason for writing dialogues in a Socratic manner would simply be to stimulate philosophical thought, as Socrates himself had tried to do.

What, then, can this tell us about Plato's development? I suggest that it tells us less than we might hope. For if Plato's aim in these dialogues is to give a portrait of Socrates, we cannot be sure that they represent Plato's own thought at the moment that he wrote them. He must at least have had enough sympathy with Socrates' position to think it worth setting before his readers, but that does not mean that he completely agreed with it; nor does it mean that he had no views of his own on topics about which Socrates professes ignorance, nor that he had no interest in topics beyond those which Socrates is seen discussing.

Talk of a Socratic period in Plato's work is dangerously ambiguous. It may mean either a period during which Plato's aim in his dialogues was to give a portrait of Socrates, or a Socratic period in Plato's *thought*, in which he shared a Socratic point of view. Often, it has been assumed that the dialogues of Plato's early period are Socratic in both these senses. Thus, Gregory Vlastos has claimed both that these dialogues are a representation of the historical Socrates and that in them Plato never ascribes to Socrates a view that he does not share.[5] But it may be thought unlikely that both these things could be true at once; one wonders whether Plato would have simply continued to follow his teacher's thought over a long period during which he produced many dialogues.

If these dialogues are intended to represent the thought of the historical Socrates, it is possible that Plato's own thought was already developing away from Socrates at the time that he wrote them; he may have developed metaphysical views about Forms and the soul, and perhaps a psychological view different from Socrates' intellectualism, while he was recording Socrates' position. Indeed, he may even have been writing, at the same time, dialogues that presented his own view: the difference between Socratic and Platonic dialogues can be explained, not by development, but by a difference in intention. (Stylistic evidence strongly suggests that the *Republic* is later than the bulk of the Socratic dialogues, but it seems not to do so for the *Symposium* and *Phaedo*, other works that express Plato's metaphysical views; see Brandwood 1992.) If this is right, while Plato's thought no doubt did develop during the early part of his career, we cannot trace that development with confidence.

Plato's development: the later phase

However, even in those works that seem clearly to express Plato's own views there are variations in style and approach, and, apparently, in doctrine. How are we to understand Plato's later development?

On one influential view, there is a contrast between the central group of works that express Plato's most famous metaphysical positions – the *Phaedo*, *Symposium*, *Republic* and, perhaps, the *Phaedrus* – and a later group of works, distinguished on grounds both of style and content, including the *Sophist*, *Statesman*, *Philebus*, *Laws* and, probably (although this is controversial), the *Timaeus*. While in the earlier group Socrates is shown putting forward positive views, he does so largely in a context of debate; in the later group ideas are presented in a more didactic way, with the chief speaker (who is often not Socrates) facing little opposition to his claims. The subjects are also more down to earth; they include logical questions (in the *Sophist*), ethical and political issues (in the *Statesman*, *Philebus* and *Laws*), and the physical world (in the *Timaeus*). While extravagant metaphysical positions are not wholly absent, they are less emphasized, except in the *Timaeus*, and even there they function as background for Plato's physical theory.

Between these two groups come two dialogues that seem to reveal a more critical and questioning position: the *Parmenides*, in which objections to Plato's central metaphysical theory of Forms are considered; and the *Theaetetus*, which, in some ways recapturing the spirit of the Socratic dialogues, investigates the concept of knowledge without coming to a definite conclusion.

On grounds of both style and content I think something like this picture of Plato's development is correct. There is a group of dialogues that can be recognized as coming late in Plato's career, including the *Timaeus*, *Sophist*, *Statesman*, *Philebus* and *Laws*. As well as a more didactic approach, there are several thematic links between these works. They take the material world more seriously than earlier works, and show a more optimistic view of it. They give the creator God a central role; and they also show a more down-to-earth, practical approach to ethical and political issues, emphasizing the point that abstract philosophical knowledge needs to be supplemented by awareness of particular facts.

What is less clear is whether the change between the central works and the later ones is a change of focus and method only, or also of doctrine. It has been argued, most notably by G. E. L. Owen (1953), that a radical shift in Plato's views took place late in his career, and that he abandoned his most distinctive metaphysical position, the theory of Forms. Certainly arguments against that theory are put forward in the *Parmenides*, and there is no explicit answer to them. However, it does not follow from this that Plato actually means us to abandon the theory; indeed Parmenides, the chief speaker of the dialogue, himself suggests that Forms are necessary for all discourse (*Prm.* 135b–c). (I shall discuss this in more detail in Chapter 3.) I suggest, therefore, that while the theory may have changed in detail, it cannot have been wholly abandoned.

What seems to be recognizably the same theory is present in dialogues normally dated later than the *Parmenides*. This is most clearly true in the *Timaeus*, where Forms play a major role; Owen had to argue that this dialogue comes earlier in Plato's career than is commonly thought. However, not only does its style link it with later works but also it shares some themes with them. The figure of God, the creator, who is central to the *Timaeus*, also appears in other late works; the theme of classification, of a world structured into genera and species, which plays a large part in the *Sophist, Statesman* and *Philebus*, can also be found in the *Timaeus*.[6] It seems likely, therefore, that Plato did continue to believe in Forms in the last phase of his career, and that there was no truly radical shift in his doctrines; and if we accept this, it is possible to see the theory of Forms at work in other places too, including the *Statesman* and *Philebus*.

Continuity and change in Plato's thought

This does not mean, however, that Plato's thought was completely static; he was open to changing his positions in response to argument. Indeed, some aspects of his thought about Forms seem to have changed. In the *Phaedo* and *Phaedrus* he says that our knowledge of Forms was gained by an experience that we underwent in a discarnate state before birth, and in this life we are trying to recover knowledge that we have lost. In the *Republic* and *Timaeus*, on the other hand, this doctrine is not mentioned, and an account of the afterlife is given that leaves no room for it; it seems possible to gain knowledge of Forms for the first time in this life. (I discuss this at more length in Chapter 4).

Again, in the *Timaeus*, Forms are said to be eternal in the sense of being timeless (*Ti.* 37e ff.); "was" and "will be" cannot be applied to them. This view does not appear in earlier dialogues, where they are simply said to exist for ever. It may well be that Plato actually introduced the idea of timelessness in response to arguments put forward in the *Parmenides*, which imply that whatever is in time must be in change (*Prm.* 141a–d, 152a–e); hence if Forms are changeless, as Plato thinks they must be, they must also be timeless.

Plato's view of the soul also seems to have changed. In the *Phaedo* the soul is something simple and indivisible, and is identified with the rational element; what we might naturally think of as mental conflict is instead seen as a conflict between the soul and the body. In the *Republic*, *Phaedrus* and *Timaeus* the soul has three elements, the rational, the spirited and the appetitive (the part where desires connected with the body are found), and conflict between them is possible. In the *Phaedrus* the whole soul is immortal; the *Republic* and *Timaeus* compromise by making only the rational element immortal.

Another example of a change in Plato's view concerns the origin of the soul. In the *Phaedrus* he insists that it is ungenerated (*Phdr.* 245d); he can also be seen as implying this in the *Republic*, since there he claims that everything that is generated will be destroyed (*Resp.* 546a), which means that if the soul were generated it could not be immortal. However, in the *Timaeus* (34c ff.) and the *Laws* (892a and elsewhere) he refers to the soul as being generated; and in the *Timaeus* (41a ff.) he seems specifically to renounce the view that everything generated will be destroyed, saying instead that while everything generated is *destructible*, some things are preserved in being by the will of God.

Not only are Plato's views not unchanging, but it is not clear that they develop in a linear way. It is quite possible that he sometimes abandoned a position and later returned to it. Indeed, as I noted in Chapter 1, the dialogue form means that Plato need not commit himself to all the views that his chief speakers express, even if he clearly intends to present them favourably.

Nevertheless, we can see some stability in Plato's central ideas; the existence of Forms and of a creator God, the immortality of the soul and the centrality of virtue are convictions that remain with him through most of his career. We must be cautious in assuming that what is said in one dialogue represents Plato's settled position; but it is possible to see some unity in his ideas, and discuss his thought as a whole.

THREE

Plato's metaphysics: the "theory of Forms"

One of the best-known aspects of Plato's thought, and one of the most pervasive, is his belief in "Forms":[1] that is, very roughly, in essences shared by those things that (in our terms) belong to a single kind or possess a single property. For instance, there is in his view something, the essence or nature of goodness, that all good things have in common; this is what Plato calls the Form of the good. Likewise there is an essence that all large things have in common, one that all living creatures have in common, and so on. Plato has a distinctive conception of these essences, central to which are the claims that they are eternal and unchanging, that they are grasped by pure reason rather than by perception, and that they do not depend for their existence on their perceptible instances.

Plato does not, in fact, always use the term "Form" to denote these essences; his most common expression for them is "the so and so itself" (e.g. "the good itself", "the living creature itself" and so on); on some occasions he also uses abstract nouns to describe them (e.g. "justice itself"). However, he does sometimes refer to them by two Greek words, *eidos* and *idea*, both of which can be translated by the English word "form"; and this way of referring to them, which is particularly useful when speaking of all the Forms as a class, has become standard in later writers, beginning with Plato's pupil Aristotle in his discussion and criticism of the theory. (While the word *idea* is indeed the ancestor of our modern English "idea", it should not be taken to imply, as the English word normally does, that these things are in the mind; for this reason, while older books often refer to "Platonic Ideas", "Forms" is now the more usual term.)

Plato never devotes a dialogue to the subject of Forms, with the partial exception of the *Parmenides*, the first part of which is taken up by a consideration of some criticisms of the theory; more often, it appears as part of the background to his thought on other subjects, such as the immortality of the soul (in the *Phaedo*), love (in the *Symposium* and *Phaedrus*), ethics and politics (in the *Republic*), and cosmology (in the *Timaeus*). Plato never expounds his position on the subject systematically, and, although I shall continue, for convenience, to speak of the theory of Forms, it is not clear that his views were really systematic enough to be called a theory. It may be, however, that they became more so in the course of Plato's career: in the dialogues where they first appear, Forms tend to be taken for granted; in later works we see him considering criticisms of them (in the *Parmenides*) and presenting his only explicit argument for them (in the *Timaeus*).

Nevertheless, it is clear that Plato's views about Forms were seen in his time as distinctive and controversial; they go beyond the simple thought, which might be seen as a platitude, that when many things are (correctly) described by a single term, there is in some sense something that they have in common. Plato thought that his position was worth defending, and others thought it worth attacking. The arguments discussed in the *Parmenides* seem to be based on those used by contemporary opponents of the theory; and Aristotle, who agreed with his teacher about many things (the existence of God, the presence of purpose in the world, the connection between virtue and happiness), nevertheless has a philosophy that differs radically from Plato's, largely because of his rejection of Plato's account of Forms.

In this chapter I shall first try to clarify what Plato's conception of Forms is and what is so distinctive about it, and then look at some specific problems that his account of Forms raises.

What is a Form?

A Form, for Plato, is in the first place the nature or essence shared by many things, when the same term is rightly applied to them; to know, for instance, the Form of the good is to know what goodness is – to know the essence that all good things have in common. Hence, a Form is in some ways like what in modern philosophy is called a universal; indeed, Aristotle, who introduced the term "universal" into philosophy, saw Plato's theory as a kind of anticipation of his own. Sometimes when Plato discusses Forms he is simply concerned with this aspect of them: the idea of an essence shared by many things. In the Socratic dialogues Socrates is often presented as searching for an account of what something, for example virtue, is – an account of the characteristic shared by all the people who are virtuous, and manifested in particular virtuous acts and in all the more specific kinds of virtue – and in two places, in the *Euthyphro* (6d–e) and the *Meno* (72c–e), he calls what he is looking for a Form.

In the *Phaedo* Plato's Socrates claims that Forms are causes or explanations of things having a certain property (*Phd.* 100c ff.); for example, the Form of large is the cause of things being large. This can be read as meaning not that the Form actually acts on things to make them large, but that by understanding what largeness is we can come to understand why things are large. It is rather as we might say "This is a square because it has four equal sides and four equal angles"; knowing what a square is enables us to know why a particular object is a square.[2] This, again, echoes the Socratic dialogues, where Socrates claims that it is *because of* a single Form – for instance, that of piety – that individual pious acts are pious (Pl. *Euthphr.* 6d).

Plato clearly believes that these essences have a real and objective existence that we can discover; this is parallel to what we would now call a realist theory of universals. This is by no means uncontroversial; many philosophers, called nominalists, have held that there is nothing over and above the particular things that we touch and see. But the realist view is nevertheless a widespread one; Plato's acceptance over it does not in itself make his metaphysical views unusual. However, his account of Forms has some more distinctive features.

One of the most notable aspects of his theory is the so-called separation of Forms. In the *Parmenides* he refers to Forms existing "separately" (*Prm.* 130b ff.); elsewhere he speaks of a Form existing "itself by itself" (*Phd.* 65d; *Symp.* 211b; *Prm.* 129a), or of its not being in anything other than itself (*Ti.* 52a). Exactly what this means is rather obscure. It does not seem to mean that Forms are literally in another place than their sensible instances; strictly speaking they are not in a place at all. One thing that the language of separation seems to imply is that Forms are not affected by what happens to their instances. Another possible implication is that they do not depend on their instances for their existence; there would be a Form of beauty, for instance, even if nothing beautiful existed in the world. That Plato did indeed believe this is implied by the *Timaeus*, where we are told that Forms existed before the world was made (*Ti.* 52d), and were used as a model by God as he brought things in the world into existence (29a and elsewhere).

Another aspect of Forms that was clearly important to Plato is that they are eternal and unchanging. The contrast between unchanging Forms and the constant change of the sensible world is drawn in the *Phaedo*, where it is argued that the soul is more akin to Forms and is therefore likely to be immortal (*Phd.* 78c ff.); and again in the *Timaeus*, where it is seen as a reason for thinking that there can be knowledge, in the strict sense, of Forms and not of sensible things (*Ti.* 27d ff.). In the same dialogue Timaeus, the chief speaker, takes the further step of saying that whatever is in time is in change, and hence Forms, if they are truly changeless, must also be timeless (37e ff.).

A third important feature of Forms is that they are not perceptible, and that it is through reason, not through the senses, that they are known. This point is emphasized in the *Phaedo*, where it is argued that the soul does not make use of the body in gaining knowledge of the Forms, and is, in fact, better equipped to contemplate them in separation from the body (*Phd.* 65d ff.), and in the *Republic*, where a contrast is drawn between the realm revealed through the senses and the realm (of Forms) grasped by the intellect, and we are urged to practise mathematics as a way of reducing our reliance on the senses (*Resp.* 523a ff.).

All these features of Forms are certainly controversial; but none of them seems wholly unreasonable. The idea of separation – of universals that do not depend on their instances for their existence – is unpopular in modern metaphysics, but it was held by philosophers such as Bertrand Russell and G. E. Moore; and for some properties it does not seem too implausible. Perhaps this is particularly true of moral properties; it makes sense to say that there is such a thing as justice even if no one is actually just. Likewise with some mathematical properties; one might say that there is such a thing as circularity even though nothing is perfectly circular.

The changelessness of Forms is also quite a plausible claim; while particular things may become, for instance, larger and smaller, what largeness or smallness *is* is always the same, and does not change when the instances change.

Finally, we may well think that Plato has underestimated the role played by perception in our gaining knowledge of the natures of things, if he thinks this can be achieved without any perception at all; but it still seems right to say that we do not directly perceive many properties of things, and that perception alone cannot give us knowledge of their natures, but rather reflection is required. This would be true, again, of moral properties, and also of extremely abstract properties such as being, sameness or difference. (I shall explore this question further in Chapter 4, in discussing Plato's theory of knowledge.)

None of these features of the theory of Forms, then, explains why the theory seems so striking, and why it has made so strong an impression on some philosophers, and seemed so alien to others. To understand this, we should look at another aspect of the theory, the evaluative one: the way in which Plato sees the Forms as ideals of which the sensible world falls short.

Plato sees Forms as having a special value, which other things do not share; this reveals itself in two ways. First, it is good to understand and to contemplate Forms. This is something to which we should aspire and from which, when it is achieved, we will get pleasure; it will also have a good effect on our soul, stimulating us to virtue. This is perhaps made apparent most dramatically in two dialogues, the *Symposium* and the *Phaedrus*, which have the theme of love. In both of these it is argued that the ultimate object of love is the Form of beauty, and that love of beautiful people is valuable in so far as it stimulates us to look for this Form. The Form, therefore, is an object of emotion similar to, but stronger than, what we ordinarily feel for our beloved (*Symp.* 210e ff.; *Phdr.* 250b ff.). A similar thought is found in the *Phaedo*, where the philosopher is shown looking forward to death because this will enable him to understand Forms more clearly without the distraction of the body (*Phd.* 65d ff.), and in the *Republic*, where the philosophers who are rulers of the ideal state prefer to spend their lives in contemplation of Forms, and need to be compelled to take part in government (*Resp.* 519c ff.).

Secondly, it is also good to resemble Forms. Forms are paradigms, models or patterns that we may look to in shaping things in the world, and a thing is in a better state the more closely it corresponds to them. This is especially apparent in two places: in the *Republic* philosopher rulers are described looking to the order and harmony of the realm of Forms, and trying to produce a similar order in the state they are governing (500b ff.); in the *Timaeus* God, in the same way, looks to a Form as he makes the world, and seeks to make his product as perfect as possible by making it resemble the Form as closely as possible (*Ti.* 30c ff.).

This brings to light an important aspect of Forms; things can instantiate them to a greater or lesser degree. In saying that there is a Form of beauty, Plato means not simply that there is an essence that all beautiful things share, but that there is an essence that things share *to the extent that* they are beautiful; and as things can be more or less beautiful, they can share in the Form to a greater or lesser extent. But in fact Plato seems at points to go further than this. It is not just that things *can* fall short of the Forms, but that things in the sensible world necessarily do so: they can, by divine or human efforts, be brought closer to the perfection of the Forms, but will never fully attain it. This produces a contrast between the perfection of the Forms and the imperfection of the sensible world, and gives the Forms an importance they would not otherwise possess.

In a way, I suggest, it is not so much Plato's actual view of Forms that is so distinctive, but his view of the inadequacy of the material world, which leads him to contrast it with Forms. It is this contrast that is the really striking aspect of his theory; but this turns as much on his theory of material things as his theory of Forms. In the next section I shall look more closely at his account of the material world, and ask in what way it falls short.

What is wrong with the world?

How does the material world fall short of Forms? I want to suggest that there are several ways in which it does so, and it is dangerous to concentrate on one of these ways to the exclusion of others. In particular, it may be that it falls short in different ways in relation to different Forms.

According to a traditional reading of Plato, things may fall short of Forms by possessing the properties of which they are the Forms in an imperfect way. For instance, a person or a society may fall short of the Form of justice by not being perfectly just; a diagram may fall short of the Form of circularity by not being perfectly circular. This view is not wholly wrong, but we should be cautious in using it to interpret Plato.

Clearly, Plato thought that the material world does in many cases fall short of Forms in this way; and it seems plausible that he thought it necessarily true that it does so. At the end of the *Republic* Plato's Socrates seems to conclude that the ideal state is not actually achievable, but is "an example laid up in heaven" to which people can look in guiding their own lives (*Resp.* 592b). Also in the *Republic* he suggests that the movements of the heavens, because they are visible, cannot be wholly unchanging and without deviation (530a–b; although it is possible that he later changed his mind about this, as he came to give more significance to the universe and its maker[3]).

However, this cannot be the only way in which the world falls short of Forms, for with some Forms it is hard to make sense of the idea of a thing possessing a property imperfectly. For instance, consider largeness. It is in a sense true that nothing is perfectly large, but this is not because we have a concept of perfect largeness and nothing happens to instantiate it; it is because "perfect large-ness" does not make sense. "Large" is a comparative term, and for anything we see as large, we can always imagine something larger. When we call something large we normally have some comparison in mind. For instance, a small elephant is one that is smaller than other elephants; it will still be large in comparison with land animals generally. Plato often makes use of relative terms such as "large" in drawing attention to the contrast between Forms and things. The point here is not that material things' instantiation of Forms is *imperfect* but rather that it is *qualified*; what is large in one way will be small in another.

In the case of largeness, the obvious way in which a thing's instantiation of the Form may be qualified is by comparison: the thing is large in comparison with one thing, small in comparison with another. But there are other possibilities. For instance, in the case of unity something might be unified in one respect, multiple in another (by having many parts or many properties). In the *Symposium*, Diotima (the chief speaker in the central portion of the dialogue) lists a number of ways in which the beauty of something may be qualified: it may be beautiful in one respect, ugly in another; beautiful in comparison with one thing, ugly in comparison with another; or beautiful in one context, ugly in another (*Symp.* 211a).

One might wonder why it should be seen as a *defect* of things that they possess their properties in a qualified way. Certainly this could be used to show that there is a *distinction* between Forms and things; we can hardly identify largeness itself with the class of large things if they are only qualifiedly large. It might also be used to show that we do not get our *knowledge* of Forms from things (at least completely). We cannot come to understand what largeness is just by looking at an elephant, since the elephant is also in some respect small; we need to use reflection, interpreting our experience in the light of concepts that do not derive from experience. But why should it make things less perfect, less valuable, than Forms?

I think that it does so precisely because it makes them unsuitable as a source of knowledge. For Plato knowledge is something valuable, and one reason that Forms are more valuable than sensible things is that they are appropriate objects of knowledge; if we seek knowledge we must not focus on the sensible world, but on Forms.

In this context it is worth noticing that in the *Symposium* Diotima also refers – apparently as a gloss on the point about different contexts – to the possibility that something might be beautiful to one person, not to another. This is rather surprising, since Plato normally defends objectivity in the realm of values; one would expect him to say that if two people disagree about whether something is beautiful, one of them is wrong, and so its beauty is not really qualified. One possibility is that he is thinking not just of a difference in taste but about two people with different purposes: an object may be well made, and so beautiful, when considered in relation to one purpose, but not when considered in relation to another. But alternatively one might read the passage as meaning that when people disagree about whether something is beautiful then, even if it is truly beautiful, it is inadequate as an example of beauty because it is not an appropriate source of knowledge. We cannot learn what beauty is from an example, if we cannot even agree whether the example is really beautiful.

While in many cases it seems clear that Plato thinks of sensible things falling short of Forms because their possession of properties is qualified, this way of falling short will again not work for all Forms. In particular, it will not work for the Forms of natural kinds, such as human being and other animals, or fire and water. There is no obvious way in which our status as human beings is either imperfect, or qualified. Is there, then, a way in which we fall short of the Form?

Once again the *Symposium* provides a clue, for it mentions a fourth way in which things may fall short of perfect beauty, besides respect, comparison and context. They may also be beautiful at one *time*, ugly at another. Plato, then, seems to think of change as one of the ways in which material things fall short of Forms. Things can of course change in respect to beauty, and size, shape and other qualities that correspond to Forms: but they can also, for Plato, change in respect to their natural kind. The *Timaeus* makes it clear that the physical "elements" can turn into one another (*Ti.* 49b ff.): water, for instance, turns into air when it evaporates, and air may condense into water. Something similar can be true of species of living creature. When I die, my body will turn to dust, while my soul, for Plato, will go on to live another life, either out of the body or in another body, and may no longer be human. Hence, being human is a temporary property of me, and in this way I fall short of the Form of human being.

As we have already seen, Plato saw change as pervasive in the material world, and thought of this as one of the central contrasts between that world and the Forms. What is less clear is just what, in his view, the extent of this prevalence of change was. In the *Phaedo* he claims that sensible things "one might say, never remain the same" (*Phd.* 78b). In saying this he seems to be accepting what is commonly called a theory of flux: a theory that in his time was associated with the Presocratic philosopher Heraclitus, who is credited with the famous sayings "Everything is flowing" and "It is impossible to step into the same river twice". Aristotle tells us that as a young man Plato was influenced by the thought of Heraclitus, and that this is what motivated him to believe in separated Forms. We cannot, he thought, have knowledge of sensible things because they are in constant change, so, if there are objects of knowledge they must be separate from the sensible world (Arist. *Metaph.* A 987b1 ff.). Certainly, as both the *Phaedo* and *Timaeus* imply, Plato accepted the view that there was some kind of flux in sensible things, but just how extreme was the kind of flux in which he believed?

In the *Theaetetus* Socrates discusses a very extreme theory of flux (apparently more extreme than Heraclitus' own) according to which things are changing in *all* respects *all* the time, and never remain the same in any respect (Pl. *Tht.* 179d ff.). This theory is rejected, and it seems unlikely that Plato ever thought that it was true of the sensible world. For one thing, it has very strange consequences: it implies – as the *Theaetetus* shows – that we can never hope to speak the truth about any sensible thing, because it will already have changed while we are speaking. Clearly, Plato – even if he believed we have no *knowledge*, strictly speaking, of the sensible world – thought we could speak meaningfully about it. For another thing, in the *Timaeus* the constant change of the sensible world is described as something that we *see*: yet we clearly do not see things changing in all respects all the time.

What then does Plato mean when he speaks of the world being in constant change? There are two possibilities, both of which may be aspects of his view. First, he may have thought that everything is changing in *some* respect all the time, even if in other respects it remains stable enough to be recognizably the same entity. This is a possible reading of *Phaedo* 78b, and is also supported by the *Symposium*, where Diotima describes both our body and our soul as being involved in constant change (*Symp.* 207d ff.). While it is not a directly observed fact – many things we see have no visible change going on in them – it is supported by many scientific theories; there are constant processes of change maintaining the visible stability of things.

Secondly, everything is *liable* to change in all respects, and perhaps *will* sooner or later change into something of another kind. This seems to be the point being made in the *Timaeus*, where the elements are described changing into one another: it is not that all fire is constantly changing into air (although perhaps some fire, somewhere, is always doing so) but that all fire is *liable* to change. Although this passage is one of the most puzzling in Plato's work, and there is much dispute about its philosophical point, it can be read as meaning that what we see is not *essentially* fire, since it is capable of changing into something else: fieriness is just a quality that it has. If I point to my desk and ask "What is that?", it would not be appropriate to answer "brown", although it is brown, because brownness is just a quality it has and might lose. Plato is suggesting that those predicates, such as "fire", that we might naturally think of as identifying the object in question, are really similar to "brown": they really only ascribe qualities to things.

This is the aspect of change that is most directly relevant to the question how things fall short of Forms. Ever since Aristotle it has often been thought puzzling why the fact that something possesses a property at one time but not at another should be taken to mean that it possesses it less than perfectly. But Plato may have felt that if something is at one time beautiful, at another not, and so beauty is not essential to it, this means that it cannot *be* beautiful in the fullest sense, because beauty is not part of what it *is*; it is, rather, something it happens to possess because of its relation to something else.

In any case, it seems clear that Plato did see the changeableness of the sensible world as an important part of the contrast between it and Forms, and as one of the ways in which it falls short of them, however he worked this out in detail. He saw stability and reliability as good qualities, and so was disturbed by the constant change of the world around him. Because of this, the fact that Forms are unchanging – that what justice, beauty and so on are is always the same – not in itself a particularly surprising claim, took on for him a special significance.

Forms, bodies and space

In the *Timaeus*, Plato gives a fuller account of the nature of bodies and their relation to Forms. We have seen that the attributes that physical things owe to Forms are treated there not as part of their essence, but rather as qualities that might change; and these attributes include not only things such as colour and shape, but also attributes such as fieriness, which define bodies as the distinctive sort of thing they are. This raises the question whether there is any element in physical things that is not liable to change in this way. It turns out that according to the view presented here there is: this is a mysterious entity that is described by a number of metaphorical terms, of which the best known is the "the receptacle of becoming" (*Ti.* 49a). Plato clearly finds the receptacle puzzling and difficult to explain; it is not understood through reason, as Forms are, but neither is it directly perceptible; nevertheless he thinks we have to admit its existence. While bodies such as fire and water can properly only be called "such and such", not "this" – they are only qualities, not things in their own right – the receptacle can be called "this": it is the real thing that we are pointing to when we seem to be indicating a body (49d–50a). While at first it is mysterious just what the receptacle is, in the end it is identified with space (52a–b).

The passage of the *Timaeus* that deals with the receptacle is very obscure, and almost anything that can be said about its interpretation is controversial. But it is possible to see the receptacle as in some way underlying and composing bodies, so that bodies come into being when parts of the receptacle take on qualities derived from the Forms. Thus, for instance, fire comes into existence when a region of space becomes fiery. Sometimes the fire seems to be identified with the qualified region of space (51c) and at other times it is identified with the quality it takes on (49d ff., 52c), but the basic conception of what happens is the same in either case.

An analogy that may illuminate the relation of bodies to the receptacle is the relation of a wave to water. The wave comes into being when water takes on a particular form, but the wave may move through the water, so that different parts of the water take on the form in turn. In the same way, when a body moves through space we can interpret this as different regions of space taking on the quality, for example fieriness, that is distinctive of that body.[4]

Why does Plato introduce the receptacle into his theory? One reason may arise from his view of change. It is possible to argue that in every change there must be a factor that remains unchanged. Otherwise it is not really a change, that is, an object changing from one state to another; rather, it is just one object being replaced by another. For instance, if a man turns into a pig something must have remained throughout the change, or else we cannot say that *he* has turned into a pig, but only that a man has disappeared and a pig appeared. What remains through the change cannot be *in itself* either human or porcine; it has those qualities at different times, but they cannot be its essential properties, in terms of which it is identified.

In ordinary changes, as of shape or colour, it is normally easy to pick out the thing that persists through change, and the properties that identify it. But the most fundamental kind of change, that between the physical "elements", fire, water and so on, involves *all* sensible qualities. So if there is something that persists through this change, it must have no sensible properties of its own.

These thoughts have led some philosophers to posit something that has no properties of its own at all. This theory, the theory of "prime matter", is sometimes ascribed to Aristotle, and was certainly held by later Aristotelians. But it is an uncomfortable view. If the underlying thing has no properties of its own, how do we identify it?

Plato, by identifying the underlying thing with space, overcomes this problem. Space has properties of its own – its three-dimensional structure – but it has no *sensible* properties, such as colour, sound, heat and so on. Hence it can be seen as what underlies sensible change. When one object is transformed into another, this can be seen as a change in space; the region of space persists through the change, but is transformed from one quality to another.

However, there is another reason why Plato posits the receptacle; this has to do with the status of bodies as images. At 52d, Timaeus says that we ordinarily believe in the existence of space because we think that everything that exists must be in something; this is not in fact true of realities (Forms), which do not exist in anything other than themselves, but is true of images. Because an image derives its nature from something else, it must also exist in something else. The point seems to be that images are relational entities. An image of Socrates, for instance, is constituted by the relation of resemblance something bears to Socrates. Relations of this kind cannot exist on their own; there must be something that has the resemblance.

Is it generally true that images must exist in something other than themselves? The passage is sometimes read as referring specifically to mirror images, which clearly do exist in a medium distinct from themselves, the mirror. But it can also be read as covering more substantial images, for example a bronze statue, if the image is identified not with the figured bronze but with the figure in the bronze. An image of Socrates exists in bronze; it exists because the lump of bronze bears a relation to Socrates. In the same way bodies exist in space; they exist because a region of space bears a relation to a Form. Forms and space are the ultimate existents (at least in relation to the sensible world, although a full account of what exists would also have to include God and souls); bodies are constituted by the relation between them.

How many Forms?

One puzzle to which Plato's theory gives rise is just which general terms have Forms corresponding to them. Plato faces this problem

40

directly at one point, at the beginning of the *Parmenides* (130b ff.). This dialogue is generally thought to have been written after those, like the *Phaedo* and *Republic*, where the theory of Forms is first developed at length. In it Socrates, as a young man, is shown proposing a version of the theory of Forms, and facing criticism from Parmenides, the greatest philosopher of the previous generation. Parmenides raises the question what Forms Socrates believes in. His answer is that he definitely believes in two classes of Forms: those for extremely general predicates such as like and unlike, one and many, rest and motion, and those for moral or evaluative predicates such as just, beautiful and good. He is less certain whether there are Forms for natural kinds, such as human being, fire and water, and he definitely rejects Forms for "worthless" things such as hair, mud and dirt.

Parmenides, however, replies that Socrates is saying this because he is young, and that as he grows older and is more "gripped by philosophy" he will see none of these things as beneath his notice. It seems that Parmenides wants to expand the realm of Forms to cover a wider range of predicates. Perhaps we should see Socrates as too focused on the *contrast* between Forms and the sensible world, thinking of Forms as something exalted of which sensible things fall short; the emphasis on evaluative Forms encourages this way of thinking. If he were to take more seriously the fact that the sensible world is an image of Forms, he would recognize that the kinds of thing we find in the sensible world also have Forms corresponding to them. Certainly in the *Timaeus* Forms of natural kinds are present, both the "elements", such as fire and water (*Ti.* 51b–e), and kinds of animal, of which human being is an example (39e–40a). While he does not explicitly mention a Form of hair, he does discuss the place of hair in the scheme of creation, making it something that might appropriately have a Form (76b–d).

It seems, then, that Plato accepts at least three classes of Form: those of extremely general properties, those of moral and evaluative properties and those of natural kinds. The first two are more dominant in the earlier works that feature Forms. The evaluative Forms are Plato's central concern, while the extremely general Forms such as unity, largeness and equality often feature in arguments intended to reveal the contrast between Forms and sensible things. In later works the extremely general Forms become more of an object of interest in their own right, while the natural kind Forms also become important.

Plato sometimes refers to a fourth class of Forms: those of arte-facts, such as a weaver's shuttle or a bed (*Cra.* 389a–c; *Resp.* 596b ff.). He suggests that craftsmen, when they create these things, work with the relevant Form in mind. Some have felt that in these cases Plato's language should not be taken seriously. But in fact it seems appropri-ate, given Plato's general outlook, that there should be such Forms, for there is, for him, no fundamental difference between the works of craft and those of nature. Both are produced by intelligence, in the one case human intelligence, in the other divine, and the maker of the universe, himself described as a craftsman, looks to a Form in making the world, just as human craftsmen do in producing their works.

It seems, then, that Plato accepts quite a wide range of Forms. But is the range unlimited? Is there a Form for every meaningful predicate? One line that suggests there is can be found in Book 10 of the *Republic*: "we usually posit a single Form in connection with each of the many things to which we apply the same name" (*Resp.* 596a). That is, it seems, if there is a class of many things to which the same name (i.e. the same general term, such as "good" or "shuttle") is applied, there is a Form. However, it is possible to read this with the emphasis on "posit", in which case it may mean not that there actually *is* a Form in every such case, but that it is reasonable to start by assuming that there is; however, this assumption may turn out to be wrong.

In what circumstances might it be wrong? A clue is given by a pas-sage in the *Statesman*, where the chief speaker, the Eleatic Stranger, says that there is no Form corresponding to the term "barbarian", meaning a human being who is not Greek (*Plt.* 262d); this is because it is not appropriate, in classifying human beings, to begin by divid-ing them into Greeks and everyone else. As we shall see in Chapter 4, in several dialogues Plato discusses the classification of things in the world, and distinguishes between natural and arbitrary ways of classifying things, insisting on the importance of "dividing at the joints" (*Phdr.* 265e). It seems possible, therefore, that he thinks there is a Form for every predicate that corresponds to a natural, rather than an arbitrary, way of classifying things.

Self-predication

One of the most puzzling aspects of Plato's discussions of Forms is that he often seems to think of them as instances of themselves; for example, the Form of the good is described as something good (*Resp.* 532c), the Form of living creature as a living creature (*Ti.* 30c), and so on. This raises many problems. For one, some Forms, if they are instances of themselves, will turn out to have properties that are not appropriate for Forms. An obvious example is the Form of change (discussed in the late dialogue, the *Sophist*; e.g. *Soph.* 255d); if it is an example of itself it must be in change, but it is central to Plato's conception of Forms that they do not change. Another example is provided by Forms of artefacts, such as bed or shuttle. One might well feel that it is essential to these that they were *made* by a crafts-man, but it seems to be essential to Forms that they are ungenerated. (In Book 10 of the *Republic* Socrates does actually suggest that the Form of bed was made, by God [*Resp.* 597b], but this seems hard to fit into his overall theory.)

Another problem is posed by Forms of relative properties such as largeness. As we have seen, the contrast between these Forms and the things that share in them turns largely on the thought that nothing is large without qualification; a thing must always be large in comparison with one thing, small in comparison with another. If the Form is predicated of itself, then presumably it *will* be large without qualification, but this seems not to make sense; the idea of something large without qualification is not just one that happens to have no instances in the world, but one that is incoherent.

Yet another problem is one of concreteness. If, for instance, the Form of human being is a human being, it must have specific concrete qualities of the kind all human beings have: it must have hair of a particular colour, a nose of a particular length, and so on. If this is so, actual people will resemble the Form more closely, and so come closer to perfection, the closer they are to having these particular qualities. But this is implausible. It is more natural to think of the ideal for human beings as something more abstract, which does not fill in every detail; and certainly Plato gives no sign of thinking there is a completely specific ideal for human beings, or for any other kind of thing. (Another problem arising from self-predication, the "third man" argument, will be discussed later.)

These problems have led some to suggest that Plato's use of self-predicative language should not be taken seriously. One suggestion (Vlastos 1972) is that Plato is using the idiom found, for instance, in Chapter 13 of Paul's *First Epistle to the Corinthians*, where he says "Love [or in some versions 'Charity'] is kind and long-suffering". This clearly does not mean that love is itself kind, in the sense in which people are kind, but rather that, necessarily, everyone who loves is kind. As a limiting case of this, one might say that love is loving, since it is true, although unexciting, that everyone who loves is loving.

Certainly some of Plato's uses of self-predicative language might be explained in this way; and the fact that this idiom exists may be part of the reason why he found it natural to use this language. However, it does not seem that this can account for all Plato's uses of this language; for in some places it seems to be important to him that the Form *itself* has the property in question, and because of this it *explains* the possession of the same property by its instances.

An alternative view, put forward by Michael Frede and others,[5] is that statements of the form "*X* is *F*" (e.g. "justice is virtuous") can be understood in two ways: one in which they mean that *X* has *F*ness as a property; the other in which they mean that *X* has *F*ness as part of its nature. For instance, we might say that justice is virtuous, meaning that being virtuous is part of what it is to be just. Another example of this kind of predication is something like "The porpoise is a mammal". This statement is not about an individual porpoise, but about the species, and does not mean that *it* literally *is* a mammal – that it has warm blood, suckles its young, and so on – but rather that being a mammal is part of what it is to be a porpoise. It is this second kind of predication that is relevant to Plato's account of Forms. When he says something like "justice is virtuous", this can be taken to mean that being virtuous is part of what it is to be just, and, once again, "justice is just" can be read as a limiting case of this; being just is the whole of what it is to be just. (In other cases Plato can be seen as using the first, more ordinary kind of predication in connection with Forms. When he says, for instance, that Forms are eternal, this means simply that they have eternity as a property.)

This account makes sense of much of what Plato says, and may be seen as implicit in much of his discussion of Forms. If we now want to defend something like a theory of Forms, this would seem to be a good path to follow. Nevertheless, I am doubtful whether Plato ever himself clearly recognized this distinction between kinds of predication. There are some things in his work that do seem to require that Forms should be seen as literally instances of themselves, possessing themselves as a property. In the *Symposium*, it is central to the argument that the Form of beauty is itself something beautiful, an appropriate object of love, the contemplation of which is worth aspiring to and gives satisfaction. In the *Republic* the Form of the good is described as the best of realities (*Resp.* 532c). Moreover, in many places the relation between Form and instance is described as a relation of *likeness*, and the Form is described as a model (*paradeigma*; e.g. *Ti.* 29a), of which the instances are copies; this is most simply understood as meaning that the Form itself has the same property that the instances possess, and they have the property by resembling it. Likewise, the claim that instances fall short of the Form is most straightforwardly understood as meaning that they do resemble it, having a property in common, but not perfectly.

An interesting way of making sense of much of this language without accepting the stranger consequences of self-predication has been proposed by I. M. Crombie (1962–3: vol. II, 274–5), who suggests that a Form should be seen as something like a design: the relation of instances to Forms is like the relation of, say, a house to the design on which it is built. (Of course, the comparison should not be pressed too far; the design was made by someone for the sake of the house, while a Form is ungenerated and does not exist for the sake of material things.) The design does not literally *possess* the properties of the house, for example being made of bricks, or being three storeys high; but these properties are *contained* in the design. We can talk of the actual house as resembling the design, and indeed as resembling it more or less closely, as falling short of it. Much of the language Plato uses about Forms can be understood in the same way. Moreover, it is reasonable to think that the design of something beautiful will itself be beautiful. (The special puzzles raised by the Form of the good will be discussed in Chapter 7.)

I do not want to suggest, though, that Plato had a well-worked-out theory along these lines, but only that this will help to make sense of much of what he says. The distinction between this view and literal self-predication is quite easy to miss unless one is actually looking for it, and Plato may not have fully distinguished them. It certainly seems that in some places he sees Forms as standards, of which particular things may fall short; the Form of justice, say, is not just the quality common to all just people or states, but the *standard* of justice, to which people and states may approximate more or less closely. But "standard" can mean either an abstract standard – a principle specifying what a truly just person would be like – or a standard object – something that is itself truly just. It is the first notion that the idea of a design seeks to capture, but Plato may not have clearly separated it from the second. He wants to affirm that the Form of justice represents perfect justice, contrasting with imperfectly just individuals; but then it is easy to fall into thinking of the Form as a perfect *example* of justice. However, I hope I have shown at least that something that is recognizably a theory of Forms can survive without this implication. Certainly, if we emphasize this aspect of Forms we will end up with a deceptive picture of the theory; the realm of Forms will come to seem too much like a literal other world – just like ours, only more perfect. It seems to have been this aspect of Forms that repelled Aristotle. He could not see any point in the theory if it just duplicated our world (e.g. Ar. *Metaph.* B 997b5 ff.). It is better to see the realm of Forms not as a literal other world, but as a pattern, providing standards against which our world can be judged.

Forms and reality

Another striking aspect of the theory of Forms is that Plato often refers to Forms as having "being", by contrast with sensible things, which are sometimes described as "becoming" (e.g. *Ti.* 27d–8a), while in the *Republic* they are referred to as "between being and not being", in that they "are" in one way but "are not" in another (*Resp.* 478d ff.). What does "being" mean here? It seems unlikely that it means existence; Plato is not saying that the sensible world does not exist, that it is an illusion. It seems plausible, rather, that Plato is talking of the predicative sense of "being": the sense in which it is used in "being large", "being beautiful" and so on. Indeed, this is borne out by the *Republic*, which spells out the claim that sensible things are "between being and not being" by saying that the many beautiful things will in a way be ugly, the many just things in a way unjust, and so on. One may think, then, that Plato is using "being" as shorthand for "being so and so"; to say that only Forms have being in the fullest sense is to say that only they possess properties in an unqualified way.

Yet this does not seem to do justice to everything Plato says about the being or reality of the Forms. For instance, in the *Phaedo* Socrates warns us not to see sensible things as "being", although the pleasure and pain they produce may force us to do so (*Phd.* 83b ff.). This can hardly mean that we should not think they *exist*; how, if they did not exist, could they produce pleasure and pain? But nor does it plausibly mean that we should not think they have properties, such as size, equality and so on, in an unqualified way. Why should pleasure and pain lead us to think they have being in this sense?

There are a number of things that Plato may have in mind when he speaks of the Forms as "being" in a way in which other things are not, and I think it would be wrong to choose one of them to the exclusion of others. First, as Vlastos (1965) has pointed out, the words for "being" (*on, ousia*) can also be translated as "real", or "reality". "Reality" can be used in a way equivalent to "existence", as when we contrast what is real with what is imaginary, but it can also be used in another sense, of a genuine example of some kind of thing, as when we contrast real with imitation pearls, or like the Velveteen Rabbit in the story by Margery Williams, who wanted to be real, that is to be a real, living animal. "Real" can also sometimes have evaluative implications; we speak, for instance, of a car that we admire as "a real car" in a way that suggests that a defective example of a kind is not a real example.

If we ascribe reality in this sense to Forms, it is indeed a kind of predicative being, but not any old predicative being, but one in connection with an especially important predicate: the one by reference to which something is identified as the kind of thing it is. In saying that something is real, we do not mean just that it has some property without qualification, but that it is, genuinely, the sort of thing that it claims to be or by reference to which it is defined. So, if we are looking for real beauty, for instance, we should look at the Form rather than at sensible beautiful things; this may be important both from a cognitive point of view, if we want to know what beauty is, and from an evaluative one, if we see beauty as something valuable that we aim to possess. In this case sensible beautiful things will indeed lack real beauty *because* their beauty is qualified in some way. But the mistake Plato is warning against is not simply thinking that their beauty is unqualified, but rather thinking that they are the most genuine, most fundamental, examples of beauty.

Secondly, Plato sometimes contrasts being with becoming (e.g. *Resp.* 509b); he may think, therefore, that things in the world lack being because they are involved in constant change, and so are always becoming something new. This can be seen as contrasting with the constant being of Forms: "being" can here be taken both in an existential sense, since Forms exist forever, and in a predicative sense, since they always retain the same properties.

Finally, there is a possible sense of "real" in which the most basic constituents of the world are real, and the way they manifest themselves is less real (even though it has objective existence, and is not just an illusion). As we have seen, Plato sometimes suggests that sensible things depend on Forms, along with the receptacle, for their existence;[6] Forms may therefore be seen as "more real" in the sense that they are ontologically more fundamental.

The way in which Plato emphasizes the "being" of Forms and contrasts it with the "becoming" of sensible things should not be exaggerated. He often does speak of sensible things as "being" so and so. And while in places "being" is used of something permanent, contrasting with what is constantly becoming something new, in other places the relation between being and becoming is understood in the natural way, with becoming interpreted as coming into being. However, Plato does have a distinctive way of using the concepts of being and becoming in some special contexts, and this is what we have been concerned with here.

Why believe in Forms?

It is surprising that – although Plato clearly knew that his belief in Forms was controversial – there is very little explicit argument for it in his works. In fact, in only one place, in the *Timaeus* (51b–d), does he present a direct argument for the existence of Forms, and the argument there is rather cryptic, and clearly presupposes some knowledge of Platonic philosophy. Timaeus claims that unless Forms exist as something distinct from material things, there is no difference between knowledge and true belief. He goes on to provide reasons for thinking that there is a distinction between knowledge and true belief, but the crucial premise, that there cannot be such a distinction unless there are Forms, is left unsupported. Clearly, someone who has never heard of Forms will have no reason to accept this premise; rather, it is meant to appeal to someone who already has some understanding of Forms and the role they play in Plato's system. The argument does not provide a reason to introduce a new theory; it is intended to defend an existing theory, by reminding us of the function, that of a secure ground for knowledge, that Forms have within that theory, and suggesting that nothing else can fulfil this function.

There are two other places in Plato's work where he puts forward considerations that *could* be used as part of an argument for Forms, but in neither passage does that actually seem to be his main aim.

One is in the *Phaedo* (74b ff.), where Socrates is arguing for the position known as the doctrine of recollection: that we had knowledge of Forms in a disembodied state before our birth, and in our present life are sometimes reminded of them; for instance, when we perceive two equal sticks this reminds us of the Form of equality. In the course of this argument, Socrates puts forward an argument that supports the claim that the Form of equality is different from the equal sticks that remind us of it. But his main aim does not seem to be to argue for this difference; in fact his respondent, Simmias, has already agreed this at the beginning of the discussion. Rather, Socrates' aim is to show that we do not get our knowledge of equality from perceived equal things such as sticks, but must already have some knowledge of it if we are to recognize them as equal.

The other passage is from the *Republic* (476e ff.), where Socrates argues that only things with the distinctive characteristics of Forms can be objects of knowledge, because only they possess properties without qualification; sensible things possess their distinctive properties – largeness, beauty and so on – in a qualified way. It is easy to see how this *could* be used as part of an argument for the existence of Forms. If we add the premise that knowledge does in fact exist, we can conclude that, as only Forms can be objects of knowledge, Forms must exist. In fact, this argument could be combined with that from the *Timaeus* – which does give reasons for thinking that knowledge exists as something distinct from true belief – to produce a stronger argument for the theory of Forms. But within the *Republic* this is not Plato's aim; rather, he is trying to show that as only Forms are true objects of knowledge, it is only those who pursue knowledge of them who are rightly called lovers of knowledge, and so entitled to the name "philosophers". He is seeking to rule out the suggestion that dilettantes, lovers of sights and sounds, have a right to that name; the real philosopher is someone who knows something of significance.

We know from Aristotle (*Metaph.* A 990b9 ff.) that arguments for belief in Forms were used in Plato's school, the Academy. Clearly he did think that argument in favour of the theory was possible, and sometimes useful. But it is in fact difficult to find arguments that could, by themselves, provide a motive for introducing the theory of Forms.

Some arguments seem too broad, and it is not clear why they should motivate the introduction of Forms rather than of some other entity. For instance, it is sometimes suggested that Plato introduced the notion of Forms because he thought that the objects of knowledge should be unchanging, and that, as things in the material world are clearly in change, there must be something else that plays this role. In a way, this is certainly right: Plato did think that objects of knowledge must be unchanging, and that Forms were able to play this role. And this is indeed an advantage for the theory of Forms over rival views on which everything changes. But it is not clear why this line of thought should have led Plato to posit *Forms* specifically, rather than some other kind of unchanging reality, for instance God, or atoms, the ultimate constituents of the physical world.

Other arguments seem to motivate the introduction only of a particular class of Forms, not of the wide range of Forms in which Plato seems to have believed. For instance, one might argue that we cannot gain a clear conception of some properties, such as large and small, just by looking at examples of them, since what is large in comparison with one thing will be small in comparison with another; hence, what largeness is must be something distinct from visible large things, something not perceived through the senses. But this argument will not extend in any straightforward way to other properties, such as being a human being; when we look at a human being, it seems, we can see that she is human, and nothing in our immediate experience shows us a respect in which she is not human. Indeed, Plato himself has Socrates make a point along these lines in *Republic* Book 7 (523a ff.): some properties, such as largeness and unity, are useful for reducing our reliance on the senses; others, such as being a finger, are not, since when we look at a finger our senses do not show us any aspect under which it is not a finger. Yet Socrates does not say that there are no Forms for properties such as being a finger, or that the senses do give a completely adequate account of those properties, but only that our immediate experience does not give us a reason to think they do not. And elsewhere, as we have seen, he does introduce Forms for natural kinds, such as human being, and artificial kinds, such as bed, which do not raise the same problems as properties such as largeness. If Plato first introduced the theory of Forms in response to these problems, as some think, why would he extend it to other properties that do not raise them?

I suggest that these puzzles may be solved if we suppose that Plato did *not* introduce Forms in response to an argument; rather, he had a basic intuitive conviction, perhaps inherited from Socrates, that something like Forms existed. When he began to work out his view of Forms in detail and to apply it, he found that it could help to solve various problems, and this gave it an advantage over rival views, and so was an additional reason for accepting it. This explains why arguing for Forms is not a priority with him: arguments for Forms arise incidentally in the discussion of other issues. It also explains why Plato feels able to use arguments that are limited in the ways I have discussed. He is not introducing a theory in response to problems; rather, he is claiming it as an advantage for an existing theory that it can solve certain problems. Thus it can be seen as an advantage of Forms that they perform a certain role, even if something else *could* perform that role, and it will also be an advantage of the theory if one group of Forms helps to solve a particular problem, even if other Forms are not relevant to it. The main reason for adopting the theory lies not in any one specific argument, but in its coherence and its general usefulness.

There is a clear shift between the Socratic and Platonic dialogues in their attitude to Forms, but this can be seen as a change not so much of doctrine as of perspective. Plato is not introducing new entities; as we have seen, Socrates does believe in universal essences such as virtue itself, holiness itself and so on, and even occasionally calls them Forms. Nor is Plato exactly ascribing new characteristics to Forms; it is quite likely that, if Socrates had been made to reflect on the Forms in which he believed, he would have agreed with many of Plato's distinctive views about them. It is quite reasonable to say, for instance, in the light of the way he discusses virtue, that for him the nature of virtue does not change, and that we know it through reasoning rather than through the senses. Even the aspect of Forms that is often seen as most distinctive of Plato, separation, can be seen as implicit in Socrates' thought; he might well have agreed that virtue itself does not depend for its existence on particular virtuous people, especially as he was doubtful about whether there were any really virtuous people.

But in the Socratic dialogues these aspects of Forms are never emphasized. Socrates' concern is not with the general claim that Forms exist, and their status, but always with the particular Form that he is investigating on each occasion, and its ethical implications. Plato, by contrast, reflects on Forms as such, and the way they contrast with sensible things, and begins to think systematically about them. For him it is important, for instance, that they are unchanging, that they are objects of knowledge and that they have no imperfection about them: all respects in which they contrast with the material world.

Problems for Forms

In the first part of the *Parmenides*, as we have seen, Plato shows Socrates, as a young man, proposing a version of the theory of Forms; he then faces criticisms of the theory from Parmenides. These criticisms are not answered within the dialogue, although it does not follow that Plato thought them unanswerable. Here I shall discuss two of the problems that Parmenides raises.

The first of these is commonly called the "third man" argument (*Prm.* 132a–b). It seems to have been a well-known argument in philosophical circles at the time; Aristotle refers to it in his *Metaphysics* (A 990b15), and Alexander in his commentary on the *Metaphysics* makes it clear that this was the same argument which we know from the *Parmenides* (Alex. Aphr. *in Metaph.* 83.34 ff.). It is to them that we owe the name "third man", since they discuss a version of the argument that uses as an example the Form of man. The *Parmenides*, however, uses instead the Form of large.

Parmenides begins by getting Socrates' agreement that although there are many things that we call by one name, "large", there is *one* thing, the Form, in virtue of which they are all large. He then argues that if we consider the Form and the other large things together, there must be *another* Form in virtue of which *they* are all large. (So if an ordinary large thing is the "first large", and the original Form the "second large", this will be the "third large".) However, there is no reason to stop there; if we look at this "third large" together with the original Form and the other large things, there must be a further Form, a "fourth large", in virtue of which all these are large. And so *ad infinitum*: an infinite series of Forms is produced.

This result is obviously disturbing, not only because it produces an infinite number of Forms for each predicate, when Socrates' original proposal is that there is *one* Form in virtue of which, for instance, all large things are large, but also because the intention is to *explain* why large things are large by their relation to the Form. If we then have to posit another Form to explain why that Form is large, yet another Form to explain why *that* is large, and so on, we have an infinite regress of explanation, and it is often felt that this is not genuinely explanatory: it leaves the fact with which we started basically unexplained. So, if the theory of Forms leads to this conclusion, it may seem best to abandon the theory.

However, are we forced, just by believing the basic principles of the theory of Forms, to accept Parmenides' argument? In fact, it looks as if his argument rests on some assumptions that could be questioned. One we are already familiar with is the self-predication assumption: that the Form of large is itself something large, and likewise for other Forms. Parmenides says that we should consider the Form of large and *other* large things together, and then we will discover another Form in virtue of which *they are large*. If the Form in virtue of which things are large is not itself large no problem arises; there is no need to introduce anything else to explain its largeness.

However, this is not the only assumption we need to make the argument work. Why should we not say that the Form of large is large in virtue of itself, although other large things are large by relation to it? To block this move the argument needs some further assumption. The assumption that fulfils this function is normally called a non-identity assumption. There has been some dispute about just how the non-identity assumption is best formulated, but the simplest formulation is one proposed by Gail Fine (1993: 206): nothing is large in virtue of itself (and likewise for other predicates, at least those that have Forms corresponding to them). Parmenides seems to be making some such assumption as this when he claims that there must be *another* Form in virtue of which the original Form and its instances are all large.

These assumptions are not obviously unreasonable; it is plausible that someone who believes in Forms might accept them. As we have seen, Plato's language often suggests that he believes in self-predication, and it is essential to the theory that, at least in ordinary cases, something like non-identity is true: ordinary large things are not large in virtue of themselves, but through a relation to the Form. However, nor is it obvious that either assumption should be accepted. We have seen that some have interpreted Plato in such a way that he is not committed to self-predication, while there may also be reasons to reject non-identity when this is applied to the Form itself. Fine (1993: 226–8) has argued that ordinary large things cannot be large in virtue of themselves precisely because their largeness is imperfect or qualified; the same need not be true of the Form, which is large in an unqualified way.

It seems possible to give up one or other of the assumptions. If we maintain both we face a damaging regress, but either on its own does not pose a problem (or at least this particular problem). Another possibility, however, is to see some kind of ambiguity in the terms in which the problem is stated. If this is right, both assumptions might be true in a way, but on different interpretations of the terms. One way of achieving this result has been suggested by Constance Meinwald (1992). It turns on the distinction between two kinds of predication mentioned above (§ "Self-predication"). On ordinary predication, where an object possesses a property, self-predication will be false (the Form of largeness does not have the property of being large) but non-identity will be true (each thing that has the property of being large has it in virtue of something else, the Form). On the special kind of predication where an object has a property as the whole or part of its nature, self-predication will be true (the Form of largeness is large in that largeness is its nature) but non-identity will be false (something that has largeness as its nature need not have it in virtue of something else).

Another possible solution, which also turns on ambiguity, can be found if we compare Forms with standard weights and measures.[7] The Form of large can be seen as a standard of largeness in the same way that something can be a standard for a particular weight or measure, for example the (former) standard metre as a standard for the property of being a metre long; other things are large by resembling the Form. This raises a problem over how we are to use the word "large". On the one hand, we might well suppose that if other large things *resemble* the Form, then it has the same property that they have, so it is large; in this case self-predication will be true, non-identity false. On the other hand, in saying things are large we are *comparing* them with the Form, and the Form cannot be compared with itself; it does not literally resemble itself, so it seems wrong to call it large. Both views seem to have some intuitive power, but we cannot maintain both of them at once without paradox. However, which one we accept – how we actually use the word "large" – may in the end be just a matter of choice. The problem seems to be one about how the word is to be used rather than about what Forms are really like.

Interestingly, a parallel puzzle exists in modern philosophy about standard measures, such as the standard metre that at one time existed in Paris. The metre was defined in such a way that other things were a metre long if their length was the same as that of the standard. Some philosophers, such as Ludwig Wittgenstein (1953: 50), have argued that the standard should not itself be described as a metre long, since in saying things are a metre long we are comparing them with the standard, and it cannot be compared with itself. Others, such as Saul Kripke (1981: 54), hold that, as the standard has the same length as other things that are called a metre long, it must be right to say that it, too, is a metre long. One thing that we can be certain of, though, is that the standard existed; the fact that there was a puzzle about how to speak of it does not mean that we need to deny its existence, or in general to think that weights and measures cannot be defined by reference to standards. Something similar may be true of Forms.

Before leaving Parmenides' arguments, we should note that while the third man argument is the one that has stimulated most discussion, it is not the one that Parmenides himself thinks is the greatest difficulty for Forms. He gives this title to an argument that seeks to show that knowledge of Forms is impossible (*Prm.* 133b ff.).

This argument turns on the claim that Forms are related, in the distinctive way that their names imply, not to ordinary things, but to other Forms; conversely, ordinary things are related to other ordinary things, and not to Forms. Thus, for instance, human slaves are slaves of human masters, not of the Form of master, and human masters are masters of human slaves, not of the Form of slave; the Forms of master and slave, however, are what they are in relation to one another. If this reasoning is extended to knowledge, Parmenides claims, it will follow that only the Form, knowledge, can be related to truth itself, and the Forms of specific knowledges (i.e. branches of knowledge) to specific realities, that is, Forms. Our knowledge, on the other hand, will be related to ordinary realities, not to Forms.

There is no space here to explore this argument in detail. A full treatment would have to show not only how it might be answered, but also why Parmenides sees it as so intractable. It is certainly the case that Forms do not typically stand to us in the relation that their names indicate: the Form of master is not our master, the Form of statesman not our ruler, the Form of bed not something we could lie on, and so on. It does not obviously follow from this that we cannot stand in *any* relation with Forms. Knowledge may be an exception; so, as we have seen, may love. Perhaps the problem is one of giving a principled criterion to distinguish the relations that we can stand in with Forms from those that we cannot. One may also suspect that the puzzle arises from an excessively literal application of the thought that the Forms constitute a distinct world. One might think that if they do not stand to us in relations like master this is because they are not part of our world but are located elsewhere; but if this is true it is hard to see how we could have any access to them. But as I have suggested, this may not in any case be the best way to look at the realm of Forms.

Plato's response to these problems

What was Plato's own response to these problems? Some have thought that they were so devastating that they led him to abandon the theory of Forms altogether. But the language of the passage does not suggest that. As we have seen, Parmenides calls the problem of the unknowability of Forms "the greatest difficulty", yet he insists that it *can* be answered, although only an exceptionally gifted person would be able to follow the answer (*Prm.* 133b, 135a–b). Later, he says that if we simply refuse to accept that Forms exist, we make all discussion impossible (135b–c). In addition, dialogues that most scholars see as later than the *Parmenides* – most notably the *Timaeus* – include discussions of Forms, and not just as common essences that things share, but as paradigms that they resemble, while necessarily falling short of them (e.g. *Ti.* 37d): one of the clearest statements of the classic conception of Forms.

Did Plato, then, have definite answers to the problems in mind? No such answers are stated in the *Parmenides*, but perhaps we are being challenged to work them out for ourselves. One possible view is that we are meant to see Socrates as holding an inadequate version of the theory of Forms (perhaps implying, also, that Plato in earlier works had expressed an inadequate version of the theory). Parmenides' arguments expose difficulties, and we have to revise the theory to overcome them, although it will remain the same theory in essentials. For instance, we can see the third man argument as depending on the assumptions of self-predication (understood in a fairly literal way) and non-identity. Perhaps the moral is that one of these assumptions must be given up.

Alternatively, we may see the problem as lying not in the actual theory Socrates holds, but in the way he expresses it. Unclarities in the way he expounds the theory give rise to misunderstandings, which allow apparent problems to be raised. In this case the moral is simply that we have to clarify the way we speak about Forms in order to show that these problems do not really arise.

However, there is another possibility: that Plato did not have any specific solution to the difficulties in mind, but nevertheless believed that one was possible, and set out the difficulties as a stimulus to future research. One might think that it would be wrong to cling to a theory in the face of such problems if one could not oneself see any answer to them. This might be right in the case of a scientific theory, put forward as a solution to a problem; if it raises difficulties that cannot be overcome, that is a reason for thinking it is not a good solution. However, I have suggested that Plato's belief in Forms was not like that. Rather, he had a deep intuitive conviction that such things as unity itself, justice itself, beauty itself, and so on exist. It might be reasonable to cling to such a conviction even in the face of problems that one cannot immediately solve. The philosopher Zeno of Elea, a friend of Parmenides, who makes a brief appearance at the beginning of the dialogue, was famous for putting forward some notorious paradoxical arguments that seem to show that there is no such thing as plurality or motion (the most famous of his arguments is probably that which turns on the paradox of Achilles and the tortoise). Some of these arguments have proved very hard to answer, but clearly the right response is not to stop believing in plurality or motion – we know, by experience, that these things exist – but to go on believing in them while seeking a solution to the paradoxes. Plato may have seen it as right, in the same way, to go on believing in Forms, and to look for a solution to the paradoxes that they raise.

FOUR

Knowledge

Our discussion of the Forms has already shown that knowledge plays a central role in Plato's thought. It is important to him that they are suitable objects for knowledge, and he sees knowledge of them as something to aspire to. In this chapter we shall look more closely at this aspect of his philosophy. I shall begin with a brief look at the one work, the *Theaetetus*, where Plato confronts the topic of knowledge, as it were, head on, asking what knowledge is. After this I shall look at a number of other aspects of Plato's view of knowledge, and in particular of the relation between knowledge and Forms.

The *Theaetetus*: Plato on knowledge

Although the *Theaetetus* is generally thought to have been written relatively late in Plato's career, in many ways it seeks to recapture the style and method of the "Socratic" dialogues. It presents Socrates, as he appeared in many of those dialogues and as he may have been in real life, examining a number of proposals rather than stating a worked-out view, and reaching no definite conclusion. Near the beginning of the dialogue Socrates introduces the famous image (which may go back to the historical Socrates) of himself as a midwife, trying to help his interlocutors to give birth to ideas (*Tht.*

150b ff.). In the course of the work he enables the young mathematician Theaetetus to come up with three proposals for the definition of knowledge, but in the end all are rejected. However, the discussion of these proposals is used as a peg on which to hang various further discussions, which go some way beyond the dialogue's official aim of defining knowledge. Among the topics discussed are: the Heraclitean theory that the world is in radical flux; the relativism of the Sophist Protagoras, according to whom "a human being is the measure of all things" (*Tht.* 152a) and whatever seems true to me is true for me; the possibility of false belief; and the relation between elements and composite wholes.

The *Theaetetus* is one of Plato's most fascinating works, but it is valuable as an example of philosophy in action rather than as a source of philosophical teaching. It is far from clear what moral, if any, we are meant to take away from the reading of it. What is certain, though, is that it does not leave us with a definition of knowledge. In what follows I shall look briefly at the three proposed definitions and why they are rejected.

Theaetetus' first proposal is that knowledge is perception (*Tht.* 151e). This is rejected on the grounds that while our awareness of some properties such as colour, heat, musical tone and so on comes through the senses, there are others such as sameness and difference, likeness and unlikeness, number and, especially, being that we grasp not with the senses but with the intellect. It is therefore not perception, but belief, that enables us to grasp these things, and Socrates says that if we do not grasp being we do not grasp truth, and so do not attain knowledge (184b–6e). It is not entirely clear what Socrates means by this but, at any rate, what he says does seem to give us a reason for rejecting the definition. It would seem that, at the very least, properties such as being *can* be objects of knowledge – that we can know that something exists, that two things are different and so on – and if these properties are not grasped by the senses this is a reason not to identify knowledge with perception.

The second proposal discussed, following on from this, is that knowledge is true belief (187b). This is rejected on the grounds that it is possible to persuade people, rhetorically, of something that happens to be true, although in such a case they will not have knowledge; an orator, for instance, might persuade a jury that a certain person committed a crime, when he did indeed do so, but the members of the jury do not *know* this, as is shown by the fact that the orator could equally have persuaded them of the opposite had he so chosen (201a–c). It is somewhat obscure what Socrates thinks *would* be sufficient to produce knowledge in such a case. At one point he suggests it might be produced by "teaching", that is, presumably by going over the evidence in a rational way; the problem is that court proceedings do not allow enough time for this. Later, however, he seems to say that only an eyewitness could know who committed a crime. But in any case, it seems right to say that rhetorical persuasion can produce true belief without knowledge, so Socrates is right to reject this proposal.

Theaetetus' third proposal (201d) is that knowledge is true belief with an account (*logos*). At first sight this is much more plausible than the first two. It seems to resemble the view, much discussed in recent philosophy, that knowledge is justified true belief, since a justification for a belief might well be called an account of it. But it emerges that this is not exactly what Theaetetus has in mind. He means, rather, that to know a *thing* is to have true belief about the thing along with an account of the thing. Socrates then brings a number of criticisms against this theory, based on different interpretations of the term "account". One of his criticisms, however, although directed against a particular reading of "account" – that it means a distinguishing mark that enables us to pick something out from other objects – is of wider relevance, and poses a problem for many theories of knowledge. It turns on the question whether, when we say that true belief must be accompanied by an account, we mean true belief about the account or knowledge of the account. If the first, then it seems that the requirement that we have an account adds nothing to what is already involved in true belief; to think about something at all we must have a way of picking it out. If the second, our definition becomes circular; it uses knowledge to define knowledge (209d–10b).

This problem can be generalized: it is an objection to any theory of knowledge that sees it as true belief together with some further piece of information. If we require only true belief about this new piece of information, it is not clear why this should by itself turn our belief into knowledge. If one piece of true belief does not constitute knowledge, why should two pieces of true belief do so? (Both, after all, might have been produced by rhetorical persuasion.) But if knowledge of the new information is required, the definition becomes circular. This is not to rule out the possibility that acquiring a new piece of information might in fact enable us to turn our true beliefs into knowledge. But if it does so, it is because it brings about some change in our mental state, not because its presence is, by definition, enough to constitute knowledge. Thus in what is probably a much earlier dialogue, the *Meno*, Socrates claims that true belief can by turned into knowledge by working out the explanation (*Meno* 98a). But this need not mean that knowledge is simply true belief together with possession of an explanation, for this would raise the same problem: true belief about an explanation, or knowledge of it? Working out the explanation brings about the transformation into knowledge, but this does not in itself say exactly what the transformation involves. Plato never, in the *Theaetetus* or elsewhere, achieves a satisfactory account of what knowledge is.

Knowledge and Forms

We now turn to look at other aspects of Plato's theory of knowledge, concerned not so much with what knowledge is but with what it is knowledge of and how it is gained, and in particular with the connection between knowledge and Forms. There are three aspects of the theory of knowledge that especially deserve discussion. First, I shall look at general questions about the knowledge of Forms, what is involved in knowing Forms, and in particular the question whether Forms are the only thing we can know. Secondly, I shall consider the theory of recollection, the proposal that we gain knowledge through remembering something we have learned, outside the body, before our birth into the present life. Finally, I shall look at Plato's view of the structure of knowledge and of philosophical enquiry, and of the special part played in it by the Form of the good; Plato's account of these issues is given in the central part of the *Republic*, by means of the three famous analogies of the sun, the line and the cave.

Forms and definition

What is it to know a Form? Essentially, I suggest, it is to know what some kind of thing is: to know the Form of good is to know what goodness is; to know the Form of large is to know what largeness is; and so on. It is, therefore, the sort of knowledge that would naturally be expressed in a definition. This is not surprising, when we remember that the theory of Forms arose out of Socrates' quest for definitions. Many (although by no means all) of the Socratic dialogues are concerned with the search for definitions, and in two of them, the *Meno* (72c) and *Euthyphro* (6d–e), Socrates calls what he is looking for a Form. That quest is not abandoned in those dialogues where the theory of Forms is present in a more developed state, although, because Plato thinks this knowledge is hard to attain, he rarely gives actual examples of definition. However, one of the central aims of the *Republic* is to find a definition of justice. The definition actually given is provisional, but it is suggested that an investigation of Forms, linking it with the Form of the good, is what we need to achieve a more certain result (*Resp.* 504b–5a). This interest in definition remains in Plato's later works: the *Theaetetus*, as we have seen, is a quest, although an unsuccessful one, for a definition of knowledge, and Plato searches, apparently successfully, for definitions of the sophist and the statesman in the dialogues of those names. (A passage at the beginning of the *Sophist* [217a ff.] also suggests that Plato at one point planned a third dialogue in the group, which would have been concerned with the definition of the philosopher.)

In many places Plato uses the language of perception in describing our knowledge of Forms – he speaks of seeing or looking at the Forms, or of touching them – and this has sometimes been taken to mean that the knowledge he is looking for is not propositional. But Plato's language of perception can be seen as a metaphor, like "seeing the point", "grasping the truth" and so on. Knowledge of Forms is a kind of insight, and is clearly presented as a striking experience of a kind that can be life-transforming, but this may still be knowledge that can in principle be stated. A Form is a really existing object, and so when we know a Form there is some object that we know, but that does not mean that knowledge of Forms is acquaintance *as opposed to* propositional knowledge; it can be seen, rather, as knowledge of *what they are*.

The combination of Forms

However, definitions are not the only thing Plato thinks we should be looking for in our investigation of Forms. In later works, especially the *Sophist*, he emphasizes the importance of relations between Forms. The chief speaker of the *Sophist*, the Eleatic Stranger, draws attention to the way in which Forms can "combine" or "blend" with one another, and, in describing dialectic, the distinctive activity of philosophers, claims that they should investigate which Forms can combine and which cannot (*Soph.* 253b ff.).

Just what is meant by "combination" is somewhat unclear; it may be that Plato is using the term in a rather broad sense, so that it covers what we would think of as several different relations. He certainly seems to think that two Forms combine when one of them is predicated of the other. Thus, for instance, the Forms of motion and rest both exist or are something. This means that the Form of being is predicated of both of them, or that they have being as a property; and this is seen as a combination between these Forms and being (254d). On the other hand, the Stranger also claims that all discourse depends on the combination of Forms (259e), yet it is clearly not the case that every assertion predicates one Form of another; "Socrates is wise", for instance, does not. It may be that Plato sees combination as including not only cases where one Form is predicated of another, but also cases where two Forms are predicated of the same object. "Socrates is wise" could than be taken to imply the combination of, for instance, the Forms of human and wise. Thus, in investigating the combination of Forms, we would be enquiring into which Forms are compatible, in that they could belong to the same objects, and which are not.

The idea of combination of Forms is not a wholly new one in the later works. There is in fact a reference to Forms combining in the *Republic* (476a). In the *Parmenides*, indeed, there is a passage where the young Socrates is sometimes read as saying that different Forms do not combine (*Prm.* 129d–e), but in fact he need only be taken to mean that *opposite* Forms, such as likeness and unlikeness, do not combine. But while the basic idea is not wholly new, the focus on it certainly is. Plato's philosophy is taking a rather different direction here from that found in the classic works written earlier in his career.

In the *Sophist*, the Stranger undertakes an investigation of the relations between five very great or very important Forms – being, sameness, difference, motion (or change) and rest (or stability) – enquiring which of these can, and which cannot, be predicated of one another, but also emphasizing that they are all distinct from one another (*Soph.* 254c–7a). (These are sometimes referred to as the greatest Forms, but the Stranger does not say that they are *the* greatest; others, such as unity, may be equally important.) The method demonstrated here could no doubt be applied to other Forms as well, including natural kinds and evaluative Forms, for we have no reason to think that Plato has abandoned interest in these. Yet it is significant that Forms of extreme generality are here singled out as among the most important. It may be that Plato thinks that an understanding of them is necessary to any investigation of relations between Forms.[1]

In this passage the most notable features ascribed to Forms in earlier dialogues – their eternity and changelessness, their being grasped by reason and not through the senses and so on – are not mentioned (although changelessness is discussed in an earlier passage of the *Sophist* [248a ff.]), and the tone is for the most part drily logical, without the mystical elements found in many earlier accounts of Forms. This may lead us to doubt whether the Forms discussed here are the same as those found in earlier works. Yet even in the *Sophist* the Stranger at one point shows an attitude of reverence for the Forms he is discussing. Referring specifically to the Form of being, he calls it divine, and says that it is because of the brilliance of this Form, which blinds us when we try to look at it, that it is hard to discern the nature of the philosopher, who is concerned with being (*Soph.* 254a–b).

In fact it is possible to see the contrast between the *Sophist* and earlier works as resulting, not from a change of doctrine, but from a difference in purpose. The theory of Forms, as expounded in works such as the *Phaedo, Symposium, Phaedrus, Republic* and *Timaeus*, is primarily a theory about the relation between Forms and things: sometimes the contrast between Forms and things, sometimes the way in which Forms underlie things. It is also a theory about our relation with Forms: how we come to know them, and how we can move towards contemplation of them. For this reason it focuses on the realm of Forms as a whole, and on the characteristics that they share. But in the *Republic* Socrates describes the true method of dialectic as "proceeding from Forms to Forms, and ending with Forms" (*Resp.* 511b–c); it is not concerned with the relation of Forms to us or to the world, but with their own nature and their relations with one another. Someone doing dialectic in this way would focus not on the ideal qualities of the Forms, which set them apart from sensible things, but on the individual nature of each Form and what makes it what it is. It does not follow that these Forms should not be seen as having those same ideal qualities. The discussion in the *Sophist* of these very important Forms and their relations may in fact be the clearest example in Plato of the method of dialectic described in the *Republic*, but not actually practised there. Much of what Plato writes is practical in aim, directed either towards the guiding of our lives in general or towards moving us to do philosophy, but in this passage of the *Sophist* it is possible to see him doing philosophy itself, from a purely theoretical perspective.

Collection and division

One aspect of the relations between Forms in which Plato takes a special interest is the way they may be related as genus and species.

Sometimes, a generic Form may have a number of more specific Forms falling under it; for instance, the Forms of land animal, water animal and so on may be seen as falling under the Form of living creature (see *Ti.* 30c, 39e ff.); Forms such as justice and temperance may be seen as falling under the Form of virtue. It is worth remembering here that the most common Greek word for form, *eidos*, can also be translated "kind". This need not mean that Plato is thinking of Forms as kinds in the sense of classes of objects, but he does sometimes think of each Form as defining a kind of thing and setting it apart from other kinds of thing. The more specific Forms are sometimes referred to as parts of the more general one. This language should probably not be taken too literally, since it is hard to fit it together in detail with the idea of Forms as ideal patterns (although Plato does sometimes use both kinds of language together, notably in the *Timaeus*). The point is rather that the "parts" can be seen as more specific versions of the "whole": the Form of living creature determines, in a rather broad way, the requirements that something must satisfy to be a living creature; the Form of land animal determines a specific way of satisfying these requirements. There may in turn be more specific versions of the Form of land animal. By investigating them we can draw a classificatory tree, going down to the individual species. Investigation of these relations may move in either direction: it may start with a number of species and look for the genus within which they fall, or it may start with a genus and seek to articulate its various species.

Once again this theme goes back to an early stage in Plato's thought. The idea that Forms can stand in part–whole relations is found as early as the *Euthyphro*, where holiness is called a Form, but is also described as a part of justice (*Euthphr.* 6d–e, 12d). However, the *Phaedrus* is probably the first work to focus explicitly on the investigation of these relations. There Socrates, having made a speech in praise of love, begins to reflect more systematically on what he did in that speech, and points out that he did two things in particular (*Phdr.* 265d ff.). One was to collect or bring together a number of seemingly disparate phenomena under one name, love, and give a definition of love that fits the class as a whole. The second was to make a distinction or division within the general field of madness. Love is seen as a kind of madness, but it is important to distinguish between a bad kind of madness and a good, or divinely inspired, kind. The divine kind is then subdivided into four varieties, found in mystical initiation, prophecy, poetry and love. Socrates here introduces the famous metaphor of "dividing at the joints": there is a natural way in which to classify things, and we should not split them up in an arbitrary way.

Both these operations, collection and division, are connected with the part–whole relation. The first begins with a multitude of phenomena and seeks the whole of which they are parts; the second begins with a whole and distinguishes the parts within it. Neither operation is presented as wholly new, for Socrates says that he has always seen them as typical of dialectic; what is new is the possibility of applying them to rhetoric. Indeed, the first operation, collection, can be seen as a development of the practice of seeing the one in the many, and searching for what all examples of something, for example virtue, have in common, which is typical of the Socratic dialogues. As for division, in those same dialogues Socrates sometimes shows an interest in classification and in making distinctions, notably in the *Gorgias*, where he classifies a number of arts or skills, and also a number of knacks, based on experience rather than knowledge, which he contrasts with these skills (*Grg.* 464b ff.). This aspect of Socratic dialectic may go back to the historical Socrates, since Xenophon also ascribes to him an interest in "making distinctions according to forms (or kinds)" (Xen. *Mem.* IV.5.12). It exploits the way in which the name of the art can mean not only "art of conversation" but also "art of making distinctions". But it is the *Phaedrus* that makes explicit this double tendency of dialectic; it both seeks unity, discerning what many things have in common, and draws distinctions, recognizing many varieties within an encompassing whole. It is the *Sophist*, however, within Plato's work, that explicitly links these operations with Forms; the Stranger says that it is characteristic of dialectic to "divide according to Forms", and this is linked with enquiry into the combination of Forms (*Soph.* 253d).

The investigation of the genus–species relation between Forms might serve several different purposes. One is simply to give a map of some area of enquiry, setting out all the species that fall within some important genus, thus improving our understanding of the whole area and of the particular species within it. This aim is particularly prominent in the *Philebus*, another late dialogue connected in a number of ways with the *Sophist* and *Statesman*. The passage there in which Socrates introduces this method is extremely cryptic (*Phlb.* 16c ff.), but the general point being made seems to be that, in order fully to understand a field of enquiry falling under some general Form, we should not simply point to the wide variety of things that fall under it, but rather seek to classify the various objects in a structured way, looking first for species, then for subspecies and so on (19a–b). The examples given here include the classification of vocal sounds, of the sort represented by letters; these are divided first into vowels, voiced consonants and unvoiced consonants, and then into more specific kinds (18b–d). Socrates claims that we cannot gain knowledge of any one of the items in this scheme of classification without knowledge of the others. Later in the dialogue this method is applied to the classification of kinds of pleasure and knowledge, since the value of pleasure and knowledge, and the contribution they make to the good life, is the overall theme of the work.

Another aim of division may be to draw attention to philosophically significant differences. When two species belong to the same genus, this means that they have something in common, but also that there is some significant difference between them; it is important not to think that because one of them has a particular property the other must do likewise. Thus in the *Phaedrus*, as we have seen, two kinds of madness are distinguished; in both we are not wholly under the control of reason, yet one is harmful, the other beneficial.

However, in the *Sophist* and *Statesman* Plato links his interest in classification with his interest in definition. It is possible to define a term by showing where it fits into a scheme of classification. Thus, starting with a very general Form such as production or acquisition, one can divide it into species, then subdivide one of the species and so on, until a very specific Form, that of the sophist or the statesman, has been identified. The definition, when achieved, will show just how the Form being defined fits into a larger pattern of Forms. The search for definitions of the sophist and the statesman follows this pattern. Indeed, in the *Sophist*, the definition given at the end of the dialogue, according to which the sophist is a producer of deceptive images, lists all the Forms under which he falls, from the most specific to the most general, production (*Soph.* 268c–d), although the same pattern is not followed in the *Statesman*.

The *Sophist* and *Statesman* present a rather different aspect of division from that which we found in the *Phaedrus*. Whereas there it was concerned with making a few philosophically significant distinctions, in the later works it aims to be comprehensive, and seems more like the scientific schemes of classification associated with Linnaeus. There is, in fact, evidence that biological classification was practised in the Academy; in a fragment of Greek comedy some of Plato's pupils are shown attempting to classify a pumpkin (Epicrates, quoted by Ath. *Deipnosophists* II.59). Indeed, in the *Statesman*, the Stranger, in the course of trying to classify arts that care for animals, makes some remarks on the classification of animals themselves (*Plt.* 262a ff.). This, however, does not mean there is a radical difference in the underlying idea; the method of collection and division is equally applicable to philosophically significant Forms, and to more mundane ones.

Can only Forms be known?

In places in Plato's work, both in the *Republic* and, perhaps more explicitly, in the *Timaeus*, the suggestion is made that *only* Forms can be known. This is certainly a puzzling claim; we have to consider both why Plato puts it forward and just what he means by it. In the *Republic*, it is linked with the claim that only Forms have unqualified "being". The argument (*Resp.* 476e ff.) is a very puzzling one. At the beginning, Socrates asserts that we can have knowledge only of what is, and indeed of what "completely is": things that are "between being and not being" can only be objects of true belief, which lies "between knowledge and ignorance". The opening claim would be plausible if "is" were taken to mean "exists"; it is not an unreasonable suggestion that we can have knowledge only of things that exist. (It is perhaps true that we can know *about*, say, Sherlock Holmes, who does not exist, but one would not normally speak simply of knowing Sherlock Holmes). This, however, raises problems with the idea of "being completely". This suggests there are degrees of being, and if "being" means "existence", this must mean degrees of existence: a puzzling idea. (Alternatively, "is" might mean "is true" or "is the case", in which case we have a reasonable claim that we can only know what is true, but the idea of degrees of truth is once again puzzling, and at any rate the way the passage then develops suggests we are discussing knowledge of things, not of facts.)

At the end of the argument, however, Socrates explains that the many objects of ordinary people's attention – by contrast with the Forms – are "between being and not being" in the sense that in one way they *are* large, heavy, beautiful and so on, and in another way they are not (*Resp.* 479a–b). For this reason they cannot be objects of knowledge, but only of true belief. It seems, therefore, that they are "between being and not being" in the sense of predicative being, the kind of being involved in being large or being beautiful, although one would not have guessed this from the way the topic is introduced at the beginning of the argument.

As I suggested in Chapter 3, it is possible that when Plato speaks of ordinary things lacking being he means that they lack reality, in the sense of really being the sort of thing that they claim to be: the way in which imitation pearls, or the Velveteen Rabbit, lack reality. However, one may wonder why this should mean that they cannot be objects of knowledge. Can we not have knowledge of velveteen rabbits? It is true that they would not be a good place to look if we were seeking knowledge of *rabbits* – live ones – and by the same token, it may be that sensible beautiful things are not a good source for knowledge of the Form, beauty itself. But it is not obvious that they cannot themselves be known. It may be, then, that Plato has made a false inference by slipping between the various possible senses of "being"; he has moved from the plausible claim that we cannot know what does not exist, or what is not true, to the less plausible claim that we cannot know what lacks "reality" in this distinctive sense.

In the *Timaeus*, we are again told that Forms are objects of knowledge, and sensible things only of perception and belief, but here this is linked with the claim that the sensible world is in change (*Ti.* 27d ff.). As I suggested in Chapter 3, this need not mean that, for Plato, the world is in such constant change that nothing stays the same long enough to be observed. Rather, his point is simply that everything is liable to change. The idea that we cannot have knowledge of things that are liable to change clearly implies an extremely high standard that something will have to meet in order to count as knowledge; but it is not completely implausible. Plato clearly sees knowledge as something that is itself secure, and cannot be shaken. But any belief based on things that change, one might think, is liable to be lost. A belief about *particular* changeable facts, based on observation – for example, that my desk is brown – will not remain true forever, and when it is no longer true, we will no longer be able to establish, by observation, that it used to be true. A *general* belief about the changeable – for example, that all swans are white – is always vulnerable to the possibility of an example turning up that falsifies it. Hence, we might argue, the only beliefs that are completely unshakeable, and so can count as knowledge, are beliefs about necessary truths, beliefs about what is unchanging, and these beliefs, of which mathematical beliefs are perhaps the clearest example, are gained by reasoning, not by perception. For Plato, they will be beliefs about the eternal natures of things, Forms.

Does Plato really want to restrict the scope of knowledge so radically? In a number of places, in order to illustrate some point about knowledge, he does refer to knowledge of mundane matters: in the *Meno* to knowing who Meno is (*Meno* 71b), or knowing the road to Larisa (97a); in the *Theaetetus* to knowing who committed a crime (*Tht.* 201a–c). It is possible to see him, in these passages, as using "know" in a more relaxed way, for something he does not think should count as knowledge in the strictest sense. However, it is clear at least that he is not proposing a general scepticism, a policy of radical doubt: he does think some beliefs about the sensible world are perfectly reasonable and well founded, or else he would not be able to describe them as knowledge even in a relaxed sense. Still, they do not have the complete security that our knowledge of Forms has.

Sometimes, this reading of Plato is objected to on the grounds that Plato clearly sees knowledge as having practical relevance, but our actions are concerned with things in the sensible world; if we have no knowledge of things in the sensible world, how can our knowledge guide our actions? (See e.g. Annas 1981: 214.) In fact, however, it seems that knowledge of abstract matters can be relevant to action. We can, for instance, know what justice is, and this will be relevant as we seek to act justly. It is true that we will not strictly speaking *know* the particular situations in which we try to act justly, but we can perceive and form beliefs about them, and then act in them in the light of what we do know. An example of this is found at *Republic* 501b–c, where the philosophers who rule the ideal state are shown looking alternately at the ideal – the Forms – and at the community that they are trying to mould as an image of the Forms. Their knowledge of the ideal guides what they do in the actual world.

In the *Meno*, Socrates claims that true belief is converted into knowledge by working out the explanation (*Meno* 98a); and Plato often uses a word for knowledge, *epistēmē*, which can also be translated "understanding". This may suggest that what Plato is really interested in is understanding, rather than simply knowledge or certainty, and it may seem more reasonable to restrict *understanding* to general truths, grasped by reason, than to restrict knowledge as such. With mathematical or logical truths, for instance, it is plausible that we come to grasp them by seeing *why* they are true, while for particular matters of fact this need not be the case. I might come to know that there is a dog in the next room by hearing it barking without having any idea of why it is there.

I think the kind of knowledge Plato has in mind is indeed one that involves understanding: that in coming to know Forms we come to see why they are as they are, not just that they are as they are. But this does not mean that *all* he is saying is that we do not have understanding of particular matters of fact. In the same passage of the *Meno* he claims that knowledge is "tied down", made secure, by explanation; explanation is important because it gives beliefs a stability they would not otherwise have. This is presumably because the kind of explanation he has in mind shows why these things *must* be true; and once we have seen that something must be true, there is no evidence that can count against it. There can, of course, be explanations of particular matters of fact, but they do not show in the same way that something must be true. For this reason our beliefs about the sensible world remain fallible.

Recollection: the *Meno*

One of the most striking claims about knowledge put forward in Plato's works is that we acquire it by remembering something we have learned, in a discarnate state, before we were born into our present life: this is commonly called the theory of recollection. Plato introduces this theory in a number of works, from rather different perspectives. Probably its first appearance is in the *Meno* (80d ff.). There, Socrates and Meno have been discussing the question "What is virtue?", and have found that they are completely stuck. Socrates insists that he is not deliberately trying to confuse Meno, but, just like him, does not know at all what virtue is. This prompts Meno to raise the famous paradox (sometimes called "Meno's paradox" or "the paradox of enquiry"): if you do not know at all what a thing is, how can you look for it, and how will you recognize it if you find it?

Clearly in some cases this is not a serious problem. Often the knowledge we need to understand a question, and see what evidence might be relevant to answering it, is quite different from the knowledge we need to give the answer; consider, for instance, the question "What was the date of the Battle of Bannockburn?" But with an abstract question such as "What is virtue?" there does seem to be more of a puzzle. While Socrates and Meno are unable to give a definition of virtue, they seem to have some awareness of what it is, which enables them to understand what they are searching for and to see what evidence might be relevant, but it is not clear how they would explain what they know about it, or how the knowledge that enables them to start the enquiry differs from the knowledge they are seeking.

Socrates, in answering this question, appeals to a religious tradition, according to which we have lived many lives, seen things here and things in Hades (i.e. the world of the dead), and so have learned everything. Having once known what virtue is, and so on, we are able to recover that knowledge. It is not made entirely clear how this helps to solve the paradox. How does the fact that we *once* knew something help us to enquire about it now, if we have lost the knowledge? The thought is presumably that while we no longer have explicit knowledge of what we once learned, we do have some kind of implicit awareness of it, which enables us to direct our search, to accept some claims about virtue and reject others when they are presented to us, and so to move towards an explicit account.

Socrates then gives a demonstration of this with a slave of Meno's, guiding him, by careful questioning, towards the solution of a geometrical problem. At the end the slave is able to give a correct answer to the problem, although at the beginning he did not know it. Socrates claims not to be "teaching" the slave, that is, actually telling him the right answers; rather, the slave is finding out the answers for himself. It is often felt that, in fact, Socrates is giving the slave too many clues, by leading questions, so that the slave could have reached the right answer just by following Socrates' suggestions. But it seems that what Socrates is trying to illustrate here is at least possible, although perhaps it really needs a longer demonstration than Plato has space for within the *Meno*. When asked the right questions we can see for ourselves that some answers are right, others wrong, although we did not know this before; we need guidance to make sure that we go in the right direction. But we do not accept the answers just because the teacher gives us them; we are working them out for ourselves. This seems to be true of both mathematical and philosophical learning. It contrasts with other areas such as history, where we do have to accept what people tell us.

Socrates claims that, within the dialogue, the slave has only achieved true belief about the answer to his problem, but that with more questioning he will be able to achieve knowledge (presumably because he will not only be able to give the right answer, but also explain why it is the right one). He will have found this knowledge within himself and, Socrates claims, recovering knowledge from within oneself is recollection (*Meno* 85d). Thus, the theory of recollection is established.

However, Socrates' argument here is questionable. It may be true that the slave is finding knowledge within himself in the sense that he is not actually acquiring it from anyone else, but this may mean not that it was actually present in him, but merely that he has a capacity to work things out for himself, to see how concepts are connected to one another, and so on. Alternatively, the knowledge may have been present in him in some sense, but not because he had actually learned it in the past or once known it consciously; he may just have innate, implicit knowledge. In this case it would be odd to describe what he was doing as "recollecting".

One puzzle that this argument raises is just what we are supposed to be remembering. Explicitly, we are told that we are remembering things that we have learned in previous lives. But it seems that the emphasis is on the discovery of abstract truths, including mathematical truths (which are what the demonstration with the slave focuses on) and philosophical truths such as the nature of virtue (which is the theme of the dialogue as a whole). It is knowledge of this kind, not knowledge of empirical matters, that we can reasonably be said to recover from within ourselves. But it seems implausible that we could have learned these truths by ordinary experiences in previous lives, here or in Hades, given that we do not learn them by experience in this life. The *Phaedo* is going to make it clear that what we are recollecting are Forms, and that we gained the original knowledge by contact with Forms while in a discarnate state. Although this is not explicit in the *Meno*, it is compatible with what is said there: the context is an enquiry into the question "What is virtue?", and virtue is described earlier in the dialogue as a Form (*Meno* 72c). So we can see Socrates and Meno as having had some knowledge of the Form of virtue before their birth.

Recollection: the *Phaedo*

In the *Phaedo* (73a ff.), Socrates discusses recollection again, but presents it in a rather different way. In the *Meno* recollection is prompted by questioning, and what it produces, when complete, is explicit knowledge, involving the ability to give an explanation. In the *Phaedo* it is prompted by perception, and (although this is controversial) it seems that what it enables us to do is to recognize examples of a Form, to acquire a general concept or see the one in the many. For instance, by looking at pairs of sticks that are equal (in length) to one another, we may acquire a concept of equality; and this, Socrates argues, means that we are remembering the Form of equality, which we knew before birth.

Socrates' argument is that when we see sticks or stones that are equal to one another, this makes us think of equality itself, and this means that we are being reminded of equality; this, in turn, implies that we have known it before. Why should we think that this is a case of being reminded? To begin with, Socrates argues simply that the equal sticks and stones are distinct from equality itself, and that when, perceiving one thing, we are made to think of something else, this is a case of being reminded. This, as a general claim, does not seem plausible; perceiving one thing might stimulate us to invent something new; for instance (in an example suggested by David Bostock [1986: 63]) James Watt, seeing steam coming out a kettle, was stimulated to come up with an improved design for a steam engine.

However, Socrates goes on to say not merely that equal sticks and stones are distinct from equality itself, but that they *fall short* of it (*Phd.* 74d), and that when we see them we recognize this. This seems a possible basis for a rather stronger argument for recollection. When, say, I see a picture of Socrates, and this not only makes me think of Socrates, but also question to what extent it is like him, this does imply that I already have some knowledge of Socrates and am being reminded of him; I could not judge that the picture fell short without some prior knowledge of what it falls short of.

What is meant by saying that sensible equal things fall short of the Form? As we saw in Chapter 3, this could mean either that their equality is *imperfect* – they are not, in fact, precisely equal, only approximately so – or that it is *qualified* – they are equal in one way but not in another (e.g. equal in length but not in thickness). In the case of equality both these ways of falling short may be in play. In the case of other Forms mentioned in this passage, one may be more relevant than the other: for instance, with largeness the point may be that things are large in a qualified way (since it does not makes sense to think of anything as perfectly large), but with justice the main point may be that people and societies are imperfectly just.

Although this point is never made wholly explicit, one can see Socrates as arguing that we cannot simply get our notion of equality from sensible equal things; our concept of equality cannot just be that of "what these sticks have". Rather, we bring a conception of equality to the sensible equal things, although we do not have that conception consciously until we encounter the sensible equals. This is why we can speak of the sensible equals reminding us of equality. This can be supported by reference either to imperfect possession of properties, or to qualified possession of them. If we recognize sensible things as approximating to, but falling short of, equality, we must already have some idea of what equality is. Likewise, if their equality is qualified we must already have some conception of equality, to distinguish the respect in which they are equal from the respect in which they are not.

It also seems (although here there is some dispute about the translation) that Socrates refers to the possibility of disagreement about whether two sensible things are equal (*Phd.* 74b). This can be seen as supporting the same point; we cannot be getting our conception of equality just from the sticks if we disagree about whether the sticks are equal, but agree on what equality is, and can distinguish it from its opposite.

All these points tend to support the view that our concept of equality is not derived just from perception of its instances; rather, we already have that concept, and bring it to perception. However, once again, it does not follow that we acquired it by some past experience, before birth. Socrates, in drawing this conclusion, is going beyond what his argument warrants. It might be innate in us, or we might have acquired it by some unconscious process during this life.

Recollection: the *Phaedrus*

A third dialogue in which recollection features is the *Phaedrus*. Once again, as in the *Phaedo*, it is made clear that the objects of recollection are Forms. However, it introduces some interesting new ideas concerning the question what recollection enables us to do.

Recollection in the *Phaedrus* seems to have two aspects. On the one hand, we are told that a soul cannot be incarnated as a human being (as opposed to a lower animal) unless it has, before birth, a vision of the Forms, since human beings have to "understand the language of Forms, proceeding from a multitude of perceptions to a unity gathered together by reasoning" (*Phdr.* 249b–c). This seems, as in the *Phaedo*, to refer to an ability that all human beings exercise (although this has been disputed). But about just what ability this is, Plato's language is ambiguous. It could refer, once again, to seeing the one in the many, forming a general concept. We have many individual perceptions of trees, and we come to see them all as belonging to a single *kind*, but we could not do this unless we had some inner, unspoken, awareness of the Form. But it could also refer to the way we become aware of even one tree: from many individual acts of perception we come to see it as a single unified *thing*. Plato may here be suggesting that we could not do this unless we had an inner awareness of the kind of thing it is.

However, the principal use that the *Phaedrus* makes of recollection is different. The theme of the central speech in the *Phaedrus* is the praise of love, and in it Socrates describes the experience of falling in love: the result produced in us by the vision of beauty (*Phdr.* 251a ff.). He says that when we see a beautiful person this reminds us of the Form of beauty, which we perceived before our birth, and wakens in us a desire to regain that heavenly vision; the metaphorical wings of our soul, lost at birth, begin to grow again. What is distinctive of this account of recollection is that in it we recollect the experience; we are not just enabled to give an account of Forms, or to recognize instances of Forms, but rather we remember what it was *like* to contemplate the Forms, and so we are moved to want to recapture that experience. This gives recollection a mystical aspect that it does not have in other places where it occurs. Beauty plays a special role here because its instances – unlike the instances of other central Forms such as goodness and justice – are visible; but once visible beauty has stimulated our desire for the vision of the Forms, we can pursue the other Forms as well. Hence, beauty plays a central role in moving us to philosophy.

The significance of recollection

One important question that arises in connection with recollection is how widespread it is. On a traditional view, which I have followed, in the *Phaedo* and the *Phaedrus* it is very widespread indeed, being something we all do whenever we deploy concepts. In the *Meno*, however, it is more restricted, and happens only when we engage in a conscious process of learning. The kind of learning in which the slave is shown engaging is indeed very common; many of us must have experienced recollection while studying mathematics. But it is plausible that recollection of things such as the nature of virtue is much less common, and indeed is confined to philosophers. In the light of this it has been suggested (see Scott 1987, 2003: chs 1–2) that the *Phaedo* and *Phaedrus* too should be interpreted so as to make recollection more restricted, and that they refer not to the acquisition of concepts, but to the achievement of conscious knowledge of Forms.

It is true that in the *Meno* the name "recollection" is restricted to what happens at the end of the process, the actual achievement of conscious knowledge, but our implicit awareness of the nature of virtue and similar matters seems to be at work before that. It is what enables us, first to ask the question "What is virtue?", then to see what evidence might be relevant to the answer. Socrates does not suggest that the search for an answer should begin by ignoring our ordinary beliefs about virtue. On the contrary, he makes use of such beliefs, both general beliefs such as "virtue is beneficial" (*Meno* 87e), and beliefs about examples, such as that justice and temperance are virtues (73d–4a). Indeed, until we achieve knowledge of what virtue is, such beliefs must be provisional (this will be discussed later in the chapter, when we look at the method of hypothesis), but they cannot be abandoned entirely; they do guide us in our search, and it is by reflection on them that we are led to the truth. This makes most sense if they are themselves derived from our prenatal awareness of the Forms, which is present, although only in an implicit way, when we begin to form the concept of virtue.

In the light of this, it is not implausible that in the *Phaedo* recollection is seen as being involved in the actual formation of concepts. This is not inconsistent with the account given in the *Meno*; it may be that we have a latent knowledge of Forms, acquired before birth, that enables us first to recognize examples, then, when stimulated by questions, to move towards a more articulate account. But if that is right, "recollection" is being used in the two dialogues as a name for different stages in the process (see Crombie 1962–3: vol. II, 143–4). In the *Phaedrus*, "recollection" refers both to the formation of concepts, and to the process, stimulated by the vision of beauty, that brings us to conscious knowledge of the Forms.

The claim that all of us have some implicit awareness of the Forms, and manifest this in our daily life, might be taken to support the view that all are capable of philosophy, as Socrates in the Socratic dialogues seems to have believed. However, I am not sure how close the connection between these views in fact is. Certainly the *Phaedrus*, although it insists that all human beings must have had the prenatal vision of Forms, still implies that only some are capable of philosophy, which suggests that even if we all have latent knowledge of Forms, some extra capacity is needed to make this knowledge explicit.

A second significant question about recollection is how important it is to the theory of Forms. In the *Phaedo*, they are clearly presented as inseparable (*Phd.* 77a); Socrates claims that the existence of Forms stands or falls with the existence of the soul before birth, apparently because it implies recollection. However, it is not obvious that they must be connected so closely. The theory of recollection seems to have two aspects. First, our knowledge of Forms in some sense comes from inside us; we do not gain it straightforwardly from perception, or from a teacher, although both perception and teaching may stimulate us to achieve active knowledge. Secondly, this knowledge was acquired by an experience in a discarnate state before birth, and is now being remembered. The first element seems essential to Plato's thought, but the second is less so; might we not simply have an innate capacity to grasp the nature of Forms when appropriately stimulated?

Plato's doctrine of recollection has often been compared to the modern concept of *a priori* knowledge: knowledge which is gained by reasoning rather than by experience. In a way this seems right; he is pointing to a kind of knowledge that does not depend simply on sense-experience. But he may nevertheless be making it too like empirical knowledge if he thinks it was gained by an experience before birth; he writes as if we must actually have met the Forms to have knowledge of them, and this must have happened before birth, since we clearly do not directly perceive them in this life. But if our knowledge of the Forms rests on an intellectual grasp, not a literal seeing, it ought to be possible to gain that knowledge in this life as well.

It is, in fact, possible that Plato moved away from the doctrine of recollection. In two dialogues, the *Republic* and *Timaeus*, we are given accounts of the afterlife that do not include the vision of Forms that is needed for recollection. What is more, the *Republic* urges us to pursue wisdom in *this* life in order to be able to make correct choices in the afterlife (*Resp.* 619d–e) and the *Timaeus* gives an account of the origin of the soul that points to a different explanation of our capacity to know Forms; the soul is made by God in such a way that its nature is similar to that of Forms, and so is able to know them on the principle that like knows like (*Ti.* 35a ff.). It seems, then, that recollection is not essential to the theory of Forms, and we should not assume that Plato believed in it throughout his career.

Philosophical enquiry

Our last topic in this chapter is the nature of philosophical enquiry. How does Plato think we should go about it?

This question is addressed most fully in Book 6 of the *Republic*, in the passage that introduces the famous simile of the divided line (*Resp.* 509d–11e). The passage is complex, and seems to be making many points at once, but its principal aim is to introduce a view of philosophical method, and in particular the difference between philosophical and mathematical enquiry. Socrates asks us to imagine a line, apparently vertical, divided into two unequal parts, each of which is then subdivided in the same ratio as the whole. Thus, when the division is completed, the line will have four sections.

When the line is first introduced we are told that the different sections represent different kinds of object: the two sections making up the lower line represent the realm of visible things – ordinary sensible objects – while the two sections making up the upper line represent intelligible things, a class that at least includes Forms. Of the two sections that make up the lower line, the lowest represents images, such as shadows and reflections, in the visible world and the other represents concrete objects, such as animals, plants and manufactured things. However, when we reach the two sections of the upper line, we are not told that they represent different objects; rather, they seem to represent two kinds of enquiry, the lower of the two sections standing for the kind of enquiry typical of mathematics, while the other, the highest section of the line, stands for that typical of philosophy or dialectic.

It is odd that while in the lower line we are introduced to two kinds of object, in the upper line we are told only of two kinds of enquiry. Many readers of the passage have supposed that the two sections of the upper line should indeed be seen as standing for different kinds of object, with which the two kinds of enquiry are concerned: dialectic will be concerned with Forms, mathematics with some other kind of object. There is evidence from Aristotle that Plato did at some point in his career believe in special objects with which mathematics deals (Ar. *Metaph.* A 987b14–18). However, here

Socrates seems to say that mathematical reasoning *is* concerned with Forms: "the square itself and the diagonal itself" (*Resp.* 510d–e). The intended correspondence between parts of the line should be seen as relating not so much to objects as to states of awareness: mathematical reasoning is related to dialectical reasoning in the same way that perception of images is related to perception of concrete things. The underlying thought seems to be that while mathematicians are thinking about Forms they are doing so indirectly, just as someone looking at a reflection of trees in water is perceiving the trees but indirectly. Mathematicians do not have the direct grasp of Forms that philosophers have, and which is implied by the term "knowledge".

Why is mathematicians' grasp of Forms inadequate? Socrates gives two reasons. One is simple: they use visible diagrams. Although they are indeed thinking of "the square itself", not of the particular square that they have drawn (since they intend their conclusions to be universal), they cannot grasp the Form by pure thought, as it should be grasped, but need to rely on visible diagrams to get a clear idea of it.

The other difference between mathematicians and philosophers is more obscure; it is that mathematicians rely on hypotheses. This means that they have concepts associated with certain basic mathematical terms – the odd and the even, kinds of shape or of angle – of which they cannot "give an account"; this may mean both that they cannot explain further what these concepts amount to – that they cannot give a definition of them – and that they cannot give reasons why these concepts are correct. Later, Socrates is to compare the state of mind of someone who cannot give an account of some term with dreaming (*Resp.* 533b), and he thinks of dreaming as mistaking an image for the reality (476c). The mathematicians have in their minds a conception – an image, in an extended sense – of what, for instance, a square is, and because they take this conception for granted and cannot explain or justify it, they do not have a real grasp of the Form of square, even though that is in some sense what they are thinking about. Hence, once again, their state of mind is like that of someone looking at shadows or reflections rather than concrete things.

How, then, is the philosopher to move beyond this state of mind, and come to know Forms as they are? To answer this we must look more closely at Plato's use of the concept of hypothesis, which he has already introduced in earlier works.

The method of hypothesis

In two places, in the *Meno* (86e ff.) and *Phaedo* (100a ff.), Socrates recommends a method of enquiry – derived from mathematics – that starts from hypotheses. By this he seems here to mean statements that are plausible, so that it is reasonable to accept them as a starting-point for enquiry, even though they are not *known* to be true. If enquiry had to start with something that we knew for certain, it is not clear that it could ever get off the ground. Thus in the *Meno* Socrates implies that we cannot know whether virtue has any particular quality – specifically, whether it is teachable, the official topic of discussion in the dialogue – unless we first know what it is (*Meno* 71a). But how can we discover what it is without making reference to its qualities? The concept of hypothesis allows us to break this circle; starting from a plausible claim about its nature we can make inferences about its qualities, even without knowledge. There is some dispute about just how Socrates is using the term "hypothesis" in this passage, but on what seems the most plausible reading he adopts the hypothesis that virtue is knowledge, and infers from that that it is indeed teachable; the claim that virtue is knowledge is itself supported by reference to a further hypothesis, that virtue is good (i.e. advantageous). Likewise in the *Phaedo* the existence of Forms is taken as a hypothesis, and used as a basis for arguing to an account of the explanation of becoming and perishing, and finally to the immortality of the soul.

A hypothesis is not, on this account, primarily a claim put forward to be tested; it is something that the participants in a discussion find plausible and are therefore able to use as a basis for further discussion. But, since hypotheses are not *known* to be true, they *may* be challenged. In fact, in the *Meno* the hypothesis that Socrates and

Meno first agree on, that virtue is knowledge, is later challenged (*Meno* 89d ff.); in the *Phaedo* the actual hypothesis used is not challenged, but the possibility is explicitly mentioned (*Phd.* 101d). If this happens, we may either abandon the hypothesis, or find some more basic claim, on which agreement can be reached, on whose basis it can be defended.

However, this form of reasoning is widely seen as unsatisfactory; even if we do in fact manage to achieve agreement, the method will only expand our stock of plausible beliefs; it will not give us knowledge, since if the starting-points of reasoning are not known, what is derived from them will not be known either.

Hypothesis in the *Republic*

In the *Republic*, as we have seen, Socrates criticizes mathematicians for using hypotheses as starting-points and failing to give an account (*logos*) of them (*Resp.* 510c ff.). It is not wholly clear that the kind of hypotheses he is discussing here are the same as those discussed in earlier works, for in them hypotheses were propositions, while here he refers to mathematicians as hypothesizing things: the odd and the even, figures and kinds of angles. Yet it seems plausible that when Socrates speaks of mathematicians hypothesizing these things he means, at least in part, that they assume the truth of some claim about them: either that they exist, or an account of their nature. In this way the account of hypotheses here will harmonize with that found in earlier works. In saying that they fail to give an account of the things they hypothesize, he may mean that they fail to give either a proof, or an explanation of why these things should be so, but for Plato these two ideas will be closely linked, if he thinks, as is suggested in the *Meno*, that we attain knowledge of something by working out the explanation. It may well be that Socrates also means that mathematicians cannot clearly state what they mean by these central terms. If this is right then any belief they hold about what the square and so on are will be held only implicitly. But it seems that we should see them as holding some belief about the nature of these things, which might be true or false, but which lacks justification.

The problem with the mathematicians is not that they use hypotheses, but that they see no need for anything further; they fail to recognize that a method that starts from hypotheses, giving no proof or explanation of them, cannot give us knowledge. By contrast the method of dialectic, which Socrates recommends, seeks for a more secure starting-point on the basis of which our hypotheses can be established (*Resp.* 511b ff.). No doubt some hypotheses will be rejected in the course of this enquiry; others may remain but, having been established on a firmer basis, will no longer be hypothetical.

As we have seen, the *Meno* and *Phaedo* accepted that hypotheses would sometimes be challenged, and would then need to be grounded on a firmer basis. In the *Republic*, however, this is not treated just as something that may happen occasionally in the course of discussion, but as an essential part of philosophical method; a philosopher should not remain content with hypotheses but should seek for a further ground on which they can be established. What is more, this process will end not simply with another hypothesis with which our partners in discussion will agree, but with an "unhypothetical starting-point": something that is not merely hypothesized, but known, and so is able to serve as a ground for further knowledge. It seems, moreover, that there is a *single* first principle that is able to serve as the starting-point for *all* knowledge.

How is this search for a first principle meant to work? It seems likely that the process is gradual; we do not look, at once, for a first principle that will ground all our beliefs, but rather move by stages towards it, first finding propositions that will support our initial hypotheses, then propositions that will support them, and so on. But what motivates our acceptance of a proposition? If we are right in thinking that a foundational claim gives the explanation of what follows from it, this will help to structure our search; we will look for propositions with explanatory power. If, moreover, the ultimate end of our search is a single first principle for all branches of knowledge, it is likely that as we progress towards it we will find more general claims that enable us to unify various areas of enquiry. Indeed, later in the *Republic* Socrates says that the dialectician is someone able to take a synoptic view (*Resp.* 537c). The first principle, when we discover it, will be a claim of great explanatory power over a wide range of branches of knowledge.

This, however, is not to say that our acceptance of the first principle is grounded simply in its explanatory power. Since the claims we are setting out to explain are not initially known, it is not clear that we could come to know a principle just through its power to explain them; it seems possible that there might be different systems of propositions, each coherent and each containing a first principle that explains the others, but only one of them can be right. It is likely that Plato sees the first principle as something that, although it is hard to discover, once we have found it will be self-evident; something that, once it is understood, cannot be rejected.

The distinctive feature of this account of philosophical enquiry is the twofold process that it envisages; first the way up, moving from our accepted beliefs to the first principle; then the way down, returning from the first principle to more specific areas of enquiry, of which, in the light of the principle, we can now gain knowledge. (While I have written, in line with the usual way of thinking today, of the first principle as a foundation and as grounding other claims, Plato actually sees it as "higher" than other claims, which are envisaged as hanging from it, and this metaphor guides the way he describes the process of enquiry.) On the way down we will be going again over material we had already traversed on the search for the first principle, but now with knowledge, not just provisionally; knowledge of the first principle may also enable us to make new discoveries. This twofold process was clearly important to Plato; Aristotle tells us that he often used to ask his pupils to clarify whether they were moving to or from first principles (Ar. *Eth. Nic.* 1095a30–b1).

This allows us to begin our enquiry with common beliefs, but not to accept them uncritically; the starting-points for enquiry are not the same as the starting-points for demonstrative reasoning. It differs, therefore, from the traditional understanding of foundationalist views, which require us to begin our enquiries with things that are indubitable; these are often identified with facts known through perception. Nevertheless, Plato's view does posit a foundation; it does not suggest that beliefs are validated simply by the way they hang together. But for Plato the foundation – since it is the starting-point not for enquiry, but only for demonstration – may be something quite abstract, the discovery of which requires much thought. A similar view is found in Aristotle, who distinguished between "things better known to us", which are the starting-points of enquiry, and "things better known in themselves", which are harder to find but, when found, can serve as a foundation for knowledge (Ar. *An. post.* 71b33–72a5). But for Aristotle there are different principles for the different sciences, and a number of principles in each of them; for Plato there is just one first principle for all the sciences.

A real-life analogy for the kind of structure that Plato has in mind may be provided by the axiomatic geometry that was worked out, a couple of generations after his time, by Euclid. Euclid starts with a small number of postulates from which he derives the various theorems of geometry; but of course he did not actually begin his enquiry with these postulates; rather, already being aware of various geometric proofs, he searched for the axiomatic structure that would enable them to be brought into the simplest and most coherent system. But while the structure here is similar to what Plato had in mind, he would not have accepted Euclid's postulates as first principles, but would have insisted on the search for a more fundamental principle that would explain them.

Knowledge and the good

One question remains; what is the unhypothetical first principle? We are never told in so many words, but the context strongly suggests that it is the Form of the good or perhaps, strictly, a statement of the nature of that Form. Immediately before the image of the divided line, in which Socrates contrasts mathematicians with philosophers, he introduced the image of the sun, in which the Form of the good is presented as the source of knowledge and reality (*Resp.* 507a ff.). Socrates says that as the sun both promotes the generation and growth of sensible things and enables us to see them, so the good is responsible both for the being or reality of Forms, and for our knowledge of them. The dialectical method is concerned with Forms, so it is reasonable to see the good, which gives us our knowledge of Forms, as the first principle in that method.

However, the claim that both the reality of Forms and our knowledge of them derive from the good is clearly an obscure one, and Socrates says little to make it clearer. Indeed, it is reasonable to see the two claims as going together; if the Forms are what they are because of the good, it is plausible that knowledge of the nature of the good will enable us to understand the other Forms as well. But how, exactly, can it be responsible for their reality?

In the *Phaedo*, Socrates refers to the view that things are as they are because it is best that they be so. He thinks that if this could be shown, it would be the basis of a good explanation of things, although he does not think that any explanation of this kind has in fact been achieved (*Phd.* 97d ff.). Might Plato be thinking along the same lines in the *Republic*, now applying this thought not to sensible things but to Forms?

Perhaps Plato is suggesting that Forms exist, and have the nature they have, because it is best that they should do so. In this way they could be said to owe their reality to the good, and we could gain knowledge of them by understanding what is good. Socrates does indeed describe the system of Forms, at *Republic* 500c, as ordered and divine, free from injustice and so on, so he does seem to see it as in some sense good. Alternatively one might also suppose that instances of the Forms are good; justice, for example, is a Form, and it is good that instances of justice, just souls and communities, exist in the world. One might, therefore, explain what justice is not by reference to the way in which the existence of the Form itself is good, but rather to the way in which its instances are good. Or one could combine these two lines of thought, suggesting that the way the Forms themselves are ordered is good, but also that things are good to the extent that they instantiate the Forms, and that both these relations to the good may be involved in explaining the nature of a Form.

Working out what this would amount to in detail is still problematic. It is true that for some Forms in which Plato believes, a connection with the good is reasonably clear. These include the moral or more generally evaluative Forms, for example justice and beauty; we can see justice as either a kind of goodness or a state of character that promotes the good, so we can come to grasp its nature through understanding the good.

With other Forms the link may be through teleology, the idea that things exist for a purpose: we come to grasp the nature of things by grasping the purpose that they serve, how they promote the good. This applies most straightforwardly to artefact Forms such as that of bed. But if we believe, as Plato did, that natural things – for instance the elements, or kinds of animal – are in the world for a purpose, it can also apply to them. This, however, leaves unexplained other Forms that Plato certainly recognized. These include the mathematical Forms, and also the extremely general ones such as being, sameness and difference.

Can Plato have thought that these Forms are in some sense good? Certainly some have felt that beauty or appropriateness is to be found in mathematical systems, and Plato may well have shared this attitude. He does, for instance, refer to the sphere as the most perfect of shapes (*Ti.* 33b), and he thinks that certain numbers stand in relations of harmony with one another, independently of the sounds they produce when applied to strings of the lyre (*Resp.* 531e). We may find this implausible. We may hold that if the relations between mathematical concepts are logically necessary, goodness cannot be relevant to them. But Plato may not have shared this attitude.

One other possibility deserves mention: that the good should be connected, not with each individual Form, but with the harmonious *system* of Forms. Some have even suggested that the good *is* that system, but it may be more plausible to see it as a property that the system possesses, although other things may possess it as well. Certainly Plato's language at *Republic* 500 implies that the system of Forms, as a whole, is something good, something harmonious. It can be seen as fitting together somewhat in the way that we might describe a beautiful or elegant mathematical or scientific theory as doing. In this case, we may suppose that to understand the nature of each Form we must understand how it fits into the system, and to understand how the system fits together we need to know the nature of the good that it instantiates. In this case not all individual Forms need be seen as contributing to the good as such; it is as part of a system that they do so. One advantage of this view is that it explains how, despite linking Forms with the good, Plato occasionally refers to Forms of bad things such as injustice (e.g. *Resp.* 476a). We can say not that injustice itself contributes to the good, but that it is good that there is a system of classification in which things such as injustice have their place.

These are just a few attempts to explain something about which Plato's words are, as he recognizes, extremely cryptic. What is clear is that he places the good at the centre not only of his ethics, but of his metaphysics and epistemology. For him, therefore, philosophy cannot be divided; the most abstract metaphysical studies are relevant to the way we govern our lives and the state.

The image of the cave

Before we leave this section of the *Republic*, we should look at the third important image that is introduced here, in one of the most famous passages in Plato: that of the prisoners in the cave (*Resp.* 514a–17a). The passage goes over much of the same ground as the images of sun and line, in a more graphic form, but it also introduces some significant new points about the practical consequences of the theory outlined there.

Socrates first asks us to imagine a group of prisoners in a cave, chained in such a way that they cannot turn, and can see only the wall of the cave in front of them. Behind them is a fire; between them and the fire are people carrying statues, the people hidden behind a wall, while the statues protrude above it. The prisoners can see only the shadows cast by the statues, in the light of the fire, on the wall in front of them. The people carrying the statues sometimes speak, and the prisoners hear the echo of their voices from the wall. Since the prisoners have no knowledge of what is behind them, they think that the shadows on the wall are real people and things, and that the noises coming from the wall are their voices.

Socrates next describes one of the prisoners being freed, and turned around to face the fire, so that he sees the actual statues; such a person would be dazzled by the light of the fire and would have difficulty adapting to this new way of seeing things. If he then were led out of the cave into the sunlight, he would have even more difficulty adjusting, and would at first not be able to look at real things in the world outside, but would have to start by looking at shadows and reflections. Later, however, he would be able to look at real things in the outside world, and in due course would look at heavenly bodies, and last of all at the sun.

Finally, we are asked to imagine such a person returning to the cave, in the hope of liberating the prisoners who still live there. Whereas at first he had difficulty adjusting to the light, he would now find it equally difficult to adjust to the darkness. As a result, those in the cave will think that his eyesight has been ruined; they will not want to leave the cave, and if he tries to liberate them they will kill him.

This story is often seen as expressing Plato's theory of the sensible world, according to which everything we perceive is an illusion, like the shadows on the walls of the cave. But in context it seems that Plato's aim in introducing this story is epistemological and political, not metaphysical; in the initial description of the prisoners he is describing a particular state of mind and society, not the sensible world as such. It is true that Socrates says that the cave represents the world revealed by sight, and the fire within the cave the sun. But even within the cave it is possible to turn towards the fire and see solid objects; although the things we see in the sensible world are images of something further, the Forms, this does not mean that they are illusory. As for the escape from the cave, it does not mean a literal escape from the sensible world. It is something we can achieve in this life, while still literally living among sensible things: it is a change of the focus of our attention, from the visible to the intelligible.

If the story is read in this way, some parts of it are quite easy to interpret (see *Resp.* 517b ff.). Those in the cave are those whose minds are concerned wholly with the sensible world; the escape from the cave represents the turn from these concerns to intelligible realities. The person who, on first emerging from the cave, looks at shadows and reflections in the outside world, represents the mathematician, whose awareness of Forms is indirect. Socrates is about to go on to recommend mathematics as a preparation for philosophy, and in particular as a way of turning our attention away from the senses (521c ff.). The person looking at real objects in the outside world represents the philosopher contemplating Forms, while the vision of the sun represents the contemplation of the Form of the good.

What is harder to interpret is the distinction of levels within the cave. There are two different situations within the cave; that of the prisoners, who see only shadows, and that of those who have turned towards the fire, who can see the actual objects of which they are shadows. If we insist on a precise correspondence between this image and that of the line, it seems that the first should represent looking at (literal) shadows and reflections in the sensible world, the second looking at concrete objects. Yet this is hardly plausible; the prisoners are described as "like us" (515a) but we do not spend our lives looking at literal shadows and reflections. The condition of the prisoners is clearly meant to represent something philosophically significant; and the shadows they look at are said at one point to include "shadows of justice" (*Resp.* 517d), showing that literal shadows cannot be all that is meant.

It seems that Plato wants to distinguish, among those who are concerned wholly with the sensible world, between two groups: those whose lives are governed by illusions, and those who have some reasonably reliable true beliefs (perhaps because they are guided by philosophers). The second group, perhaps, although they have no real understanding of the nature of justice, might generally be able to recognize examples of it, while the first cannot get beyond appearances, supposing, for instance, that people are just if they are rich and so able to repay debts.[2] It is reasonable that Plato should want to make this distinction, since it seems that, by the time he wrote the *Republic*, he did not think that everyone was capable of philosophy, yet he does not seem to have thought that most people were condemned to a life of radical illusion. But if he is drawing the distinction in this way, he nowhere makes it explicit, so the image remains hard for us to interpret.

At one point it seems that the cave represents a corrupt state, such as Plato thought existed in his time. When the philosopher, returning to the cave to liberate its inhabitants, is put to death, this clearly recalls what happened to Socrates at Athens. Later, however, we are told that even in the ideal state the cave is still present: when philosophers in that state are required to leave the life of contemplation to take part in government, they are described as returning to the cave (*Resp.* 519d). Here the cave seems simply to be the world of practical concerns. Perhaps we can associate the two levels in the cave with these two aspects of it: the prisoners described at the beginning are the deluded inhabitants of a corrupt state; those who have been freed but are still within the cave are like the lower classes in Plato's ideal state, and have reached the highest level of which ordinary people, without intellectual interests, are capable.

Two morals in particular emerge from the story of the cave. One we have already seen: while it is hard for the person who has been brought up thinking of mundane matters to adjust to abstract thought, it is equally hard for the person devoted to abstract thought to adjust to the mundane again. This is why philosophers are often failures at practical politics (see *Resp.* 517d ff.). They have difficulty applying their knowledge, at least at first, until they have become used to mundane affairs; but it does not follow that their knowledge is not relevant to practical matters.

The other moral is that a conversion is necessary if we are to gain knowledge of the intelligible realm. The prisoners must be turned round and led up to the outer world before they can perceive the things there, and in particular the sun; in the same way the soul must be turned towards the intelligible realm and especially the good (see *Resp.* 518b ff.). Socrates says that education is not putting knowledge into the soul. In context, the point is not to deny that it is putting *information* into the soul (although Plato would indeed reject this) but to deny that it is putting the power of knowledge into the soul. One cannot put the power of sight into the eye, but one can turn the eye to the light. In the same way we already have the power of knowledge, but we must be turned towards the good. But, Socrates goes on, the eye cannot be turned unless the whole body is turned, and in the same way the intellect cannot be turned unless the whole soul is turned. We must be motivated to pursue truth, and only if we have the right motives shall we discover it.

FIVE

The soul

Plato's conception of the soul

The Greek word that is commonly translated "soul", *psuchē*, means the principle of life in a living thing. It does not necessarily imply dualism: the view that the soul is something distinct from and independent of the body. Nevertheless, Plato's conception of the soul *was* dualist; he regularly distinguishes and opposes soul and body. This seems to have been quite normal in his time. Even philosophers whose general view of the world was materialistic often thought of the soul as a special kind of body, rather than a state or aspect of ordinary bodies. Plato's Socrates does at one point, in the *Phaedo* (85e–6d), discuss a theory that is closer to materialism in a modern sense, according to which the soul is the "harmony" of the body, the way in which the constituent elements in it are combined, but this theory is quite swiftly rejected (91c ff.). Most of the time dualism is taken for granted. However, Plato does not see dualism as immediately implying that the soul is immortal. This is a further claim that for him needs argument.

Plato's position on what functions and capacities belong to the soul varies from one work to another. In the *Phaedo* he assigns only rational activities to the soul; perception, irrational desire and even belief belong to the body, and for this reason there can be a conflict between soul and body (94b). This is one of his reasons for rejecting the claim that the soul is the harmony of the body. In other works, however, including the *Phaedrus*, *Republic*, *Timaeus* and *Laws*, this view is abandoned; the soul also includes non-rational elements, in particular the elements of spirit (anger, daring and ambition) and appetite (bodily desire – that is, desire for things connected with the body) (*Phdr.* 246a ff.; *Resp.* 435e ff.; *Ti.* 69c ff.; *Leg.* 896e–7a). In some dialogues these elements still arise in some way from the body, either being derived from it, as in the *Republic* (611b ff.), or being created by the gods, but in order to cope with bodily needs, as in the *Timaeus* (69c–d). Elsewhere, however, most clearly in the *Phaedrus*, they seem to exist independently of the body.[1]

In any case, the capacities that Plato assigns to the soul are in general ones that we would now class as mental: thinking, perceiving, feeling, desiring and so on. He does not, like Aristotle, think of biological functions such as breathing and digestion as belonging to the soul.

In what follows, I shall look in more detail at three aspects of Plato's view of the soul: his definition of the soul as a motion that moves itself; his belief in immortality; and his conception of the soul as divided into three parts, reason, spirit and appetite.

Self-motion

In two places in Plato's work, in the *Phaedrus* (245e) and in the *Laws* (895e–6a), a definition of soul is offered; it is a motion that moves itself.[2] Given that Plato is generally reluctant to commit himself to definitions, the fact that he returns to this one is quite striking. In the *Phaedrus* the definition is used in an argument for immortality, and in the *Laws* in an argument for the existence of gods, and it is most often discussed in the context of these arguments. Yet it seems to have a wider relevance. In both places the idea of soul as self-motion is accepted as if it were already well established, suggesting that it formed a fairly stable part of Plato's view of the soul; it is only the specific uses to which it is put that are presented as new. (This, of course, does not mean that Plato held it throughout his career; it is not clear, for instance, if it can be reconciled with the view of the soul adopted in the *Phaedo*, where its unchanging nature is emphasized.) In addition, Plato makes use of the concept of self-motion in the *Timaeus*, although it is not there presented as a definition (*Ti.* 37b, 46d–e, 77b–c, 88e–9a); there it is linked with rationality, giving it a wider relevance in Plato's thought.

In adopting this definition of soul, Plato seems to be making use of a widespread view in ancient Greece that it is characteristic of living things to move themselves; it is notable that in the *Laws* this information is volunteered by Cleinias, the (not particularly philosophical) respondent, not by the Athenian Stranger, the chief speaker in that dialogue (*Leg.* 895c), although it is the Athenian who argues that this can be seen as a definition. Moreover, both Cleinias and the Athenian agree that we *see* that living creatures move themselves; it is because we see a thing being moved from within that we recognize it as alive. However, for Plato, as a dualist, it is strictly speaking the *soul* that moves itself; it then sets the body in motion, so that living bodies can be described as moved from within, but not, properly, as moving themselves. (However the living thing as a whole, body and soul, can be described as moving itself.)

The term translated "motion" (*kinēsis*) can be applied to change more generally, although Plato does seem to think of motion in space as in some way primary; it is the fact that living things originate their own spatial motions that makes it plausible to call them self-movers. Plato does sometimes use language that implies that the soul has a position in space and performs spatial motions, but even if we do not accept the spatial conception of the soul, it is possible to think of it as moving itself as it performs its mental functions of thinking, feeling and so on.

What precisely does Plato mean by the claim that the soul moves itself? What feature of soul or of living things is this meant to capture? On one view, soul for him is something like energy or motive force: the power of moving without being pushed. However, this seems too weak to express what Plato means. Many things that are not alive at least seem to move without being pushed – rising flames and falling stones, rivers moving towards the sea, or magnets – but Plato does not ascribe soul to them. (He does ascribe it to the stars, but this, I shall argue, is not merely meant to bear witness to the fact that they move without being pushed, but rather to account for the apparent rationality of their motions.) Hence, when we recognize living things as moved from within, we cannot simply be recognizing that nothing pushes them.

While this view of self-motion is too weak, there is another that, I suggest, is too strong. On this view something is not self-moved if its motion is in any way dependent on anything beyond itself; hence what is self-moved must be ungenerated. Once again, how-ever, this does not seem to harmonize with the claim that we recog-nize things as living when we see them being moved from within. We certainly do not see the ungenerated status of soul, and indeed *prima facie* the soul or principle of life in a living thing *is* generated, by its parents. It is true that – since the soul is not just something that happens to move, but something that is essentially in motion – what generates it can be seen as setting it in motion, so that if it is generated it is in one respect moved from without. But it seems possible that it should be moved from without in one respect but move itself in another, if it sustains itself in motion, so self-motion need not imply being ungenerated.

What, then, is central to the concept of self-motion? I suggest that the core of the concept is the power that animals have to *control* their own movements, to take initiative, by contrast with lifeless bodies, which simply move as they are caused to move by external forces. This is indeed a feature that we can recognize in animals and that distinguishes them from other things. Self-motion, so understood, will imply at least some rudimentary directedness or purposiveness, although it will not by itself imply rationality or choice in the full sense.

For Plato, of course, it will not strictly speaking be the visible movements of the animal that are examples of self-motion, but the inner movements of its soul, which cause the visible movements; but the fact that animals control their own movements can be seen as giving evidence of the self-motion of soul.

The significance of self-motion

What follows from Plato's conception of the soul as something that moves itself? First, it is essentially something active; its primary function is that of a source of motivation, and its other activities, thinking, perceiving and so on, are significant largely because of the contribution they make to motivation. When Plato divides the soul into parts, this is done on the basis of the different motivations it can have. Secondly, the operation of the soul is never purely mechanical. External things do indeed move us to action, but they do so in virtue of the way we think of them or perceive them. We are responding to them, rather than just being caused to act by them.

As we have seen, Plato's speakers draw specific consequences from the definition of the soul as self-motion in a number of places. We shall consider the *Phaedrus* later in this chapter, and the *Laws* in Chapter 8, when we consider Plato's cosmology. Here we shall look briefly at the use made of the concept in the *Timaeus*. In that work, at several points, the idea of self-motion is linked with that of reason. The passage that makes the point of this connection clearest is 46d–e, which argues that only soul is capable of intelligence or of acting for a purpose, because, implicitly, it moves itself, whereas material things are moved from outside, and pass on the motions they receive *of necessity*. Material things, because they are moved by external causes, cannot act, in any particular situation, in any way other than that in which they do act. Hence, they will act as they do whether or not there is a reason for it: whether or not it serves some purpose or promotes some good. The soul, on the other hand, because it controls its own motions, can respond to reasons, and so can act for the sake of the good.

Plato's thought here – that only what is free from determination by physical causes can act for a purpose – stands at the beginning of a tradition linking freedom and rationality, which was to be very important in the history of philosophy. Versions of the view are found in Descartes, Kant and Hegel. This kind of freedom is not exactly the same as free will as we normally understand it, since this is often taken to imply that we are free at the moment of choice, and that our actions are not determined by our beliefs, desires and thoughts; for Plato action can indeed be determined by beliefs, desires and thoughts, but these are themselves not wholly formed by external causes. Moreover, this freedom is not a freedom to choose between right and wrong; Plato holds that if we are truly rational we will always choose the good. Wrong actions are produced when reason is obstructed in some way, either by ignorance – a failure of reasoning – or by some other power, such as anger or appetite, opposing reason. (We shall look at this in more detail later in the chapter when we consider the division of the soul.)

At several points in Plato's later works we find the claim that *nous* (reason or intelligence) is found only in soul (*Ti.* 30b, 46d; *Soph.* 249a; *Phlb.* 30c). This, I suggest, should not be taken to mean simply that the actual activity of thinking happens only in the soul, but rather that only the soul can act *for* a reason or pursue some purpose. Of course, bodies can serve a purpose, but only when they are under the control of soul (directly in the case of living bodies, indirectly for others). In taking this view, Plato's vision is very different from that of Aristotle, for whom purpose was found in the (unthinking) processes of nature as well as in the mind. Plato's view is much closer to an early modern one, in which bodily nature acts in a mechanical way, and needs to be brought under the control of the mind in order to serve a purpose. We shall see some of the use Plato makes of this idea in Chapter 8 when we look at his concept of God.

Immortality

Probably the best-known aspect of Plato's view of the soul is his belief in immortality; this was clearly important to him, as he returns to it in many works. The *Phaedo* is largely taken up with arguments for immortality, and they can also be found in the *Meno*, *Republic* and *Phaedrus*. He also makes use of the idea, although without arguing for it, in the *Gorgias* (524a ff.), *Timaeus* (41a ff.) and *Laws* (903d ff.).

In only one work does Plato seem to show doubts about immortality: the *Symposium*. In the central speech of that work (given by a priestess, Diotima, although recounted by Socrates) it is argued that the only way in which human beings can attain a kind of immortality is through their offspring (*Symp.* 207d ff.); these may either be physical offspring, our actual children, or spiritual offspring, if through education, legislation or the creation of works of art we are able to influence the minds of others. At the end of the speech it is possible, on one reading, to see a hope of personal immortality being held out to the philosopher, but not to people in general (212a).

Elsewhere, however, Plato seems to believe that the very soul that lives in us now will live forever. Yet this belief seems to have caused him some difficulty. He tried numerous arguments for it, none of which were wholly successful, and in his later works he may be seen as abandoning argument and rather believing in immortality on the basis of faith.

Before looking at some of Plato's arguments we should notice that it is in general the rational element in us that he sees as immortal, even in those works where he allows a non-rational element into the soul (although the *Phaedrus* is an exception to this). However, even if only the rational element is immortal, it does not follow that only it survives death; other elements may live on for a while after separation from the body, although not forever.

Arguments for immortality: the *Phaedo*

In the *Meno* (86b) Socrates suggests that the theory of recollection is a basis for belief in immortality; and when the theory is first introduced in the *Phaedo*, it seems that he intends to use it in the same way. According to this theory (discussed in Chapter 4) the soul acquired some important kind of knowledge in a discarnate state before this life; this implies that it *can* live in separation from the body. However, it is pointed out by Simmias, one of Socrates' interlocutors in the *Phaedo*, that, even if the theory is true, this is all it shows; the soul has existed in separation from the body and so *could* do so again, but we cannot tell that it will live forever (*Phd.* 77b).

In response to this, Socrates produces two other arguments for immortality that are worth looking at. The first (78b ff.) turns on the similarity between the soul and the Forms. The argument is complex, but the central point seems to be that both soul and Forms are everlasting because they are simple or incomposite, that is, they do not have parts. It is not unreasonable to think that what is composite is likely to perish and what is incomposite is likely to last for ever, for destruction can be seen as the dissolution of a thing into its component parts; this, rather than sheer disappearance into nothingness, is what destruction normally comes to in our experience.

This conception of destruction, with the consequence that what is composite is destructible, does indeed seem to have been a persistent feature of Plato's thought. But it can be used to support the soul's immortality only if the soul is seen as simple, and it seems that Plato did not persist with this way of thinking. In the *Republic* the soul is seen as composite, since it has non-rational parts, but the rational soul still seems to be simple; however in the *Timaeus* even the rational element in the soul is composite, having one part that contemplates Forms, another that makes perceptual judgements (*Ti.* 36d ff.).

The other argument in the *Phaedo*, which comes towards the end of the dialogue, is an extremely complex one, involving the theory of Forms and the nature of explanation, but at the heart of it there seems to be a simple point: the soul is what produces life in us, hence it should itself be seen as essentially alive, something that cannot die.[3] This depends on a conception of causation that has a long history in philosophy, but is often seen as problematic: a thing produces a quality in something else by passing on that quality to it, and therefore must itself have that quality. This clearly fits some examples of causation better than others. The example that most clearly illustrates it – and which Socrates does indeed mention in this passage – is that of heat. Fire is essentially something hot, and is also the cause of heat in other things. It does not fit other cases so well: the stone that breaks a window need not itself be broken.

But in any case, even if we accept this argument in relation to the soul, it does not give us the conclusion that Socrates wants. Fire is essentially hot in that it cannot continue to exist while being cold. If soul is a parallel case, it is essentially alive in that it cannot continue to exist while being dead. This claim, if we can make sense of it, is not implausible; it is hard to imagine a lifeless soul, as we can a lifeless body. But still fire can be quenched, and so it would seem that soul might still be extinguished. Socrates seems on the point of recognizing this, but in the end insists that whatever is deathless (or immortal) is also indestructible (*Phd.* 106d). This is true if "deathless" has its normal sense; but within the context of this argument it means only something that is essentially alive, that cannot exist while being dead. Hence this argument, like the previous one, cannot be seen as an effective proof of immortality.

Arguments for immortality: the *Phaedrus* and *Republic*

In the *Phaedrus* (245c), Socrates identifies the soul with "what moves itself", and claims that what moves itself, "because it never lets go of itself, never ceases to move". It is not wholly clear whether this is meant as an argument for immortality or just as an explanation of it. But it can be read as an argument, similar in spirit to the last one in the *Phaedo*, but perhaps somewhat stronger. While in the *Phaedo* the soul was seen as essentially living and a source of life, here it is seen more specifically as essentially moving and a source of motion. The thought seems to be that bodily things will cease to move when they lose their source of motion; but the soul, being its own source of motion, has no reason to cease to move. This is not, of course, conclusive; even if it is its own source of motion something might extinguish it and so bring its motion to an end. But it has some inclining force; the obvious reason for death in the case of bodies is not present in the case of the soul, leaving it unclear why it should perish.

There is another, more complex, argument for immortality in the same passage of the *Phaedrus*, also turning on the idea of self-motion (*Phdr.* 245c–e). Socrates begins by affirming that what moves itself is the source of all motion. This assumption is in fact open to question. It seems true that if we can trace a series of motions to a source, that must be a self-mover. Clearly something that is (in all respects) moved from outside cannot be the *source* of a new series of motions; and, on Plato's assumptions, an unmoving thing cannot cause motion. But it is not obvious that every series of motions must have a source. Could it not just go back infinitely into the past?

In any case Socrates, having affirmed that what moves itself is the source of all motion, draws from this the consequence that it is ungenerated; for if it were generated, the thing that generates, not it, would be the source of its motion. From this, in turn, he concludes that it is immortal, since if the source of all motion were to perish it could not be generated again, and the universe would come to a stop. These arguments have some force; but the most they can show is that soul, the genus, is ungenerated and immortal. As we have seen, an individual soul might move itself in one respect while being moved from outside in another; hence it might be generated by something else, although once it exists it sustains and directs its own motion. But the genus soul, if it is the source of *all* motion, cannot be moved from outside in any way; hence indeed it cannot be generated by anything else. Likewise, an individual soul could perish, and might be replaced, since there would be other souls still available to act as generators; but the genus soul, being the source of all motion, could never be replaced if it perished as a whole. If this is (as it seems to be in context) an argument for the immortality of the individual soul, then, like other such arguments, it fails.

Yet another argument for immortality is found in the *Republic* (609a ff.). Most things are destroyed by their own defects: the human body by disease, wood by rot, metal by rust and so on. But the defects of the soul – ignorance and vice – do not seem to destroy it, so there seems to be no reason why it should perish. It is not clear why bodily defects should destroy the soul, except perhaps by causing defects in the soul, which they do not appear to do. (Plato is, of course, assuming that the soul *can* exist independently of the body; if this is so, destruction of the body will not of itself cause the soul to perish.) Once again this argument has some inclining force; it suggests that there is no reason to think that the soul will be destroyed, since the obvious reasons for perishing are not present in its case. But it is not conclusive.

It is striking that in works that are thought to belong to Plato's later years, he moves away from arguments for immortality. In the *Timaeus* there is an episode where God, the creator, says that everything that is generated (which in the *Timaeus* includes the soul) can be destroyed, but in fact things made directly by him (which include at least the rational part of the human soul) will not perish, but be preserved in being by his will (*Ti.* 41a ff.). While in the immediate context this refers to the stars, it can also be applied to the human soul, suggesting that Plato now sees the immortality of the soul not as part of its nature, which can be demonstrated by reflection on its nature, but as a divine gift. In the *Laws*, although he makes use of the idea of immortality in defending the goodness of the gods, he does not argue for it (although he has argued for the existence of the gods and the fact that they are concerned about us); the part of the dialogue in which immortality figures is called a "charm" rather than a logical argument (*Leg.* 903a–b). Finally, in a letter ascribed to Plato that, if genuine, must come late in his life, we are told that we should accept immortality on the basis of a sacred tradition (*Seventh Letter* 335a).

It seems likely that Plato was never wholly satisfied with his arguments for immortality; it is interesting that in the *Phaedo* he makes Socrates say that he is advancing these arguments to convince himself when faced with the prospect of death (*Phd.* 91a). While belief in immortality was a more or less constant feature of his thought, he never found a truly satisfactory argument for it, and it is not surprising that later in his life it became for him more a matter of faith.

Why immortality matters

Plato's position on why immortality is important also seems to shift. In the *Phaedo* and *Phaedrus* the soul's true destiny is the contemplation of Forms, and this is best achieved outside the body because of the distracting effects of perception and bodily desire; being in the body is a misfortune (*Phd.* 64d ff.). In the *Phaedrus* it is compared to being in a tomb or in prison (*Phdr.* 250c), and the tomb metaphor is also found in the *Gorgias* (*Grg.* 493a). We should, according to these works, look forward to death; in the *Phaedo* philosophy is seen as practice for death (*Phd.* 64a, 67c). What a philosopher achieves after death is not simply a *reward* for a virtuous life, but the actual fulfilment of the purpose for which he has been living.

In other dialogues, however, our present life is seen in a more positive way. In the *Republic* the principal benefit of virtue, including contemplation of Forms, can be achieved in this life. Only in the last book, when Socrates goes on to deal with the additional rewards of virtue, which it gets if it is recognized both by human beings and by the gods, does he introduce the topic of immortality (see esp. *Resp.* 612b–c). Part of the significance of the afterlife is that in it we make choices for our next life on earth (619b ff.). It is true that the prison metaphor is used in the *Republic*, in the famous analogy of the cave (514a ff.), but here escape from the cave does not represent death but only conversion to a philosophical life; the philosophical ruler is envisaged as returning to the cave – that is, taking part in the day-to-day business of government – after contemplating the realities in the world outside. Likewise in the *Timaeus* the soul has a purpose within this world, helping to complete the scheme of creation.

Even in these dialogues immortality remains significant, but for a different reason; it helps to vindicate the claim that the world is well ordered, and so defend the goodness of its rulers, the gods. This has two aspects. On the one hand, it is simply, as the *Timaeus* makes clear, bad for something well ordered to perish (*Ti.* 41b). On the other hand, life after death enables the virtuous to be rewarded and the guilty punished, which does not always happen in this life. While the truest reward of virtue is an internal one, it is desirable that the virtuous should also receive external rewards, if the gods are just. This emphasis on reward and punishment is found in both the *Republic* and the *Laws* (*Resp.* 612e ff.; *Leg.* 903b ff.).

The divided soul

Another important aspect of Plato's thought about the soul is his account of the division of the soul into three parts or elements, commonly referred to as the rational, the spirited and the appetitive or desiring parts. This division is not to be found in every work of his where the soul is considered – as we have seen, in the *Phaedo* non-rational elements are assigned to the body – but it seems to have become a fairly constant element in his thought, found in the *Phaedrus* (246a ff.), *Republic* (435c ff.) and *Timaeus* (69c ff.) (although it is not clear that his conception of the three parts is exactly the same in all these works).

Plato seems to be motivated to divide the soul in this way by his aim, in the *Republic*, of linking ethics and politics; he wants there to be parts of the soul that are parallel to the classes he identifies in the ideal state, so that the harmony between these parts can constitute virtue in the soul in the same way that harmony between classes constitutes virtue in the state. The three classes in the state are rulers (later identified as philosophers), warriors and working people (farmers and craftsmen); reason, spirit and appetite are the corresponding part of the soul. However, it is possible that Plato's division of both state and soul was inspired by an earlier distinction – thought to have been current before Plato's time, and sometimes ascribed to Pythagoras – between three kinds of life that people can live, governed respectively by the love of gain, the love of honour (ambition) and the love of wisdom (philosophy) (see *Resp.* 581c).

The rational element in the soul includes the actual power of reasoning; it is sometimes called the calculative part (439d). This, as the *Timaeus* makes clear, includes both philosophical thought about Forms and more mundane reasoning about perceptible things (*Ti.* 36d ff.; cf. 41d ff.). It also includes rational desires. At first, when this part is introduced in the *Republic*, this means the desire for what is good for the person as a whole, which it is the job of reason to discern (*Resp.* 441e), and this aspect of it is not abandoned. Near the end of the work we are told that the lower parts, those that aim at honour and money, will also achieve their proper pleasures most effectively if guided by reason (586d–e). But later this part also comes to include the philosophical desire *for* knowledge or truth (581b).

The "appetitive" part is said at one point to be extremely various (580d), and is compared to a many-headed monster (588c ff.), but it is regarded as primarily the seat of bodily desires, such as those for food and drink, and sexual desire. It is also seen as the seat of the love of money, which Socrates claims is sought primarily in order to gratify these desires (581a). In this way this part can be linked with the life dominated by love of gain, and with the money-making class in the city.

The third part, the "spirited", which is seen as intermediate between these two, is more puzzling. The word translated "spirit", *thumos*, can also mean "anger", and when Socrates first distinguishes this element from reason and appetite it is indeed of anger that he is thinking (439e ff.). However, it can also be the seat of pride in one's own good deeds (553d) and shame at one's bad ones (*Phdr.* 254a ff.),[4] of respect and admiration for the achievements of others (*Resp.* 553d), of the love of honour (ambition) and the love of victory (581a–b), and it is characterized by a natural aggressiveness that, when it is governed by reason, also makes it the seat of courage (442b–c). It might perhaps be described as the self-assertive element; it brings together a number of mental activities that, while not exactly rational – they are certainly found in people not much given to reasoning – also do not arise from simple desires, but rather from a conception of the self. It is seen as dominant in the life of ambition, in the warriors of the ideal state, and also in actual states, such as Sparta in ancient Greece, which are governed by a military ideal.

The rationale of the division

It will be clear at once that this is not, in the first instance, a division of the soul into faculties, of the kind that has been common in philosophy ever since Aristotle; the rational part is not the faculty of reasoning, nor the appetitive part the faculty of desiring. Rather, it is in the first place a division into sources of motivation, which can oppose one another; it is introduced, in the *Republic*, to make sense of the phenomenon of mental conflict. Hence the distinction of reason and appetite is nothing like Hume's distinction of reason and passion; what Plato calls reason has passions of its own. (It is sometimes suggested that the second function of Plato's rational part, pursuing what is good for the person as a whole, is similar to the Humean picture of reason [see Annas 1981: 133], but this is not clearly so; pursuing the interest of the whole need not, for Plato, be reducible to working out how to satisfy the desires of the various parts; it can still be a source of motivation in its own right.)

On the other hand, we should not suppose that the division covers only kinds of motivation; other mental states are also assigned to the various parts. Most obviously, the actual process of reasoning belongs to the rational part, while sensations of pleasure and pain are assigned to the appetitive part (*Ti.* 77b). On the other hand, it is not clear where Plato would locate all mental states that he recognizes; emotional states, in particular, cause a problem. While many emotions, such as anger, pride, shame and respect, are naturally located in the spirited part, this is less clear with others, such as pity and fear.

What is meant by the expression "part" of the soul? It certainly means more than just an aspect. When Socrates argues for the division of the soul (*Resp.* 436a ff.), he means more than that it can engage in different activities, for he accepts this at the beginning of the argument, but then goes to some lengths to show that it performs these different activities with different parts. The main ground for calling them different parts is that they can oppose one another; reason can oppose appetite, as can anger, and reason can also restrain anger. Socrates argues that one unified thing cannot possess opposite attributes at the same time, so if there are two conflicting motives in the soul it must be divided. One may question whether this argument strictly works in logical terms, in particular whether conflicting motives really are opposite properties in quite the way that is needed to make the argument work. But we may think that talk of division makes sense simply as a metaphor for the possibility of conflict; when different sources of motivation in the soul conflict, they are in a way like different people engaged in a dispute.

On the other hand, it is also possible that Plato understood the concept of parts in a more literal way. Nowadays we tend to take it for granted that if the soul is not bodily it is also not located in space, so cannot have parts in the way that a material object has. Plato, however, quite often speaks of souls as having spatial location and performing spatial motions;[5] it seems he sees the distinction between body and soul as depending on whether something is perceptible, rather than on whether it is located in space. In the *Timaeus* the parts of the soul are given locations, the rational part being in the head, the spirited in the chest, and the appetitive in the belly (*Ti.* 69d–70a).

One may wonder why, if the point of the division is to allow for mental conflict, Plato recognizes only three parts. Is not conflict also possible within these three broadly defined parts of the soul: between two bodily appetites, say, or between anger and pride? Plato seems to recognize this at least in the case of appetite; the later parts of the *Republic*, which describe degenerate souls, do show conflict taking place between the appetites. The image of the appetitive part as a many-headed monster may be seen as pointing to this, the various heads representing the possibly conflicting motives within the appetitive part. In addition, in the *Republic* Socrates does at one point suggest that there may be more than three parts to the soul when he compares harmony in the soul to a musical harmony between "high, middle and low notes and *however many there may be in between*" (*Resp.* 443d, emphasis added). It may be that, while Plato is confident of the three parts he names as constant features of human nature, he does not really want to rule out the possibility of further division.

Mental conflict

The point of the divided soul is to allow for the possibility of mental conflict. Indeed, even in the *Phaedo*, where the soul is not divided, what we would call mental conflict is accepted but is treated as conflict between soul and body. In other dialogues, perhaps more intuitively, the conflicting elements are all located within the soul.

This view seems to represent a step away from that found in the Socratic dialogues. According to Socrates there, all desire is for the good; hence, if I pursue something it must be because I judge it to be good. It is not clear that this way of thinking can really accommodate the phenomenon of psychological conflict. The later dialogues, by contrast, allow different springs of motivation, not directed to the good as such, but to such things as honour and pleasure, so making conflict possible.

This also helps us to deal with the puzzling phenomenon of *akrasia* (variously translated "incontinence", "weakness of will" and "lack of self control"): of acting in a way that is contrary to one's better judgement, overcome by desire, anger or the like. Socrates' view as found in the Socratic dialogues seems to rule this out, and indeed in the *Protagoras* he does deny the possibility (*Prt.* 352b ff.). If all desire is for the good, we can only pursue something that is not *actually* good if we have made a mistake about the good. The explanation of wrongdoing, therefore, is ignorance; knowledge of the good secures good action, and can be identified with virtue. The theory of the *Republic*, by contrast, allows *akrasia*; there are springs of action other than reason, and we can be overcome by them. (In the *Laws* [863a ff.], we are explicitly told that there are three causes of wrongdoing: ignorance, *thumos* – anger or spirit – and pleasure.)

However, while Plato certainly seems to believe that one can act contrary to a specific rational judgement, it does not follow that for him a truly wise person could act wrongly; it may be that, for him, to become truly wise we need a desire for knowledge or truth that is able to overcome distracting desires. In this case, wisdom can still be seen as bound up with the other virtues.[6]

Problems of the divided soul

Plato's account of the divided soul leaves us with two problems. First, while it clearly accounts for mental conflict, can it really make sense of mental harmony? Plato wants us to think that a virtuous soul is in a state of harmony,[7] with the parts in agreement under the rule of reason; but if their aims are so different, can they really agree? Here, there seems to be a difference between the two lower parts of the soul. Plato sees the spirited element as a natural ally of reason (*Resp.* 440b, 441a), and this seems plausible. Our feelings of pride, shame, admiration, indignation and so on are often based on judgements about what is right or wrong, good or bad, so are indeed responsive to reasoning, although they do not always respond immediately, so that conflict is still possible. The appetitive element, on the other hand, seems to have objects of its own – bodily pleasures – that do not depend on reasoning, and that it has such aims seems to be essential to its identity as a part. So can it really be in agreement with reason?

It may be that all that Plato can really defend here is not genuine agreement, but only coincidence of aim; we might educate our appetites so that they aim at things that reason judges are good for us – things necessary for survival, and harmless pleasures – although they are not aiming at those things *because* they are good. If this is right, it seems that Plato's analogy between a virtuous soul and a well-ordered state is not perfect, since for him the lower classes in a well-ordered state do have the power of reasoning and are able actually to agree that the decisions of their rulers are good for them (see *Resp.* 431d–e).

The other problem posed by Plato's theory of the divided soul is whether it can make sense of the idea of choice, and of an action that is genuinely one's own rather than that of some element within one. The picture suggested by Plato's account is that when we act rationally, our reason is in control; when we act irrationally it is overcome by one of the other elements. There seems no place for an act by which we decide between the rational and irrational aims. In what part of the soul might that decision be located?

Plato does sometimes write as if the self were something distinct from the various elements, which chooses between them (see e.g. *Resp.* 588e ff.). But often he seems prepared to accept the implications of the theory of the divided soul. For many ancient thinkers, the true self can be identified with the reason, and what we choose is what seems good to us; if we pursue something that is actually bad, this is either because we mistakenly think it is good, or because we have been overcome by something, for instance appetite or anger, which prevents us acting in accordance with our choice. Neither of these is ultimately under our control. It seems that, much of the time, Plato shared this way of thinking. Even in the *Timaeus* we are told that "no one is willingly bad" (*Ti.* 86d–e), and in the *Laws* that "no one acts unjustly except against his will" (*Leg.* 860d). These statements echo the claim found in the Socratic dialogues that no one does wrong willingly, but their significance has changed; for Socrates wrongdoing was always caused by ignorance, whereas for the later Plato it may be caused either by ignorance or by *akrasia*, being overcome by anger or appetite. What is still excluded is the conscious villain, the person who *chooses* to do what is bad, knowing it is bad. But while this idea has some intuitive appeal, it is indeed hard to make sense of, and Plato is not alone in the ancient world in rejecting it.

But even if, for Plato, we are not ultimately responsible for our bad deeds, which are caused by something other than our true self, it does not follow that our decisions are of no significance or that there is no point in giving ethical advice (as Plato's speakers, of course, frequently do). This would be so only if our actions were caused by something else in a way that bypassed our decisions. But this is not so: our decisions do have an effect on action. In the case of wrongdoing caused by ignorance, it is clear that our decision leads to action; the problem is that we do not possess the knowledge that would enable us to make the right decision, and here ethical advice can directly help us. In the case of wrongdoing caused by anger or appetite, our rational part has no *immediate* control over our action; but our desires can be educated, so that their strength and direction depends on decisions made by our rational part. Hence, this kind of wrongdoing may in part be due to decisions made by the rational part in the past. In any case, reason has work to do in educating our desires, and ethical advice can be relevant here.

SIX

Politics

Plato's views on practical issues form a central part of his thought. They embrace both questions about the good of the individual – ethics – and about that of the community – politics; and any attempt to separate these is rather artificial. His most significant work in this field, the *Republic*, is concerned with both, and they are closely intertwined. Nevertheless, I shall focus on his political views first, before going on to discuss his ethical views in Chapter 7. I take them in this order simply because, in the *Republic*, Plato's Socrates expounds his views on the ideal state first, before turning his attention to the individual, and it seems appropriate to follow this order of exposition. This chapter will be concerned primarily with views put forward in the *Republic*, but will go on to consider Plato's later works in the same field, the *Statesman* (sometimes called the *Politicus*, from the Greek word for statesman) and the *Laws*.

Plato's political views are perhaps the most controversial aspect of his thought. His picture of the ideal state has struck readers, from Aristotle onwards, as unattractive; few would want to live there. This is partly because of some features it has in common with other Greek city states; indeed, in some respects, notably in connection with the position of women, Plato does seem to progress beyond the ordinary attitudes of his day. But other unattractive features of the ideal state are distinctive of Plato. Nevertheless it is worth looking to see how

Plato reaches his conception of the ideal state, and what kind of principles he uses to justify it.

We saw in Chapter 1 that there is some uncertainty about the extent to which Plato sees his ideal state as a practical proposal. But he certainly sees it as a genuine ideal: a state that would be worth living in if only it could be achieved, not just as a way of illustrating moral truths at the individual level (although it is that as well). Later, in the *Laws*, where he has quite definitely given up any hope of achieving the ideal state, and is more concerned with what can be achieved in practice, a state resembling that of the *Republic* is still treated as an ideal (*Leg.* 739c ff.); the state actually being planned in the *Laws* is seen as second best. We must therefore take the proposals of the *Republic* seriously as a reflection of Plato's views (although, as always, this does not mean that he must be seen as committed to all of them in detail).

The plan of the *Republic*

As the *Republic* will be our main source for Plato's ideas in the next two chapters, we should begin with a brief outline of its arguments. They are concerned primarily with two questions: what justice is, and whether and in what way justice is beneficial to the just person.

The first book, which is written in the style of the Socratic dialogues, shows Socrates discussing the nature of justice with two other speakers: Polemarchus, who defends a conventional view of justice (*Resp.* 331e ff.), and Thrasymachus, who holds that justice is simply the result of laws imposed by rulers, and that it is neither advantageous nor a virtue (336b ff.). Socrates succeeds in arguing Thrasymachus into a corner. However, in the next book two new speakers, Glaucon and Adeimantus (Plato's brothers), claim that Socrates' arguments have not produced real conviction, and ask for a more careful consideration of the issues, challenging Socrates to show that justice is worth having, for its own sake, not just for the sake of the rewards and reputation it brings (357a ff.). Socrates accepts this challenge, but, in a way typical of the Socratic dialogues, begins the enquiry by considering what justice is.

Socrates points out that justice can be found both in a state or community, and in an individual soul, and suggests that justice in the state may be easier to discern (368d ff.); this leads into his well-known sketch of an ideal state, which gives the work its name.[1] This lasts from the middle of Book 2 to that of Book 4. Having determined what justice, and the other virtues, are when they are manifested in the state (427e ff.), he goes on in the last part of Book 4 to give a parallel account of the virtues in the soul (434d ff.). Book 4 ends with the discovery of the answer to the first question, the nature of justice.

At this point we enter what is initially presented as a digression, although in fact it contains much material relevant to the main questions. Beginning with a consideration of the place of women in the ideal state (449c ff.), Socrates moves on to consider whether the ideal state is really achievable. The answer turns out to be that it is, but only if philosophers are entrusted with the task of government (473c ff.). This leads to a discussion of the nature of philosophy, and of philosophical education. (Some aspects of this discussion have been considered above in Chapter 3 and 4.) This whole discussion occupies Books 5–7.

In Book 8 the main line of argument is resumed. Having described a just society and a parallel just soul in Book 4, Socrates now describes various forms of unjust societies and parallel unjust souls. Finally, in the last part of Book 9, he compares just and unjust lives and gives reasons to think that the just life is happier (576c ff.). Book 10 is something of an appendix. It deals with two main themes, the place of poetry in the ideal state (to be discussed in Chapter 9), and the external rewards of justice, including those achieved after death, and includes a discussion of the immortality of the soul.

The ideal state

As was usual in ancient Greece, this community is envisaged as a city state. The central principle on which Socrates' account of it turns is that each person should perform a distinct function. This is first introduced at 369 ff. as something we need in order to have a state or community at all; rather than each person being self-sufficient, people have different jobs and exchange goods and services, depending on one another. But Socrates quickly turns this into a normative principle. First, he insists that each person do the job for which he is best qualified (370c). Then he applies it in ways that would not normally be accepted in ancient Greece: first to the army (374a ff.), and then to rulers (412b ff.). Normally in Greece all citizens were expected to do military service. As for ruling, this was indeed restricted in some states: whereas in a democracy all (free male) citizens took part in government, in an oligarchy the opportunity to do so would be restricted on the basis of wealth, and in the Spartan system on the basis of completion of a programme of military training. (The Spartan system was commonly seen as an oligarchy – which it certainly was in the simple sense of government by a restricted group – but Plato regards it as something separate from the wealth-based oligarchies, giving it the distinctive name "timocracy" [545b].) In any case, Socrates establishes what is probably a much smaller class of rulers than any actual Greek state had; and, quite exceptionally, he sees it as a job to be done on the basis of expertise.

Socrates refers to the army as "guardians" of the state (374e), and since the governing class is chosen from among the army, the term also applies to them. Sometimes, however, he restricts the term "guardian" to the rulers, referring to the soldiers as "auxiliaries" (414b). Many of his provisions relate specifically to these two classes.

At 375 Socrates says the guardians should be both spirited and philosophical – although "philosophical" is here used in a rather attenuated sense, referring to a sensitivity that enables them to distinguish friends and enemies. He then gives a lengthy description of the education – in gymnastics and "music" (including poetry) – which is suitable for the guardians (376d ff.). (Part of this will be discussed in Chapter 9.)

Socrates proposes that the division into classes be justified to the citizens by means of a myth – the so-called "noble lie"[2] – according to which the people of the ideal state originally rose out of the earth, making the land their mother, and so are all kinsfolk, but nevertheless are of fundamentally different natures, the rulers having gold in their bodies, the warriors silver, and the craftsmen and farmers bronze and iron (414d ff.). This may well give the impression that the qualities that determine what class one belongs to are inherited, and indeed Socrates says that this is normally the case. However, he insists that it is not so invariably; a child fitted for one class may be born to parents of another (415b–c). Members of the classes are shown as being selected on the basis of ability (for the warriors, 374e ff., 423c–d; for the rulers, 412b ff., 537a ff.). Warriors would need to be recruited at an early age, as their education is strictly regulated, but the characteristics desired in them, being spirited and "philosophical", swift and strong, are perhaps visible at an early age. The qualities required in rulers – knowledge, aptitude for learning and love of the city – do not become apparent so early, but this is not a problem as the training of rulers does not begin until they are twenty.

Socrates argues that the guardians should not have private property, or even private dwellings, but should live like soldiers in a camp and be supported by the rest of the population (who, as farmers and craftsmen, sometimes referred to as "money-makers", do have property of their own) (416d ff.).

Later, returning to the subject in Book 5, he argues – very surprisingly in ancient Greece – that some women should be guardians, since everyone should do the job for which they are best fitted, and some women will have the skills needed for fighting and government (451c ff.). Although this is one of Plato's most striking proposals – and one of the most controversial in his time – we should note that it is very restricted in scope; it applies only to the two upper classes, and women of the farmer and artisan class are not given equality in the same way. Moreover, Plato's speakers often take a rather negative view of women; even in this passage, while insisting that individual women may be better qualified than some men, and so should not be excluded from fighting and government, Socrates is still made to claim that women are on average less able.

He also introduces the notorious "community of women and children": the proposal that there should be no permanent marriages (among the guardians), but arranged pairings at special festivals, and that children should be brought up in state nurseries, not recognizing any particular people as their parents (457c ff.).

Unity in the state

In all this there is an emphasis on the unity of the state. The principle of specialization is taken to promote this (*Resp.* 423d), presumably because it makes all parts of the state dependent on one another. Extremes of wealth and poverty must be avoided, as they tend to divide the city, and the city must not get too large, as it will then break up into separate groups (421d ff.).

Socrates also especially emphasizes the unity of the guardian class, which he thinks will promote unity in the state as a whole (465b). The absence of private property is thought to promote this, by removing causes of quarrelling (418a–b), and the "community of women and children" has the same effect, by making people see one another as relations (462b ff.). Socrates sees unity as the greatest good for the state, and indeed as necessary if it is to *be* a state at all. A state divided against itself is not one state but a collection of states (422e–3b).

Socrates aims at a state where everyone is concerned about each other, and sees their interests as coinciding; just as the whole body is pained when one finger is injured, so the whole state should be pained when one of its members is injured (462c–d). The rulers should be those who most deeply identify their interest with that of the community (412d–e).

Adeimantus asks whether the guardians, living in a camp without private property, will be happy (419a). Socrates answers that what matters is not whether they are happy but whether they contribute to the happiness of the community. But later he says that they will be happy, because they are honoured and supported by the rest of the community, who owe their safety to them (465d ff.).

The claim that it is the happiness of the whole state that matters has sometimes been taken to show a lack of concern for the happiness of individuals. It may seem that Socrates is here treating the state as an organic entity with a happiness of its own, distinct from that of its members, a thought encouraged by the fact that he draws an analogy between the state and the individual soul. However, he need not be read this way; he may mean only that it is the happiness of all the citizens, not just of one group, which matters, and it is not unreasonable to ask one group to suffer a reduction of happiness if others are benefited by it.[3]

It is not wholly absurd to see the system Socrates proposes as tending to make all the citizens happy, although one has to make some rather strong assumptions about human nature to justify this view. The ordinary people are happy because they are wisely governed and effectively protected; the rulers and warriors are happy because they are supported by the people and honoured for their role in governing and protecting them. Each group gains satisfaction both from the benefits that other groups give them and from performing their own part well.

Philosopher rulers

One final provision does not emerge in Socrates' initial description of the ideal state, but only later, in Book 5, when the speakers are considering whether the ideal state is truly possible. It is that the rulers of the state must be philosophers (*Resp.* 473d ff.), not simply in the sense in which it was earlier argued that the guardians must be "philosophical", having the sensitivity that enables them to distinguish friends from enemies, but in the sense of having philosophical knowledge and training, including, as becomes clear in due course, knowledge of Forms. Initially this is mentioned as a condition for the ideal state to come into being in the first place; but later we find that the philosopher rulers are to be a permanent presence in the state, with much of the later part of the work given up to a description of their training (535a ff.).

That rulers should be philosophers follows naturally from two points. The first is that rulers should be experts: that ruling is a skill, to be assigned to those best qualified for it, those with the relevant

125

PLATO

knowledge. This is already implicit in the earlier description of the
ideal state, from the point where the principle of specialization was
made to apply to rulers. The other is that the knowledge relevant to
ruling is philosophical knowledge; and this is a reasonable claim if
we think that the central object of philosophical knowledge is the
good, and that things in general – including states – are in a better
condition the more closely they approximate to an ideal pattern. A
central passage for understanding the work of the philosopher rulers
is 500b ff., where they are described looking at the pattern of Forms
and trying to produce an image of it in the state.

Virtue in the state

At the end of his first description of the ideal state, Socrates asks
where in the state he has described its virtue may be located. He
argues that, as a well-ordered state, it must possess all the virtues, and
assumes that the virtues are those included in what was to become
a traditional list, later called the cardinal virtues: wisdom, courage,
temperance and justice (*Resp.* 427e). (The *Republic* seems to be the
first place where this list is used in a serious context, although the
Symposium, probably earlier, uses it in a humorous context in the
speech of the poet Agathon [*Symp.* 196b ff.]. However, the choice of
topics for the Socratic dialogues show that these virtues were central
concerns of philosophers at the time; the *Protagoras* lists these four
together with holiness [*Prt.* 329c–d], but the *Euthyphro* suggests that
holiness is a part of justice [*Euthphr.* 12d].)

It seems clear that the wisdom of a state is located in its rulers
(*Resp.* 428d), the courage in its army (429b). This does not mean
that no one but a ruler can be wise, no one but a soldier brave, but it
is on account of the rulers that we say that the *state* is wise, and on
account of the army that we say the *state* is brave.

In his account of temperance (431e ff.), Socrates relies on the
widespread (although not universal) identification of temperance
with self-control. He points out that this term is actually paradoxical;
it does not make sense to speak of a person (as a whole) controlling

126

himself (as a whole). What it means is that the better – the rational – element in us controls the worse elements, the unruly desires. Likewise a state, he suggests, can be called temperate when rational people are in control, and the rest of the population agree that they should rule. (This reference to agreement is important; it means that the population is not kept down by force; and it allows the virtue of temperance to be grounded in the lives of the whole population, not, as with the two previous virtues, just one class.)

Finally we come to justice. This, rather surprisingly, turns out to be identical with the principle with which we began: that each citizen should "perform his own function", meaning not just that there should be a division of labour, but that everyone should do the work for which he is best suited (433a ff.). The reasons given for this identification are, at first sight, rather weak. The main one seems to be simply that it is a virtue, as it makes an important contribution to the benefit of the state, and as it is not identical with any of the other virtues it must be justice, which is the only one left over. This obviously turns on the acceptance of the list of cardinal virtues, which one might think is by no means obvious, especially if we are engaged in giving revisionary accounts of just what the individual virtues are. Socrates also says that, in ordinary speech, we often say that justice is doing one's own work and not intruding in that of others, but here the phrase seems to have a rather different meaning: it does not mean doing the work for which you are best qualified, but rather sticking to matters that concern you or have been assigned to you – in the modern idiom "minding one's own business". In any case, whether or not the observance of this principle deserves the name of justice, it is identified as an important virtue, central to the preservation of the state.

Problems of the ideal state

Probably the feature of the ideal state that will first strike most modern readers as problematic is the exclusion of large numbers of citizens from the opportunity to take part in government. However, while Socrates in the *Republic* takes this to extremes, it was quite a common feature of Greek states; Plato is by no means alone in his rejection of democracy. Moreover, the ordinary people of Socrates' state – the farmers and craftsmen – seem to live what would generally have been seen as quite a normal life, with little government interference on a day-to-day basis; they are allowed to own property (although extremes of wealth and poverty must be avoided), to marry and have children of their own.

Much more striking are the restrictions placed on the life of the guardian class. It is notable that it is in connection with them, rather than the farmers and craftsmen, that Adeimantus worries whether they will be happy. First, there is the fact that they cannot own property (including homes) of their own, but are wholly dependent on the rest of the state for support. Secondly there is the "community of women and children"; quite apart from the unreasonable restrictions this places on personal life, Aristotle was surely right to say that it would not achieve its intended purpose (Ar. *Pol.* 1261a10 ff.). If we regard everyone in our community as a relation, the ties of kinship will be weakened; we will not come to regard everyone in the state as we currently regard our parents, children or siblings, and the aim of promoting unity will not be achieved.

Perhaps the most disturbing feature of Socrates' ideal state, however, is simply the absence of personal choice. There are three possible ways of life, to which citizens are assigned on the basis of their aptitudes, and then expected to live the kind of life appropriate to their class, which, at least in the case of the ruler and warrior classes, is quite rigidly determined. There is an assumption here that if something is beneficial to the state, government has the right to require it.

We should be careful here; to say that Socrates does not leave room for personal choice is not to say that he favours coercion. On the contrary, it is clear that he sees the citizens of the ideal state as consenting to their position. This is shown both in the description of temperance, where it is emphasized that rulers and ruled are in agreement about who should rule, and in various passages dealing with the unity of the city, and the way the various elements in it rely on one another (see e.g *Resp.* 462b ff., 465d ff.). Socrates does sometimes use the language of compulsion,[4] but this need not mean that he actually imagines coercive measures being taken; it may simply mean that certain things are required of the citizens, with the assumption that they will in fact agree. Indeed, he will later speak of the rulers themselves being compelled to take part in government (520a), but clearly they could not be physically forced to do so, and in fact it is made clear that they consent. Socrates sees tyranny, which does involve coercion, as the very opposite of the kind of state he is describing.

We are likely, in imagining the ideal state, to think of what would be necessary to achieve such a system of government in the actual world; and this would no doubt require rigorous policing, since real people are not, on the whole, like the citizens of Socrates' state, and would have to be compelled to fit into it. But according to the account given by Socrates, if such policing were necessary the state would already have failed. The state as he describes it probably involves less coercion than most states of the time. It is striking that judicial matters and punishment are hardly mentioned in the sketch of the ideal state (by contrast with the later, more down-to-earth *Laws*). Plato recognizes, of course, that most actual people would not accept life in such a state; if people are going to do so they must be educated for it. Hence we have the strange suggestion that the ideal state can be made real only if we start by sending away from the city everyone over the age of ten (540e–41a). This may be read as an effective admission that the state is not a practical possibility. But if we could achieve a community of truly rational people, Socrates seems to be saying, this is how they would choose to live.

This approach to the ideal state seems to be based on an incredible faith in the power of reason; both the reason of the rulers, in discerning the best solutions, and the reason of others, in recognizing that they are the best and consenting to them. What is problematic is not coercion as such, but the lack of recognition that different ways of life, different ways of seeing the world, may be valuable. Socrates' proposals may be seen as making sense, if we suppose not only that there is a definite, well-defined good to be sought in government, and that for each of us there is a best way of contributing to that good, but also that people are in a position to recognize this. But all these assumptions are, of course, open to question.

It is very common in Plato's dialogues for government to be treated as an expertise in the same way that, for instance, medicine or navigation is an expertise. In such cases, there is an agreed goal: health in medicine, safety at sea in navigation and so on. What distinguishes experts is their knowledge of how to achieve this goal. But is there a similar goal in politics? If there is an objective good for people and states, then in principle there can be; we all want to attain the good, and some people might be specially skilled at finding a way to achieve it. If there is not, then the business of government becomes something different, not finding the way to an agreed goal, but rather deciding on what goals to aim at. But even if there is an objective good, it does not follow at once that there are people qualified to find it, and able to convince others that they have done so, and in the absence of such people government will, in practice, have to involve deciding on goals, choosing between different conception of the good.[5]

Two features of the ideal state are particularly disturbing. One is the censorship of literature, and of the arts more generally, at first presented as part of the guardians' education, but later seen as applying to the state as a whole. This will be discussed in Chapter 9. The other is the way in which rulers are allowed to deceive the people. At 389b–d Socrates says that although in general lying is to be avoided, the rulers in the ideal state may be allowed to lie in the same way that doctors can. This picks up an earlier passage where we are told that lies are "a useful drug" that can be used to stop our friends doing something bad through madness or ignorance (382c). This – even supposing it is true of doctors – will apply to rulers only if they are seen as experts taking care of the people from a position of superior knowledge.

This manifests itself in two places. One, which we have already commented on, is the "noble lie" used to give citizens a sense of identity. However, Socrates says that he hopes the rulers themselves will one day come to believe it. We might, on the contrary, think it hard to suppose that anyone will believe it; but in that case, one might think that it could serve its purpose just as well if it were regarded simply as a useful fiction. The other place where lying is authorized, even more disturbingly, is the lies told to the warrior class as part of the programme of breeding; they believe that partners are being assigned to them by lot, but in fact they are being selected in such a way as to produce the best children (459c ff.). We would in any case find such a programme disturbing, but more so if it is brought about by deception. Once again, we have the assumption that rulers, if they are genuine experts, are entitled to do whatever is in the interest of the state.

The *Statesman*: a new approach

Later in his career, Plato returns to political themes in the *Statesman*. While the approach taken there has much in common with the *Republic*, it also introduces some distinctive new features. In particular, it places a new emphasis on the concept of law. The *Republic* has little to say on this subject, suggesting at one point that the details of legislation are unimportant, the wisdom of the rulers being what matters (*Resp.* 425c ff.). The *Statesman* gives a new importance to the subject.

Government is treated, as in the *Republic*, as a skill like medicine or navigation; but while in the *Republic* the expertise of the rulers seemed to rest primarily on their knowledge of unchanging Forms, in the *Statesman* emphasis is placed on their ability to make decisions for particular people in particular circumstances (*Plt.* 293b ff., esp. 294b). Hence, it is argued, a true statesman should not be limited by law, but left free to make what judgements he finds appropriate in each situation. Interestingly, it is also claimed that the expert ruler does not need the people's consent. However, in the absence of a true statesman – and it seems to be implied that they are in general absent from actual states – law is an appropriate second best, acting as a rough guide to what a true statesman would judge (295a ff.). Hence while it would be wrong to subject the expert in government to the requirements of law, it is even worse if a ruler who is not an expert ignores the law in order to benefit himself or do favours to others (300a–b). It follows that of the various forms of government that exist in the actual world, law-governed forms are better than lawless ones; the first group include kingship, aristocracy (perhaps here meaning the Spartan system) and constitutional democracy, while the latter include unconstitutional forms of democracy, oligarchy and tyranny.

It is hard to say whether the *Statesman* gives law a higher or a lower place than it has in the *Republic*. On the one hand, it seems that the rulers of the *Republic* govern according to unchanging principles that could well be called law-like, while here the flexibility of the statesman and his ability to deal with particular circumstances is emphasized. On the other hand, written law had no importance in the *Republic*, since the wisdom of the rulers was the guarantee of good government. Here, although written law is a second best, it is taken seriously as being often the best of which we are capable, and as superior to lawlessness.

Both these developments, however, can be seen as examples of the tendency, which appears in many of Plato's later works, to take the sensible world and ordinary life more seriously. This leads him on the one hand to emphasize the importance of particular judgement as well as universal knowledge; this is also found in the *Timaeus*, where the rational element in the soul includes not only the part that contemplates Forms but also the parts that make perceptual judgements (*Ti.* 37a–c); and in the *Philebus*, where it is pointed out that our understanding of universal Forms must be supplemented by the ability to recognize particular examples of them (*Phlb.* 62a–c). On the other hand, it also leads him to consider the needs of actual states, where no expert ruler is present, and to recognize the importance of law in those states.

The *Laws*: politics in the actual world

Plato returns to the subject of politics in what is probably his last work, and his longest, the *Laws*. The dialogue deals with the founding of a hypothetical new city in Crete, and the core of the work is a proposed legal code for the new city, prompting Aristotle's comment that "The greater part of the *Laws* consists of laws" (Ar. *Pol.* 1265a1–2); however, there is much else as well, including historical material, discussions of the nature and purpose of law, religion, education and, rather surprisingly, the benefits of drinking-parties.

The work is much more practically oriented than the *Republic*. The new constitution is explicitly presented as a second best. Although the communism of the *Republic*, including the "community of women and children", is still seen as an ideal, it is not practicable in the real world (*Leg.* 739c ff.), so the *Laws* provides for the citizens to own property and to have conventional marriages and families. Consent is still considered important, and provision is made for every law to have a preface in which the legislator tries to persuade the people of the benefits of the law; but it is recognized that this will not always succeed, so punishment also features significantly throughout the code (718a ff.).

This more down-to-earth approach may be interpreted in more than one way. On the one hand it can be seen as representing a growth of pessimism in Plato. Having at one time made proposals for a radically new kind of state, he has come to recognize that this is not possible, and is offering a second best instead. But alternatively, we may suppose that the ideal state of the *Republic* was never conceived as a real possibility. In this case, the fact that he is now ready to offer a set of practical proposals, even if they fall short of the ideal, can be seen a showing more optimism than his earlier position.

Two features of the *Laws* deserve special attention. The first is the view taken by the chief speaker, the Athenian Stranger, of the purpose of law. In fact he makes two suggestions about its purpose. One is that it exists to promote peace within the state (628c ff.); this can be seen as echoing the claims of the *Republic* about unity. The other is that the purpose of law is to promote virtue. The Athenian is inspired here by the Spartan constitution and that of some Cretan cities; these were normally seen as aimed at promoting courage in war, but he argues that they should really be seen as aimed at virtue as a whole (630e). However, he accepts that they are in fact more effective at promoting courage than other virtues such as temperance (634a ff.). Again this echoes some elements in the *Republic*, notably in the proposals for education, which aimed at encouraging virtue, but the *Laws* places more emphasis on virtue as good in itself, not just as something that ensures the good of the state (631b ff.). This idea of virtue as the aim of law was also taken up by Aristotle. The idea that it is the function of the state to promote morality is now an unpopular one, but one can see how it arises, given two assumptions, both Platonic: that it is possible to discern, objectively, what virtue is; and that virtue is a great good to those who possess it. If virtue is the greatest good we might expect the state to promote it, just as if we take, for instance, wealth or freedom to be the greatest good, we may see it as the business of the state to promote these.

The other central claim of the *Laws*, however, would be much more widely accepted even now: that law itself should be sovereign in the state (612d ff.). Here again the Athenian praises the Spartan and Cretan systems because they do not commit power to any one person or group, but, by a system of checks and balances, ensure that law itself should be supreme. For this reason he thinks they are especially deserving of the name *politeia*, "constitution", which thus comes to be used as the name of a particular system of government, as well as a term for systems of government in general. Here law seems to rise to a much higher status than it had in either the *Republic* or *Statesman*; it is described as the "dispensation of reason" and seen as something divine. Of course, law is made by human beings; it is called divine because it is an expression of reason, the divine element in us. But if we commit power to one person or group we are committing it to them as complete persons, including both reason and appetites, while if we commit power to the law we are committing it to something that can be recognized as rational. Checks and balances, in turn, ensure that the law is observed, while a single ruler or group of rulers could ignore it if this were in their interest. This idea of the sovereignty of law, and of the division of power as a way of ensuring it, has remained influential down to modern times.

SEVEN

Ethics

Ethics – the philosophical consideration of the question how we should live – is central to Plato's thought throughout his career. His thought, like that of many ancient philosophers, focuses especially on the virtues – that is, on morally admirable states of soul or character – rather than on the rightness or wrongness of specific actions, although he does, of course, sometimes consider the way the virtues are expressed in action.

While Plato devoted many dialogues to ethical questions, most of them are normally seen as Socratic dialogues, expressing the thought of Socrates rather than of Plato himself. The work in which the mature Plato presents his ethical ideas most fully is the *Republic*. Its official theme is justice, but as justice is seen as bound up with the other virtues, it does in fact present Plato's thought about the virtues more generally.

Plato continued to think about ethical issues later in his career; as we have seen, two later works, the *Statesman* and *Laws*, deal primarily with political topics, but these are, of course, bound up with ethical ones in Plato's thought, especially as he sees the promotion of virtue as a major part of the work of government. He also wrote one more work that deals directly with ethical questions, the *Philebus* (the last of his dialogues to feature Socrates as chief speaker); this addresses, rather more directly than the *Republic*, issues about the good or happy life for human beings (rather than about virtue), and considers the place of pleasure and knowledge in the good life. Much of the argument of the *Philebus* is hard to interpret, but it does give significant insight into Plato's ethical thought. Here, however, I shall focus on the *Republic*, as his central presentation of his ethical position.

The investigation of justice

As we saw in Chapter 6, the *Republic* is an enquiry into the nature of justice both in the state and in the individual. At the individual level, it addresses two central questions: what justice is and why it is beneficial. These questions will form the main themes of this chapter.

The word translated "justice", *dikaiosunē*, is one of the most important terms in ancient Greek ethics, and has a rather wider application than our modern word. It has many of the connotations of "justice", being linked with law, with fairness, with punishment and rectification, and so on, but it also shares some connotations of "honesty". Behaviour generally seen as characteristic of a just person includes telling the truth, and refraining from stealing, cheating and so on (see *Resp.* 331b ff., 442e ff., 485c ff.). We tend to use the word "just" (in connection with people, as opposed to societies, states of affairs and so on) only of people who are in a position to make judgements – judges, teachers assigning marks, and the like – whereas the ancient Greeks might use the corresponding term of anyone who acted rightly towards others.

Socrates, however, sets out in the *Republic* to find a more precise account of what justice is. In doing so he makes a striking assumption. He takes it that justice can be found both in a community and in an individual, and he supposes that justice is the *same* property in both cases; a just individual will be *like* a just state (368e ff.). Socrates does not blindly assume that this must be so; after finding what justice in the state is, he allows that justice in the soul may turn out to be something different (434d). But from the start he takes it to be *likely* that justice in the state and in the soul will be parallel. This is why he structures his enquiry in the way he does.

Since Socrates holds – plausibly – that justice in the state is a matter of the structure of that state, it follows that justice in the soul is a matter of the structure of the soul, not, at least in the first instance, of its attitude to other people or to the community. Certainly "justice" is used in both contexts, of a state and of an individual, and this is no simple ambiguity; the uses are connected. But one might well think that a just individual was one who *contributed* to a just society, rather than one who resembled one.

Socrates' point cannot just be that a word, when used in a way that is not simply ambiguous, must always stand for the same property, for "just" is used of actions as well as people and communities, and of course Socrates does not hold that a just action is one that resembles a just person; rather, it is one that promotes and preserves the just condition of the soul (443e). Instead, we can see Socrates as relying on the assumption that, in general, qualities of a community derive from similar qualities of the individuals who make it up.[1] Thus, a just person is indeed one who contributes to a just society, but he does so by passing on to it a quality that he himself possesses.

The general principle is plausible in many cases. Take, for instance, a case that Socrates considers at 435e: the love of learning. A studious community will be one that consists of studious people, and it seems that we are using "studious" in a single sense when we say this. However, it is less clear that this will be true of structural properties. If the justice of a state is found in the relations between its parts, then there will indeed be some property of the individual citizens that contributes to the justice of the state, but there is no obvious reason for thinking that this will be like the justice of the state – that it will itself be a structural property.

Virtue in the soul

In searching for an account of virtue in the soul, Socrates makes use of his account of virtue in the state, discussed in the previous chapter.

Since the virtues of the state are found in the relations between its parts, it follows that the soul must also have parts, whose relations can constitute its virtues (*Resp.* 435b–c). It is at this point, therefore, that the theory of the divided soul, outlined in Chapter 5, is introduced. The three most significant parts of the soul are the rational, corresponding to the rulers, the spirited, corresponding to the warriors, and the appetitive, corresponding to the money-makers (farmers and craftsmen). Wisdom in the soul is found in its rational part, courage in its spirited part. Temperance is the agreement between the parts that reason should rule (although, as noted in Chapter 6, it is a puzzle whether parts of the soul can really be seen as agreeing), and justice turns out to be the condition in which each part of the soul does its own work (441c ff.).

One might ask what this can mean; since parts of the soul are defined by the kind of activities typical of them, how can they fail to do their own work? Presumably, however, the point is not just that they do the kind of thing typical of them, but that they do it in a way that serves their proper purpose, for the good of the whole. For instance, in Book 8 we read of a person dominated by the love of money, whose rational part is devoted to working out how to get money, and whose spirited part admires those who have it (553d); while these parts are in a sense performing their own function (calculating and admiring), they are not doing so in a way that serves their overall purpose, as they do in a just soul. It follows that it is not enough that my soul be governed by reason in the sense of reasoning: that I act on the basis of thought-out decisions, rather than of impulse. It must be right reason, directed to right ends, that governs my soul if I am to be virtuous.

The view of virtue taken here is interestingly different from that ascribed to Socrates in the Socratic dialogues. For him, as we saw in Chapter 5, all desire is for the good; if we know what is good, we will choose it; hence the only source of wrongdoing is ignorance. Thus he was able to identify virtue with knowledge. In the *Republic*, by contrast, there are parts of the soul that can conflict; the rational part of the soul judges what is good, and pursues what it sees as good, but we can be motivated, by spirit or appetite, to pursue things we do not see as good. Hence virtue involves not only right judgement but also the power of that judgement to govern the other elements in the soul. It seems that judgement can be overcome by anger or desire, so we are only virtuous if our judgement remains in control.

In the Socratic dialogues Socrates is sometimes seen as having an intellectualist concept of virtue; for him, virtue is simply a state of the intellectual faculties. On the view presented in the *Republic*, by contrast, it involves other parts of the soul as well. But it remains fundamentally rationalist: it is the rational thought that something is good, and desire for the good, which should motivate us. It is better when our other desires and feelings harmonize with this, but they are not in themselves central to virtue.

Virtue, knowledge and true belief

Socrates' account of virtue raises a puzzle to do with the nature of reason. As we saw in Chapter 5, reason has two aspects; on the one hand it has a distinctive aim of its own, the aim of knowledge, which is most fully expressed in the philosophical life; on the other hand there is the aim of promoting the good of the whole self, which is guided by knowledge. When Socrates speaks of the virtuous soul being governed by reason, which of these aspects of it has he in mind? They are not, of course, wholly separable; it is by philosophy that we can attain the knowledge of the good that enables us to guide our lives effectively. But does this mean that no one but philosophers can be virtuous?

Certainly later in the *Republic*, in some of the arguments for the connection of justice and happiness, the just life is identified with the philosophical life (*Resp.* 581b ff.). However, it seems strange that the lower classes in the ideal state cannot be seen as just. Indeed, it is clear that Socrates sees them as contributing to the justice of the state by performing their own function; and it is plausible that this is because they have just souls, in which each part performs it own function.[2] Moreover, Socrates certainly wants the whole community to be happy (420b ff.). Can it really, for him, be happy if it is not virtuous?

It may well be that Plato wants us to see only philosophers as virtuous in the fullest sense; but he may still leave room for a lesser kind of virtue possessed by others. In the *Meno*, Socrates argued that virtue need not be constituted by knowledge, but could instead merely be true belief (*Meno* 98c ff.). While in the *Republic* he no longer holds that virtue is a purely intellectual state, so that it cannot simply be either knowledge or true belief by itself, it seems reasonable to say that it might *involve* true belief rather than knowledge; one is virtuous if one has true beliefs about the good, and one's feelings and desires harmonize with them. So in the *Republic* the courage of the warrior class is defined as "persistence in true belief about the things which are and which are not to be feared" (*Resp.* 429c). This true belief can be achieved by following the guidance of the philosopher rulers; although the lower classes do not have philosophical knowledge, they have sufficient rational powers to be able to agree that what their rulers command is best.

In later works, particularly the *Laws*, Plato's speakers suggest that people may achieve virtue by being guided by law;[3] but of course not any law will do; it must be one whose own inspiration is philosophical. What is harder to see is whether any non-philosophers in the actual world can be virtuous (or even philosophers in the actual world, since it is not clear that they have actually attained knowledge). While the *Meno* seems right to suggest that true belief can be a basis for virtue, it gives a less plausible answer to how people in the world can attain this true belief, suggesting that it is a divine gift (*Meno* 99c). This is often seen as ironic, casting doubt on whether anyone is really virtuous. Yet surely it must at least be true that some people approach closer to virtue than others, and one may wonder how this can be explained. It does not seem that Plato ever finds a wholly satisfactory answer.

The unity of the virtues

There seems, according to the *Republic*, to be a very close connection between the various virtues. In the *Protagoras*, Socrates seemed to suggest that the various virtue words – courage, temperance, and so on – were in fact names for one state: the knowledge of good and evil, which ensures virtuous behaviour (see *Prt.* 329d ff.). In the *Republic* this view has certainly been abandoned; because of the distinction between parts of the soul, there is also a distinction between the virtues, which relate to the different parts. Yet it seems that the virtues, although different in essence, will be inseparable. I, as a person, will not be wise or brave unless the parts of my soul are performing their proper function. My rational part may display cleverness or my spirited part daring, but these do not become virtues of me as a whole unless used for their proper purpose. My parts, in turn, will not be performing their proper functions unless my soul is directed by reason. Government by reason, although officially the definition of temperance, is in fact central to all the virtues, including justice.

This view, that virtues are inseparable, is implausible if they are seen just as natural tendencies to behave in a particular way; there seems no reason why a person who is naturally courageous will also be naturally temperate. However, if we see virtues as grounded in knowledge or true belief, it is reasonable to see them as going together; it is the same kind of knowledge of what is right or good that is manifested in various fields, including both running risks and controlling appetites. Aristotle also commits himself to the unity of the virtues, because he sees all virtues as grounded in practical wisdom (Ar. *Eth. Nic.* VI.13); but he distinguishes between the fully fledged virtues and natural predispositions to virtue, which are separable.

Socrates accepts that there are natural tendencies that predispose people to virtue, and he allows that these do not always go together. Indeed, he recognizes that two qualities that are desirable in guardians, the spirited and the philosophical, are hard to combine (*Resp.* 375c–d). In a similar way, at *Meno* 88b there is a reference to courage and temperance as tendencies that are not beneficial except when combined with knowledge; these are treated as not being true virtues. Likewise in the later *Statesman* (306a ff.) the Eleatic Stranger argues that temperance and courage, again probably seen as natural tendencies, do not generally arise together, and it is the job of a statesman to ensure their combination, either in one person or in a team (311a); although by themselves they may be harmful, they become beneficial when combined with right belief about what is fine, just and good (309b ff.).

Virtue and action

Socrates says that justice – and the same should go for the other virtues as well – is primarily concerned with the inner condition of the soul; just actions are those that promote and preserve this condition (*Resp.* 443c–e). In saying this, he anticipates a central principle of modern virtue ethics: that virtue, a state of character, is in some way more fundamental than moral qualities of actions. In fact it seems likely that we should take him as saying that it is more fundamental in two ways: just actions are defined in terms of the state of soul, and they are valuable because of their connection with the state of soul. Virtue ethicists often look to Aristotle as a forerunner, but in fact this view put forward in Plato's work anticipates modern virtue ethics more clearly than anything in Aristotle. Whereas for both philosophers virtue is a central concern of ethics, it is clearer in Plato that it is foundational, with actions depending on it for their moral value.

This view can also overcome a common objection to virtue ethics. It is often thought that virtue must itself be defined by reference to right action: that virtues are something like stable dispositions that enable us to choose rightly. But if this is so, we cannot go on to define right action in terms of virtue, without circularity. However, the *Republic*, by proposing a definition of the virtues in terms of the inner relation between parts of the soul, allows them to be defined without reference to right action, so that they can indeed be seen as fundamental.

Platonic justice and ordinary justice

However, this conception of justice leaves us with a puzzle. It may seem to be too far removed from our – or the ancient Greeks' – ordinary conception of justice, which is, surely, concerned with our actions towards other people. Hence, Plato has been accused of simply changing the subject (see Sachs 1963). He showed Socrates setting out to demonstrate that justice as it is normally understood was beneficial; but in fact what he demonstrates – even if his arguments are successful – is that justice in a new, revisionary sense is beneficial.

The first thing to say in response to this is that it is not clear Plato would have accepted the view that there *is* a clearly definable ordinary conception of "justice"; he may have thought that ordinary people's use of the term was fundamentally confused. Certainly in Book 1 of the *Republic* the characters search for a definition of justice that reflects people's normal understanding of the term, and is concerned with actions towards other people, but they fail to find one. They consider the definitions "paying to people what we owe them" and "doing good to friends and harm to enemies", but find these unsatisfactory (*Resp.* 331e ff.). If the ordinary use of a term is unclear or confused, it is not always unreasonable of philosophers to give it a new definition that is clearer, and that can then be used in the search for definite answers to philosophical questions.

But even if Socrates is proposing a new concept of justice that does not seek to capture precisely the ordinary use of the term, his concept should have something to do with the ordinary use of the term if it is to count as a new concept of *justice*, rather than, say, courage, or jealousy, or intelligence. A person who is just in his sense may not always act in ways we would naturally call just, but one would think that he would often do so, or at least that his behaviour has something significant in common with what we normally call just behaviour.

Have we any reason to think this? A just person's soul, according to Socrates, is governed by reason. This reason certainly enables him to pursue his own good; reason is that element in a person that takes care of the whole (441e). Does it also motivate him to respect the rights or pursue the good of others? It will motivate him to do this, if it is rational to do so: and it is natural to believe that it is. But does Socrates say anything that can explain or justify this view?

There is no doubt that Socrates is shown as holding that the just person in his sense *will* typically behave in a just way towards others. This first becomes apparent in Book 4 when he says that a person in whom each element performs its own function will himself be just and *perform his own function*; this means that he will do what he is best able to do for the good of the community (441d–e). Later, Socrates goes on to say that a person who is just in his sense will not be likely to perform any of the acts typically seen as unjust; he will not steal, break oaths, betray his friends or his country, commit adultery and so on (442e ff.). But at this point it remains unclear why this should be so.

A partial answer appears in Book 6, where Socrates is arguing for the suitability of philosophers as rulers. As we have seen, a philosopher is for Socrates the archetypal just person; and here he argues that a philosopher will not have many of the motives that lead people to act unjustly (484b ff.): he will not have strong bodily desires or love of money; and he will not think human life important, and so will not be afraid of death. In addition, he will love truth, since truth is akin to wisdom, and therefore will not normally be motivated to lie.

But while these considerations may show that the philosopher will, in general, lack motives positively to wrong others, they do not show that he will actually seek to benefit others. Moreover, they leave room for his being motivated to wrong others, when the love of wisdom itself is the motivating factor. This becomes important because of a special problem that arises later in the *Republic*.

The philosophers' choice

Socrates argues that philosophers should rule in the ideal state, but he also recognizes that they will not want to do so; they would prefer to devote their lives to philosophy. In the image of the cave, he describes a person being liberated from a dark cave in which he has been imprisoned, where he saw only shadows, and allowed to escape to the outside world, where he can see real things, finally looking at the sun (*Resp.* 514a ff.). This represents the philosopher attaining knowledge of the Forms, and in particular the Form of the good. But then, we are told, he must return to the cave – that is to the realm of human affairs – in order to take part in government (519d ff.). Obviously he will be reluctant to do so.

Socrates recognizes this reluctance, and welcomes it. He thinks a state where rulers do not enjoy ruling is a desirable one; if rulers actually love power this will lead to conflict and it is better that they approach ruling as an unavoidable duty (520d). So he speaks of philosophers being compelled to rule (520a). But clearly this does not mean physical compulsion; the rulers are told what they must do, and agree to it. Why do they agree? Glaucon says – and Socrates does not dispute it – that they agree because "we are making a just demand of just people" (520e). It is to the state that they owe the education that enables them to do philosophy; being just, they will be ready to repay that debt by serving the state.

Plato's language here, with its explicit reference to something that is owed (520b), seems to introduce a conventional conception of justice, one in which it consists of paying what we owe to others. Why should someone who is just in the distinctive Platonic sense – one in whom each part of the soul performs its function effectively – be motivated to pay debts in this way? Since such a soul is governed by reason, it will be motivated to pay debts if it is rational to do so. But why should it be seen as rational?

In fact, there are in this particular case some fairly clear reasons why the rulers should be motivated to take part in government; but they are not directly linked with the thought that this is owed to someone. In Book 4 it was argued that guardians (rulers and soldiers) should be chosen from among people who identify their interest with that of the community (412d–e). One thing this might mean is that their self-interest, in a narrow sense, is bound up with the interest of the community; and in Socrates' ideal state this seems to be true, because the division of labour that is a mark of that state makes everyone dependent on one another, enabling everyone to engage in the activities for which they have the greatest aptitude. Philosophers may be motivated to be outwardly just, in the sense of making their proper contribution to society, because if they do not make this contribution the society will be endangered, and in this case they may lose their opportunity to do philosophy.

However, the passage mentioned above can also be read in another way: not that the rulers' self-interest, narrowly interpreted, coincides with that of the city, but that they see the interest of the city as part of their own. This is supported by some of the proposals for unity in the state found later in the work, and in particular the "community of women and children". Because the guardians are related they care about one another as we do about family. We care about our children, not because our narrowly defined interest coincides with theirs – it may well not – but because we see their interest as part of ours. This is especially emphasized at 462c–e, where Socrates claims that the guardians will actually feel injury to another member of the community as injury to them. In this case, the philosopher will have a direct motive to do his part in promoting the good of the state as a whole.

However, the claim that the philosophers should take part in government because it is just seems to go beyond this. It seems that they are being asked to do this even if it is not, at least directly, in their own interest, since otherwise there would be no reason to speak of compulsion; but also that acting in this way is rational, since otherwise it would not be called just. It appears, then, that we should accept that we have reason to pursue the good of others: not, perhaps, of all others, but of others with whom we have a special connection, which may well include those who have benefited us. (Socrates says that justice requires philosophers to take part in government only in the special circumstances of the ideal state, not in ordinary states where they arise by chance [520b].) While there seems to be nothing in Plato's conception of reason to rule this out, it does not seem that he ever gives a full explanation of why it should be so.

Virtue and the good of others

The reasons given here for the philosophers to take part in government seem to apply only in the ideal state. Do rational people, in Plato's view, have any more general reason for benefiting others? After all Socrates himself, who certainly did not live in an ideal state, did not simply devote his life to contemplation, but tried to stimulate thought among the Athenians – although in the *Apology* he says his reason for doing this is that it was in response to a divine command (*Ap.* 23c).

One reason why we might want to benefit others is suggested by Diotima's speech in the *Symposium* (206b ff.).[4] This puts forward the idea that we are all seeking to leave behind something through which we can, in a sense, live on after our deaths, thus achieving a kind of immortality, and so continuing to have the opportunity to possess good things forever. One way of doing this is by physical reproduction: having children. Their life can be seen as a continuation of ours. But another way is by spiritual reproduction: influencing the souls of others. This can be done at an individual level by educating our partner in a personal relationship; it can also be done on a wider scale by, for instance, writing poems, producing laws or doing notable deeds that will achieve fame and so act as a moral example. Here, then, we have a reason to benefit others that stretches beyond the confines of the ideal state, but it is still limited; the people whose lives we affect must be connected in some way with us, so that their lives can be seen as continuations of our own.

Is there room in Plato for a more universal altruism? It is possible that he came to accept such a position later in his career. In the *Timaeus* we are told of God's motive for creating the cosmos; he was good, and what is good is not grudging, but desires everything to be good; finding the realm of matter in a confused and disorderly state, he set out to give it order (*Ti.* 29d–30a). This kind of motivation seems to be one that human beings can share as well; for the language here used of God echoes a passage in the prologue to the *Timaeus*, which includes the earliest version of the Atlantis legend. Atlantis was a tyrannical power that oppressed the people of the Mediterranean. The Athenians fought against Atlantis and regained their freedom, but then *ungrudgingly* liberated the other Mediterranean peoples as well (25c). Here the Athenians are acting to benefit people who have no special connection with them; virtue seems to have a wider scope than it has in the *Republic*. (It is interesting that in the *Republic* Socrates says that Greeks should see Greeks as natural friends [*Resp.* 470c], and only barbarians – non-Greeks – as enemies; in the *Timaeus* non-Greeks are also brought within the circle of concern.)

It is sometimes suggested that the rational person, for Plato, should be seen as pursuing an impersonal good; not just aiming to achieve the good for himself and those in some way linked with him, but to increase the amount of good in the world (see e.g. Annas 1981: 259ff.). This can be seen as following from the theory of Forms. The Form of the good is something impersonal, not the good for any one person or thing; and so the person who contemplates the Form of the good and wishes to imitate it will aim not just at his own good or that of his community, but at an impersonal good – the production of as much good as possible in the world.

However, I suggest that the theory of Forms need not be read in this way. Certainly, the Form of the good is not the good for any specific person or thing; it is the nature that all goods have in common. To know the Form of the good is not to know what is good for me or for you. This, however, is compatible with saying that each *instance* of the good is a good for someone or something. Consider the Form of father. It is not any individual person's father, but rather the nature that all fathers have in common; but each individual father is the father of someone. In the same way it may be that what is good is always good for someone or something, although there is a nature that all good things have in common. Knowledge of this nature will inspire us and help us to achieve what is good for ourselves and those dear to us.

Even if what is good is always the good of someone or something, this does not mean that we have reason to pursue only our own good; we may have reason to pursue the good of others, and this may extend more narrowly, as in the *Republic*, or more widely, as in the *Timaeus*. However, while it seems clear that Plato is committed to the thought that it is rational, and therefore just, to pursue the good of others, it does not become clear exactly why this should be. Given that some – such as Callicles in the *Gorgias* and Thrasymachus in Book 1 of the *Republic* – did challenge that view, this is a gap in Plato's arguments.

Justice and happiness: the challenge

We now turn to the second major question of the *Republic*: how justice is connected with happiness. "Happiness" here does not mean a feeling, but a life that is worthwhile as a whole. This is how the term commonly translated "happiness" (*eudaimonia*) was normally understood in ancient Greece, and it was a central concept of Greek ethics.

The relation between virtue – being a good or admirable person – and happiness – having a good or worthwhile life – was much debated in antiquity. Most philosophers saw them as going together; justice, temperance and so on are virtues and also promote happiness. Socrates, Plato, Aristotle, Epicurus and the Stoics all thought this, although they would have disagreed about just why it was so. We must be careful, however, about just how we understand this connection. On one possible reading of the relation between virtue and happiness, happiness is the more fundamental concept; virtue may be defined as a state of character that promotes the agent's happiness, or valued because it does so. This reading of the connection produces what may well be seen as an egoistic moral theory: perhaps not narrowly egoistic, if we see the happiness of others as bound up with our own, but still one that treats our own good as the most fundamental reason for action.

However, this is not the only way to see the connection between virtue and happiness. One might see virtue as the more fundamental concept, with happiness actually consisting in the exercise of virtue; or one might see the two as equally fundamental concepts, but nevertheless as linked. On such a reading, it would not in general be true that virtue consisted only of pursuing our own good, or that our most basic reasons for action always relate to our own good; they might equally well relate to the good of others. But nevertheless acting virtuously might be something that contributes to our own good, something to value and take pleasure in. On such a reading, the point of demonstrating that virtue contributes to happiness is not to give us a reason for acting virtuously when otherwise we would have none. Rather, it is to show that there is not, as one might think, a conflict involved in the good life; the requirements of virtue and happiness are not, as many suppose them to be, opposed to one another.

I have suggested that for Plato virtue does not always consist of the pursuit of one's own good; rather, it consists in the effective functioning of the soul, governed by reason. While reason is often directed to the agent's own good, it may also be directed to the good of others. Hence, when Socrates sets out to investigate the connection between justice and happiness, he is not asking what makes justice a virtue. He is not here giving an account of the foundations of ethics as we understand them, saying what makes an act right or a state of character virtuous. Hence, he need not be seen as holding an egoistic moral theory.

In the main argument of the *Republic*, it seems that Socrates is not being asked to show that justice is a virtue. It is true that Thrasymachus in Book 1 had challenged this view, but Glaucon and Adeimantus, whose speeches in Book 2 set the agenda for the greater part of the work, do not. Adeimantus, at least, or the ordinary people for whom he speaks, seems to accept that justice is a virtue; he speaks of justice and temperance being admirable, but difficult and burdensome (*Resp.* 364a).[5] Socrates is later to assume that justice is a virtue when describing the virtues of the ideal state (327e). What he is being asked to show here is that justice is beneficial to the just person.

The challenge that Socrates is here asked to answer is a plausible one. As we have seen, many ancient philosophers saw virtue and happiness as going together, and would have said that justice is both a virtue and conducive to happiness; at the other extreme there were people, represented in Plato by Callicles in the *Gorgias* and Thrasymachus in the *Republic*, who took an egoistic view, according to which justice is *neither* a virtue *nor* conducive to happiness. But between these two extremes there were many people – of whom Polus in the *Gorgias* and Glaucon and Adeimantus here are representatives – for whom justice is fine and admirable, but not good (for the just person); it is a virtue, but does not promote happiness (or at least not always, and contingently when it does). This might be seen as a common-sense view; but it is the view that Socrates here undertakes to answer.

We must now look at the challenge in more detail. In Book 2, Glaucon and Adeimantus challenge Socrates to show that justice is to be valued for its own sake, and not only for its consequences (358a ff.). Most people think that justice is in itself something burdensome, and is only valued because of its consequences; Glaucon and Adeimantus say that they themselves do not accept this view, but that it is the common view, and therefore the alternative position needs defence.

The claim that justice is to be valued both for itself and for its consequences seems to mean that it contributes to our happiness, both directly and indirectly.[6] "Good in itself" should not be read in a Kantian sense as meaning that it is admirable, independently of its effect on our happiness; it means only that it benefits us directly, through the effect that it has on our soul, rather than through something that is only contingently connected with it.[7] It can even be taken to include the case where justice is beneficial because it produces a further good thing, provided its connection with that thing is necessary. It appears that the consequences that are here contrasted with the direct effect of justice are external ones, ones that arise from other people's reaction to our just behaviour.

While Socrates holds that justice is to be valued *both* for itself *and* for its consequences, what is important is to show that it is to be valued for itself, since it is generally agreed that its consequences are valuable.[8]

Two rather different aspects of this are emphasized by the brothers. First, Glaucon talks about the origin of justice (358e ff.). He proposes – not as his own view, but as a widely held one that needs an answer – an early form of the social contract theory: people came to an agreement that they would act justly towards one another, because they found this preferable to a state in which everyone constantly has to suffer the unjust behaviour of others. What would be best for the individual is if he could act unjustly, but not expect unjust action in return; but this, in general (as opposed to some special cases) is not achievable. What is really beneficial on this view is not justice itself, but the expectation that others will act justly towards one; but acting justly is, normally, the price of this.

Secondly, Glaucon goes on to talk about the fear of punishment as a motive for acting justly (359b ff.); and Adeimantus likewise talks about the rewards that are given to just people, both by other people during life, and by the gods after death (362e ff.). But these consequences, as they point out, arise from other people, including the gods, recognizing us as just, not from justice itself; and as Glaucon says, a person who was unjust but had a reputation for justice would be rewarded, and a person who was just but had a reputation for injustice punished (361a–d). In such circumstances, is a just life still worth living? Socrates has to show that it is.

Justice and happiness: the response

At the end of Book 4, after defining justice, Socrates draws an analogy between justice and health: justice is the natural ordering of the components of the soul, as health is the natural ordering of the components of the body (*Resp.* 444c ff.). His official purpose in drawing this analogy is to illuminate the nature of injustice, and of just and unjust behaviour. Injustice, like disease, is a disruption of the natural order; just behaviour, like healthy behaviour, builds up the natural order, while unjust behaviour, like unhealthy behaviour, disrupts it. However, Glaucon points out that this analogy makes it plausible that justice is a desirable state, to be preferred to injustice, and Socrates does not dispute this (445a–b). This seems right; if the various parts in us are functioning in such a way as to preserve our natural condition, each functioning in the way it is best equipped to do, this seems a desirable state to be in.

Nevertheless, Socrates and Glaucon do not immediately draw the conclusion that justice is better than injustice, since a formal defence of this view cannot be offered until injustice itself has been examined in more detail. Because of the long digression that begins at this point, the discussion of injustice is delayed until Book 8, and it is in the latter part of Book 9 that the official arguments for the superiority of justice begin.

The first argument turns on the analogy of an unjust soul and an unjust state. As the most unjust state is a tyranny, the most unjust soul is a tyrannical one; this does not mean the soul of a tyrant, but one that resembles a tyrannized state (although a person with a tyrannical soul *may* also be a tyrant himself).[9] As a tyrannical state is dominated by one person, so a tyrannical soul is dominated by one appetite; Socrates uses the example of sexual appetite, although others are presumably possible.

A tyrannical soul, Socrates argues, is not free, because it is dominated by one desire and so cannot do what it wishes (577e ff.). It is also impoverished, perhaps because the domination of this one desire prevents it getting what it needs or wants, and fearful, presumably of what the dominating desire might force it to do. Hence, the unjust life is undesirable, by comparison with the just life, which is governed by reason. The argument here seems to depend implicitly on the idea that our rational nature is our true self; hence, when reason is in control we are free, making decisions for ourselves, while when appetite is in control we are enslaved, being forced to act in ways we do not choose.

The two remaining arguments focus on the claim that the just life is *pleasanter* than the unjust. While Plato does not approve of a life of pleasure pursued for its own sake, he never denies that a good life will be pleasant, and indeed the most pleasant; we should indeed gain pleasure from attaining what is truly good.[10] Both of these arguments turn on identifying the just life with the philosophical life, which is here contrasted (in accordance with a tradition said to go back to Pythagoras) with the lives devoted to the love of honour or gain. According to the first of these arguments (581c ff.), in deciding which life is best we should rely on the person who has wisdom and experience. The philosophical person obviously has wisdom; he also has experience, since lovers of honour and gain do not possess wisdom, while the philosopher will typically experience some of the pleasures of honour and gain during his life. And clearly, the philosopher chooses the philosophical life.

This is an odd argument. It does not seem enough to say that a life is the best if the person with wisdom and experience chooses it. This would be evidence that it was the best only if he chose it *because* of his wisdom and experience. But it does not seem that the philosopher did that; he must have chosen the philosophical life before he acquired the relevant wisdom and experience, presumably because he had a natural attraction to it. At any rate this argument does not tell us *why* the philosophical life is superior.

The last argument does so (583b ff.). It is a complex argument, but the central point is that the things that give pleasure to the mind – truth, knowledge and understanding – have a greater reality than the things that give pleasure to the body – food, drink and so on. This is because they are seen as belonging to the unchanging realm that, earlier in the *Republic*, was seen as having greater reality. Hence the pleasures derived from those things – which are the pleasures of the philosopher – are also more genuine. However, it is also argued that the lovers of honour and of gain will also achieve the pleasures most appropriate to them when guided by wisdom (586d ff.); wisdom guides us towards achieving these pleasures in the most effective way, by moderating our desires and preventing us reaching at things that are beyond our powers.

In a rhetorical conclusion, Socrates introduces the famous image of the soul as composed of a human being, a lion and a many-headed monster (588b ff.). The human being, of course, represents reason, and Socrates and Glaucon agree that it is best that it should be in control; this reaffirms the idea that our rational nature is our true self. Once again, to allow the other elements in the soul to take control is to allow our reason to be enslaved.

These arguments involve both aspects of reason identified earlier: as the faculty that plans for the good of the whole, and as an element in the soul having aims and desires of its own, for truth and knowledge. Some of the arguments focus on the latter, drawing attention to the goodness of knowledge itself, and so the happiness of the life of a lover of knowledge. But the way in which government by reason enables other aspects of the soul to achieve satisfaction is also emphasized. Finally, some arguments seem to point to the just condition of the soul as intrinsically worthwhile, independent of the achievement of any particular aim. This is true of the arguments in Book 9, which focus on the freedom of the just person in the way he controls his own life, as opposed to the enslavement of the unjust. It is also true of the considerations put forward at the end of Book 4; although not a formal argument, these suggest that the just state of the soul is desirable simply because it is a natural state, in which each part functions well.

It is important that not all the arguments put forward here turn on the goodness of wisdom itself, for not everyone can be a philosopher. Socrates wants us to think that even people without philosophical ability can be just to an extent, if they allow themselves to be guided by wisdom by submitting to philosophical government (590c–d); then they, too, will be happy. This cannot be because they enjoy the pleasures of wisdom itself, but because wisdom guides their lives in such a way as to attain the overall good.

One concern that is sometimes raised is whether the view that Socrates is defending in the *Republic* as a whole – that justice is always better than injustice for the person who practises it – is compatible with the passage about the return of the philosophers to the cave. There, the philosophers seem to be giving up what is best for them – philosophical contemplation – in response to a demand of justice; indeed, it is emphasized that it is not their happiness but the happiness of the state as a whole that matters (519e). The answer, I suggest, is that justice, as a state of soul, may always be better than its opposite, but it does not follow that every just act, considered by itself, is better than its opposite. If we take the acts in isolation, contemplation is better than taking part in government; if someone can devote his life to contemplation without injustice (as perhaps the rare philosopher outside the ideal state can) their life will be happier than that of someone who has to govern. But if a philosopher in the ideal state were to *choose* to devote his life to contemplation, he would be unjust; that means that his soul would be in a worse state than that of the just person, and so he would not be happy.

Happiness and the Form of the good

In the last sections of this chapter, I shall mention some questions that relate Plato's ethics to his larger philosophical concerns. At *Republic* 505a Socrates says that justice and everything else derives its value from the Form of the good. It seems, therefore, that this Form should help to explain what happiness is and why justice contributes to our happiness. However, within the *Republic* Socrates says relatively little about this Form, discussing it only in the central books, and there using images to describe it. Can we say how the Form of the good is relevant to the goodness of justice and the other virtues?

If we focus on justice as philosophy the answer is clear: justice enables us to contemplate the Forms, and among them the good, which is central to the system of Forms. It is the position of the good in the realm of Forms that gives value to them, and so to the knowledge and contemplation of them.

However, we have seen that justice also has a wider aspect, concerned not only with philosophy but with how we live our life as a whole; the condition of soul that justice produces is in itself a good one even if it does not lead to contemplation of the Forms. How is this related to the Form of the good? I think we must say that a well-ordered soul – one that is harmonious, in control of itself, and in its natural condition – is itself an instance of the Form of the good. This condition of the soul is therefore a good or worthwhile one to be in, and the individual virtues are good in so far as they promote this condition. Other things, too, can be seen as instantiating the Form of the good if they are well ordered, with their parts fitting together harmoniously to promote the good condition of the whole, although obviously what exactly this good condition amounts to will differ from case to case. This includes just states, as well as healthy bodies, and perhaps other things as well: artefacts that are well adapted for their purpose, and even the universe as a whole.

It may be that there is a third way in which justice is related to the Form of the good: it can enable us to be a *part* of something that instantiates the Form. This will be true in the ideal state, where the just agent contributes to the good of the whole, but also identifies the good of the whole with his own. However, because this way of being related to the good is only possible in the ideal state, it is less relevant than the other two to the project of the *Republic* of showing that justice is always more beneficial than injustice.[11]

We saw in Chapter 3 that the Form of the good is not only what all good things have in common, but also is itself a good thing: the "best of realities" (*Resp.* 532c). One may wonder how this can be. But if a good thing is something worth possessing, it seems right to say that the Form is a good thing, for contemplating it, instantiating it and being part of something that instantiates it are good states to be in, and these can be seen as ways of possessing it. Hence, while it is indeed puzzling that the nature shared by all large things should be seen as large, or the nature shared by all animals as an animal, it does make sense to see the nature shared by all good things as good, simply because possessing that nature is a good thing, worth aiming at, and worth taking pleasure in when achieved.

The nature of the good

This, however, may leave us still wondering about one extremely puzzling question; what *is* the good? What do all well-ordered things have in common? Can we say any more about it than that it is good? Socrates in the *Republic* is very cryptic about this; he points in the direction of knowledge of the good, as something that philosophers in the ideal state ought to know (*Resp.* 506d ff.), but he does not tell his listeners what it is, approaching it through images (although he does insist that it is not pleasure or knowledge [505b–d], two wide-spread views, and ones with which Socrates in earlier dialogues had shown some sympathy[12]). Does this mean that Plato himself did not claim to know the nature of the good? Or, is it, perhaps, that he thought it unsafe to commit it to writing?

We do have some evidence from outside the dialogues for Plato's view of the good, but it is hard to interpret. There is a story that he once gave a public lecture on the good; unfortunately our only report of this comes from a hostile witness, Aristoxenus (Aristox. *Elem. Harm.* II.30–31). According to him, the lecture was largely concerned with mathematics, and ended with the claim that "good is one". This could mean simply that there is one good; but it could also mean that the good is the one, that goodness is unity. If so, it fits in with an equally mysterious claim of Aristotle, who says that Plato takes unity and duality as his two basic metaphysical principles, and that he identifies one of those principle (presumably unity) as the source of good, the other of evil (Arist. *Metaph.* A.6).

Puzzling though these indications are, they do seem to fit well with a theme that is manifested in several places in Plato's work: linking the good with unity and harmony. In the *Republic* this is applied to the virtuous soul in the passage that compares it with a musical harmony: "binding all these parts together and becoming altogether one out of many, temperate and harmonious" (*Resp.* 443d–e).

Also in the *Republic*, this same idea is applied to the state in a number of places. At 422e, having urged that extremes of wealth and poverty should be excluded from the state because they tend to produce division, Socrates argues that the state he is describing is truly a state because it is unified; an ordinary community, because there are divisions between rich and poor, is really a multiplicity of states. At 462b he praises the "community of women and children" because it ensures that people have feelings in common, and this binds them together and makes them one.

In the *Timaeus* the same principle is applied to the world as a whole; the elements that make up the world are combined in a harmonious proportion, so that they may achieve "agreement" and "friendship", which makes the whole composed of them indissoluble (*Ti.* 32c). This echoes a passage in the *Gorgias*, where we are told that community and friendship hold the universe together (*Grg.* 508a).

Clearly, saying that the good is unity is not a full explanation of its nature. We would have to understand more fully the nature of the unity in question. Plato cannot have believed that anything was good if it can be described as one object, or as a whole of parts. A heap of stones is one heap, and the stones are its parts, but it is unlikely that Plato would have offered this as an example of the good. The kind of unity he has in mind is one where parts are combined harmoniously to form something that operates effectively as a whole; to gain a full understanding of this one would have to know the principles according to which they combine. But the link drawn here between goodness and unity does help us to gain some understanding of how Plato sees the good, in the state, in the soul and in the universe at large.

Philosophy and the good life

Plato clearly sees a strong connection between virtue and philosophy. This connection has two aspects. On the one hand, the pursuit of wisdom implies a disposition that is already in many ways virtuous; as we have seen, the philosopher is free from strong bodily desires and love of riches, does not fear death, and loves the truth (*Resp.* 485a ff.). On the other hand, when wisdom is attained and we have knowledge of Forms, this will inspire us to order our own lives in their image, and will give us the knowledge we need to order both our own lives and our community (500b ff.).

Because of the central place of the good in Plato's philosophy, he sees philosophical knowledge as intensely relevant to practical affairs. In this he contrasts to some degree with his pupil, Aristotle. For him there are two kinds of wisdom, philosophical and practical, and two kinds of life – both admirable, but distinct – linked with them: the political life, to which moral virtue is central, and the life of contemplation. For Plato, by contrast, it is philosophical wisdom that we need to guide our life. What is more, this wisdom does not come from a distinctively practical philosophy, separate from theoretical philosophy; the good is central to the whole of philosophy, including areas that we might see as wholly theoretical.

But while there are not two kinds of philosophy, there are two aims associated with it; the contemplation of Forms itself, and the use of the knowledge thus gained in practical life. While philosophy is worth studying for its practical value, it also gives us an aim of its own, an aim of overwhelming attraction, as it is presented both in the *Republic* and in the account of love in the *Symposium*. It is often pointed out that for ancient thinkers philosophy was a way of life. But this need not imply that it was a wholly practical kind of enquiry; while on the one hand philosophers were concerned with the question how we should live our life, they were on the other hand dedicated, as part of their way of life, to the pursuit of knowledge or truth for its own sake. In one way, for Plato, philosophy exists for the sake of practice; it aims to help us make good practical decisions, both in our own lives and in the state. But in another way, practice exists for the sake of philosophy; at least one of the aims for practical decisions is to make knowledge and contemplation of Forms possible. There remains a tension at the heart of Plato's philosophy regarding how we can reconcile these two aims.

EIGHT

God and nature

Plato's God

In many places in his work, Plato writes about a God who brings the world into being. He is often envisaged as the craftsman of the universe, and is therefore sometimes referred to by modern scholars as the Demiurge (from the Greek for "craftsman"). However, Plato often refers to him simply as "the God" (*ho theos*), and while, as we shall see, he is not exactly like the God of traditional theism, they are similar enough to make it reasonable to call them by the same name. Plato may well have played a major part in making belief in a single supreme God more widespread; philosophers after him, including Aristotle, the Stoics and later Platonists, took up the idea and developed it in various ways.

The idea of a creator God was not a widespread one in Greek thought in Plato's time. Nevertheless, there is some evidence that Socrates believed in such a God (see Xen. *Mem.* I.4, IV.3), and it is likely, therefore, that Plato had such a belief from the start of his career. Certainly the creator seems to be present in the *Republic*, although he makes only two brief appearances there, as "the craftsman of the senses" (*Resp.* 507c) and as "the craftsman of the heavens" (530a). However, it is in Plato's later works that God becomes a central figure. In the *Timaeus*, which deals with the creation of the world, he dominates the narrative; he is also present in the *Sophist* (265b ff.), *Statesman* (269d ff.), *Philebus* (28d ff.) and *Laws* (903b ff.). This seems to be related to a shift of perspective in Plato's thought – which need not imply an actual change of doctrine – in which he begins to take this world, and therefore its creator, more seriously, emphasizing the goodness of the world more than its imperfection and the way it contrasts with Forms.

In what follows we shall focus mainly on the *Timaeus*, and here a warning is necessary; in that work the chief speaker, Timaeus, says that his account is conjectural (*Ti.* 29b–d). He claims that we cannot have true knowledge of things that change, so, since his account is concerned with the changing world rather than the eternal Forms, it can be only a "likely story". However, this need not be taken to mean that it does not aim at truth; rather, it tries to come as close to the truth as possible, although it does not claim perfect success. It is therefore reasonable to use it, with caution, as a guide to Plato's views.

Why does Plato believe in God?

At the beginning of the *Timaeus* there is a simple argument for the existence of a creator. Everything visible and tangible has come into being, and everything that comes into being must have a cause. The universe is visible and tangible; therefore it has come into being, and accordingly has a cause (*Ti.* 27d–8c).

Of the two assumptions that ground this argument, the second is a widespread, although not universal, philosophical view. The first reflects Plato's own way of thinking, in which eternal and unchanging Forms contrast with transient sensible things. It is sometimes objected that even if each particular sensible thing comes into being, it does not follow that the totality of sensible things must do so. But for Plato the universe – that is the *kosmos*, whose name in Greek means "order" – is not just the totality of sensible things. It is a specific ordered state, linked with the regular motions of the heavens; and this specific state must have had a beginning. Indeed, Plato does not think that the totality of sensible things had a beginning. He believes, as we shall see, that there were sensible things, in a state of chaos, before the beginning of the ordered world.

This argument is a version of what was later to become known as the cosmological argument. By itself, however, it can prove only the existence of a cause of the world, not of an intelligent cause that deserves the name of "maker". In fact, as soon as this argument had been given, Timaeus begins referring to a "maker and father" of the world. But only later does he say anything that might justify this way of speaking.

This argument comes from a passage we have already looked at, *Timaeus* 46d–e, where a contrast is drawn between the kinds of causation typical of body and of soul. Bodies, because they are moved from outside, are governed by necessity, and this means that they cannot act for a purpose; soul, by contrast, because it moves itself, can be responsive to reasons and so can act for a purpose.[1] This claim is of quite general relevance, and can relate to the activities of human and animal souls, but in the context where Timaeus makes it it does in fact relate to divine activity in creation. If we see things in the world as existing for a purpose, as Plato does, then a soul, something living, must have ordered them so as to enable them to serve that purpose. If the universe as a whole has a purpose, then it must have a cause that is intelligent and hence living, and this is Plato's conception of God.

Much of the *Timaeus* is taken up with a discussion of the purposes that things in the world serve, and the way they contribute to the good. Like many thinkers who have argued for the existence of God, Plato is impressed with the way in which parts of human and animal bodies, and their environment, are adapted to promote survival and the continuance of the species, and also, in his view, to make intellectual activity possible. However, for him the strongest proof that the universe is well ordered – emphasized in both the *Timaeus* and the *Laws* – is the movements of the heavenly bodies; they are both regular in themselves, and form a harmonious pattern (*Ti.* 37c ff., 47a–b; *Leg.* 898c–9b). Such regular motions, Plato thinks, could not be produced by material nature on its own, but require a living and intelligent cause.

Plato does not infer the existence of a creator directly from the orderly movements of the heavens; rather, he holds that the universe and the heavenly bodies are themselves alive and rational (*Ti.* 34b ff., 39e ff.). This is another application of the claim that only soul can act for a purpose; the heavenly movements are seen as good, and so as requiring a living cause. In the first instance this is a reason for believing in souls internal to the world. But the presence of such souls is itself a good state of affairs; the universe is a living and intelligent being, which Plato thinks is the best state for anything to be in (30b). Since this state of affairs had a beginning, it must have had a cause, and since it is a good state of affairs, this must be a purposive cause. Plato's God, therefore, is not related to the universe in quite the same way as the God of eighteenth-century theism, who is often compared to a clockmaker; what he makes is alive, not purely mechanical.

Plato's argument here, from the purposive arrangement of the universe to the existence of a creator, is a version of what has come to be known as the teleological argument or the argument from design. However, it is not the same as the version of that argument most often discussed nowadays, made famous by David Hume in his *Dialogues Concerning Natural Religion*. This argument turns on an analogy: the universe and living things resemble works of human design, and there is therefore reason to believe that their cause resembles a designer. This argument is questionable, because there seem to be, in nature, causes of purposive arrangement other than design; for instance living things produce purposive arrangements by reproduction. While there may, for all we know, be a designing mind behind every natural phenomenon, acting either directly or indirectly, we do not observe this, and so cannot claim empirical justification for the claim that purposive arrangement must proceed from a mind. Plato's argument, by contrast, is conceptual. If something exists for a purpose this must have been given it by something living and intelligent, since material things cannot, on their own, act for a reason.

Of course, for this argument to have any force we must accept that the universe and things in it have purposes. This does not only mean that they serve purposes – that they are so arranged as to promote good ends – something that Plato believes, but that others might question. It also means that this is not an accident. In some cases something might produce a good although it does not exist for the sake of that good, since its cause would have produced it anyway whether it was good or not; in such a case that good is accidental. Even if things in the universe seem to have a purpose, and so call for a rational explanation, we need not accept the idea that there is a creator if we have strong enough other reasons for rejecting it.

Although this is disputed, this argument seems to show that the creator is a soul. It also shows in what respect he is like the human soul: in being a self-mover, and therefore able to act for a reason. It allows him to be very unlike us in other ways. He is a purely rational being, without spirited or appetitive elements, and it is reasonable to think that his response to reason is immediate, with no need to make up his mind. Conceptions of God often have to steer a course between the twin dangers of making him too anthropomorphic, and making him so unlike us that we cannot conceive his nature at all. Plato's conception can overcome this problem.

Plato's God and the God of theism

Plato's God, a creator external to and prior to the world, is clearly in many respects like the God of the traditional monotheistic religions, and certainly more so than some other ancient conceptions of God: Aristotle's detached "unmoved mover" or the immanent spirit of the Stoics. However, there are some significant differences.

Perhaps the most immediately striking is that Plato's God is not alone: there are other gods, his "children", who help him. The universe is a god, since it is an immortal living being (*Ti.* 34a, 92c), the heavenly bodies are gods (40a ff.), and at least the possibility of other gods is left open (40d ff.). These gods take part in the work of creation, making human and animal bodies and the lower elements in the soul (42e ff., 69c ff.).

One may ask whether Plato is a monotheist or a polytheist, but in fact it seems quite possible to be both, since monotheists and polytheists will typically use the word "god" in different ways. If "god" means a spiritual being of superhuman power and virtue, Plato believes in many of them; if it means a perfect creator and governor of the universe, he believes in only one.

Plato's creator is detached from the day-to-day workings of the universe, so if there are divine powers within it – exercising providence, answering prayers, providing inspiration to prophets and poets and so on – they must be distinct from him (see *Symp.* 202e–3a). But when Plato thinks of the whole universe as embodying a design, he naturally thinks of a single designing mind.

This detachment from the universe is another difference between Plato's God and the God of traditional theism. After the initial act of creation he withdraws, leaving the ongoing work of running the world to the lesser gods (*Ti.* 42e), probably because if he remained involved in the world this would involve him in its processes of change and so detract from his perfection.

Yet this detachment should not be exaggerated. At *Timaeus* 41b we are told that it is only through his will that anything generated can remain in being forever. In the immediate context this relates to the heavenly gods, but it must also apply to the universe as a whole and to the rational element in the human soul, which are likewise generated but immortal; it is the creator's will that sustains them in being. God does not intervene – his relation with the universe is unchanging – but he is still in a sense present.

Another striking difference is that Plato's God is not the source of all being. First, he does not create the Forms, which are uncreated and eternal. Rather, he takes the Forms as his model in making the world, trying to reproduce in the world the goodness that he finds in them (29a, 37c). The Forms, because they are timeless and non-spatial, cannot by themselves be the cause of events in time and space. God bridges the gap between Forms and the material world, producing events that happen in time and space, but using the Forms as a guide.

Secondly, God creates the world not out of nothing, but out of a pre-existing material (30a, 52d ff.). This is important, because it provides the motive for creation. God wanted everything to be good; finding the sensible realm in a state of disorder, which is not good, he set out to improve it. If all that had existed in the first place had been perfect – God himself and the Forms – it is not clear that it would have been good to create a universe, which is necessarily imperfect. But if things were originally in a bad condition, God is to be praised for making them better; and the magnitude of his achievement, even if it is imperfect, can be appreciated by comparing it with the chaos that was there before.

This brings us to our final point: it does not seem right to describe Plato's God as omnipotent. While this term is hard to define, it seems that we should withhold it in this case, for there is something external that sets a limit to what he can do. Although he controls the world and makes everything serve his purpose, there remains a disorder that he cannot overcome, an imperfection that he cannot eliminate. Thus at *Timaeus* 48a we are told that (divine) intelligence persuaded (material) necessity to guide *most* of the things that come to be towards the best, and at many places that good results were achieved *as far as possible*.

The constraint on God's power arises from the nature of the materials with which he works. An example is found at 75a ff., in the description of the creation of the human head. Here we are told that it was not possible to combine thickness (which would have given more effective protection) and sensitivity; the creator had to choose, and chose sensitivity. It does not seem that the combination would have been *logically* impossible; rather, the necessity inherent in the materials prevents it.

It is important not to overstate these limits on God's power. We must not suppose that his purpose is frustrated; his goal is to make the world as good as possible, and this is achieved. Yet there are perfections that the world cannot achieve, so that it does not perfectly represent its model. It falls short, not of the goal, but of the ideal.

Nor should we think that there is an arbitrary limit to what God can do; the limit is inherent in the project he is involved in. Any image of Forms will fall short of Forms in some respect. It will be changeable, and will be embodied in some material (see *Ti.* 52c), which will set limits to what can be done, although the precise nature of those limits may depend on what the material is.

The phrase "the best of all possible worlds" belongs to an age much later than Plato's, but it expresses well the spirit of Plato's thought about the universe. But the phrase is ambivalent: on the one hand it celebrates the goodness of the world; on the other it laments its limits. It means that the evil that is present in the world is inescapable; nothing better is possible. Both aspects of the concept are present in Plato. He sees the goodness of the world as cause for celebration, but he also sees evil as inevitable.

Plato's conception of God is an interesting one, and deserves to be taken seriously. It may overcome some problems that the traditional conception gives rise to, in particular the problem of evil, which arises in a particularly acute way if God is seen as omnipotent and as the source of all being. It is often thought that we have a choice between the traditional conception of God and no God at all. But if we accepted a Platonic God – a powerful, wise, benevolent, but limited, designer and maker of the universe – we could not dismiss the idea as unimportant; such a being would be an appropriate object of religious feeling.

Necessity

We should now look more closely at necessity, the constraint under which God works.[2] We have seen that, while only soul is capable of intelligence, material things are governed by necessity. This gives rise to two different kinds of explanation: things brought about by an intelligent cause are explained in terms of the purpose they serve; things brought about by material causes in terms of necessity, that is by showing how, given a certain event or arrangement of things, a particular result is necessary (*Ti.* 46d–e). When intelligence and necessity work together – when an intelligent being makes use of material things and exploits their powers – both kinds of explanation may be relevant. For instance, vision is explained in both these ways. At 45b–6c we have an account of the mechanism of vision. A beam of light, flowing from the eyes, picks up the motions of whatever it comes into contact with, and transmits them back to the eyes.

At 47b–e the purpose of vision is explained. Its primary purpose, Timaeus claims, is to enable us to see the movements of the heavens, study of which will move us to philosophy. Many such double explanations are found in the later part of the dialogue.

This distinction determines the shape of the *Timaeus*. The first part, which deals with the creation of the world as a whole, the heavenly bodies and the rational human soul, focuses on intelligence. The second part is concerned with materials used by God in creation and focuses on necessity. The last part tells us how these materials were used in the making of the human body, and here there are explanations in terms of both intelligence and necessity.[3]

While necessity is a constraint on the power of intelligence, it can also have a positive significance. Timaeus says that "intelligence prevailed over necessity by persuading *it* to guide most of the things which come to be towards the best, so that this cosmos was produced *by necessity* subordinated to wise persuasion" (48a, emphasis added). This, I suggest, should be taken seriously; it is necessity that guides things towards the best, and plays a part in producing the cosmos; the natural powers of things, governed by necessity, are put to positive use. Yet the references to intelligence prevailing and persuading show that necessity originally existed independently of it, and was not then a force for order.

There has been much controversy about just how we should understand Plato's use of the term "necessity" here, but I want to defend the view that it refers to what we would now call natural or causal necessity. Material things, for Plato, have natures that determine how they behave in specific circumstances.[4]

There are a number of reasons for thinking this. First, it makes sense of the original contrast between intelligence and necessity. Material things are seen as incapable of intelligence because, given the circumstances, they *must* behave in a certain way, and have no control over their movements. Next, the part of the *Timaeus* devoted to necessity bears this out. It shows that material things have definite natures (based on geometrical forms), and that these determine the ways they move and interact, the ways in which different bodies can be transformed into one another and the effect they have on us in perception (*Ti.* 53d–68c). This way of reading necessity shows how the creator can make use of material things as instruments in producing the cosmos – a tool, to be useful, must be relied on to behave in a particular way – but also how they can set limits to his powers. Finally, this reading shows how necessity can provide an explanation of a state of affairs, since we have explained an outcome if we show how it arises necessarily from what goes before.

However, the concept of necessity, so understood, gives rise to two major problems. First, Plato associates necessity with disorder. He describes it as "the wandering cause" (48a); he says that when separated from intelligence it produces "chance and disorderly effects" (46e); and he links it with the state of things before the universe was made, which was one of "discordant and unordered motion" (30a).[5] When controlled by intelligence it can be a force for order, but left to itself it is not. We naturally associate necessity with order. Can we make sense of Plato's linking it with disorder?

Secondly, we are told that intelligence *persuaded* necessity to guide most of the things that come to be towards the best; that is, the creator induced necessity to do something it would not have done of its own accord. But is not necessity unalterable? How can it be persuaded to serve a purpose?

The problem of disorder

We tend to associate natural necessity with order and regularity; and there certainly is a link. If anything is governed by natural necessity, its behaviour is regular in the sense that there is a rule to it; given specific circumstances, it can be relied on to behave in a specific way. This does not, however, mean that it is regular in the way that the heavenly bodies are (or seem to be) regular. It does not have to be periodic, returning to its starting-point at definite intervals; nor need it be easily predictable. It is plausible that when Plato refers to necessity in the absence of intelligence as producing disorder, this is what he has in mind: periodicity is a kind of stability, which is something he values, and predictability helps to make the world intelligible; their absence would indeed make the world a worse place.

We are also told that necessity in the absence of intelligence produces chance events; but this need not mean that they are wholly undetermined; it may mean only that they have no purpose and are unpredictable. That "chance" can be understood in this way is shown by the existence of games of "chance". The fall of a die is governed by deterministic laws, so that if I know the exact speed and direction with which it is thrown I can predict how it will land; but in practice it is unpredictable and so can be called a chance event.

In fact, while we generally think of the material world as, at least to a large extent, governed by deterministic laws, much of it is in practice unpredictable; the weather, the incidence of natural events such as earthquakes, or indeed health and disease in the human body, cannot be predicted in detail. For a long time, science, while not of course denying this, tended to neglect it, focusing on systems that were predictable, but recently the situation has changed, and scientists have begun to take fuller account of the disorderliness and unpredictability of the natural world; this may make it easier for us to appreciate Plato's point of view.

One aspect of this change has been the development of chaos theory, according to which some systems have sensitive dependence on initial conditions, which means that if their starting-point is changed by however small an amount, they will develop completely differently. Such systems are deterministic – there is a rule that governs their behaviour – but not periodic, and not predictable unless the initial conditions are known with perfect precision, which is not possible for a finite being.

There are also some systems that are not chaotic in the technical sense, so that they are in principle predictable, but that cannot be predicted in practice because of the complexity of the phenomena involved. Here again scientists have recently begun to focus on this area, treating complex systems as interesting in their own right rather than neglecting them in favour of simple ones.

It is clear that, much of the time, natural necessity does indeed produce systems that are in some way disorderly. Why, then, does the idea of a connection between necessity and disorder often seem alien to us?

One reason may be the fact that we are familiar with large-scale machines, and often take them as a paradigm of the behaviour of things governed by necessity; it is very natural to refer to "mechanical" necessity. Machines do indeed behave in a visibly regular and orderly way. But in fact they are not typical of things governed by necessity; they are cases where necessity has been organized by intelligence to serve a purpose.

However, perhaps the major reason why Plato's way of thinking looks alien to us is that, since Newton, we have had an explanation, in terms of necessity, of the movement of the heavenly bodies: the very phenomenon that Plato saw as evidence of intelligence (not just in the creator, but in the world itself), because they are so orderly, and necessity for him was linked with disorder. Newton showed that necessity *can* produce this kind of order. But after Newton it became easy to see the heavens as paradigms of necessity, giving rise to the sense that whatever is governed by necessity should have the same regularity and predictability. This, I suggest, was a mistake; the heavenly bodies are in fact unusual among natural phenomena, and while Plato was wrong to see them as rational beings, his view was not absurd given how different they are from most things governed by necessity. In many cases Plato was right to see necessity, left to itself, producing disorder, and intelligence introducing order.

The problem of persuasion

The other puzzle that Plato's use of the concept of necessity poses is that he refers to intelligence *persuading* necessity to guide things towards the best. Surely necessity is unalterable, in which case it makes no sense to speak of persuading it.

Glenn Morrow (1950) has proposed an answer to this problem that I think we should in essence accept. Persuasion contrasts with compulsion; whereas compelling something means making it act in a way contrary to its nature, persuading it involves exploiting its nature to bring about a desired result. In the *Phaedrus*, when discussing literal persuasion in the context of rhetoric, Socrates claims that we tailor our methods to the nature of the soul of our audience, exploiting the qualities of that soul (*Phdr.* 271b ff.).

Material things have natural powers that determine how they will act when placed in a particular arrangement. Intelligence – human or divine – can then exploit this by creating new arrangements in which the powers can interact so as to produce a desired result. This result will be explained through necessity (since, given the natural powers of the materials, it followed necessarily from the way they were arranged), but also through intelligence (since intelligence brought about the arrangement).

However, this account still leaves us with a puzzle. Before intelligence acts there will already be an arrangement of materials that, left to itself, should determine what events will follow. Hence, intelligence does not just produce new arrangements, but alters the arrangement things are already in, and in doing so it seems that it overrules the necessity that governs their movements.

This means, I think, that we have to accept that the necessity that governs material things is not absolute; it determines how things will behave *if nothing else intervenes*. From this it follows that if the material world were isolated from outside influences, its behaviour would be wholly determined; it would be as it was imagined by Plato's older contemporary Democritus, a materialist, who held that everything happens by necessity (DK Democritus 68 A1, A66), and as we have seen this would mean that nothing happened for a purpose. But for Plato the world is not so isolated; it is constantly influenced by souls, not only by God in creation but by other souls, human and divine, throughout its history

Souls, because they move themselves, are independent of material forces, and they in turn can act on the material world. They do not eliminate necessity, since material things go on behaving according to their determinate nature, but they modify its effects, creating new arrangements in which it has desirable results. If there were not souls the universe would be deterministic and so bereft of purpose; but because there are souls it is not.

The origin of evil

Although Plato believes that this world is good, he recognizes that there are many imperfections in it. In the first place, simply because it is a material thing and not a Form, it will fall short of its model in a number of ways. One of these is mutability; it cannot be unchanging as the model is. This is revealed, for instance, in the way in which it cannot possess eternity in the fullest sense, but only time, which is an image of eternity (*Ti.* 37c ff.). Another is the way in which it is necessarily embodied in some material, which will impose limits on what can be achieved (52b–c).

However, these factors mean only that some goods cannot be achieved. Plato also believes that there are some positive evils in the world: disorder in the natural world; irrationality in the soul. How do these arise?

We have seen that before God took control of the material world it was in a chaotic state of "discordant and unordered motion" (30a). While God succeeded in making the world for the most part orderly, he did not completely eliminate this disorderly motion; we are told that it continues within the ordered cosmos (57d ff.). It seems that even within the cosmos the material factor cannot be brought completely under divine control, and therefore continues to produce damaging results.[6]

Timaeus does not say much about the effect of material disorder on the world at large. (Elsewhere Plato shows some interest in catastrophes, such as the legendary flood, and their effect on history. These are discussed at the beginning of the *Timaeus*, in the Atlantis story [22c ff.], and in the *Statesman* [270c–d, 273a] and *Laws* [676a ff.].) The emphasis here is rather on the effect of material disorder on individuals. Various kinds of evil that can affect human beings are traced to physical causes. Old age and death are caused by the decay of the particles that make up our bodies (*Ti.* 81c ff.); disease is caused by imbalance among the body's material constituents (82a ff.). But material causes are also found for the evils that affect the soul.

As we have seen, there are for Plato two primary kinds of evil, or sources of wrongdoing, in the soul: ignorance, affecting the rational part of the soul, and the rebellious tendencies of the lower parts of soul, spirit and appetite. Both of these in the *Timaeus* seem to have bodily causes. At 43a ff. we are told how the rational soul, in infancy, is plunged into the flood of matter, both internal to the body (the bloodstream) and external to it (in sensation); this disrupts it, halting the operation of pure reason, disordering that of perceptual judgement. Later the soul recovers and we achieve intelligence, but we need proper nurturing to recover fully.

The lower parts of the soul are not themselves of material origin, but are created by the gods. They are described as dangerous, but necessary; presumably we need them to survive in the material world (69c ff.). However, the disorder of these parts, which leads them to behave in a rebellious manner, is later shown to have a bodily cause (86b ff.). Diseases of the soul are divided into ignorance and madness. Madness is said to be produced by excessive pleasures and pains, pleasure producing indulgence, while pain produces bad temper and melancholy, cowardice and recklessness. These pleasures and pains are themselves traced to bodily causes, and the fact that disorder in the soul has a bodily origin is used in support of the claim that "no one is willingly bad" (*Ti.* 86d–e).

It seems, then, that matter is both disorderly in itself, and a source of disorder in the soul. This harmonizes well with the *Phaedo* and *Republic*, in both of which body is seen as a cause of evil. Yet this is in some ways puzzling. For one thing, if matter has a disorderly motion of its own, going back to the primeval chaos, before soul was introduced into the world, what is the source of that motion? If self-motion is seen as a distinctive characteristic of soul – and the language of self-motion is used repeatedly in the *Timaeus* – then it might seem to follow that soul is the source of all motion. I suggested in Chapter 5 that this problem can be overcome if we are prepared to tolerate an infinite regress. If we trace a series of motions to a source, this source must be a self-mover; but it is possible that there are series of motions that have no source, but go back infinitely into the past; and the disorderly motion of matter in the *Timaeus*, which goes back to the primeval chaos, may be of this kind. Nevertheless, some readers will find this solution an uncomfortable one.

In any case, there is another problem that does not turn on a particular theory of soul; Plato's own conception of matter makes it hard to see how it could give rise to disorder. For him the material world consists fundamentally of the receptacle, space, characterized by qualities that are images of the Forms. The receptacle itself is said to be neutral and not to distort the images that it receives (50d–51b). But in this case, while it may indeed set limits to what the creator can do, it is hard to see how it could give rise to positive disorder.

There seems to be a real tension in Plato's thought here. On the one hand, as part of his general project of contrasting the material world and the Forms, he seeks to give as reductive an account of matter as possible. On the other, he wants to explain disorder in the world, without attributing it to God, and this requires a positive, active independent element. This is also required by Plato's view of the motive of creation, according to which there was once much more disorder in the material world, before God took it over, and God's aim was to eliminate that disorder.

Cosmology in the *Laws*

In Book 10 of the *Laws*, in the course of a defence of religion, Plato returns to the topic of cosmology. In some ways the position taken here is very similar to that of the *Timaeus*. There is a creator God,[7] although he remains in the background; the gods we are urged to worship are those of the heavens. The world is good and ordered for a purpose, and the regular movements of the heavenly bodies are used as evidence for this. But in some other ways, the *Laws* seems to reveal an outlook very different from that of the *Timaeus*. Since this is probably Plato's last treatment of the subject, we should briefly focus on it.

The chief speaker of the *Laws*, the Athenian Stranger, advances an argument against materialism that rests on the concept of self-motion (*Leg.* 894d ff.). Everything that moves, he argues, must be moved either by itself or by something else; and if we trace a sequence of motions back to its source, we will find that the first in every sequence must be a motion that moves itself. For this reason it cannot be true, as materialists think, that the soul is just an epiphenomenon of material changes; it is something fundamental to the universe.

The Athenian claims that if soul is the source of all motion, it is the source of all good and evil; and there must be more than one soul at work in the world, since there is at least one soul producing good and one producing evil (896d–e). He goes on to argue, however, on the basis of the heavenly movements, that the souls that are most powerful in the universe are good ones, and can be identified with the gods (898c ff.).

It will be seen that the Athenian's argument turns on an assumption that might be questioned: that there cannot be an infinite regress of motions. Timaeus (and the Stranger in the *Statesman*) seemed prepared to accept an infinite regress, tracing material motion back to the primeval chaos (*Ti.* 30a, 52d ff.; *Plt.* 273b–c). In the *Laws*, by contrast, the Athenian starts from an assumption, which he says many materialists share, that the world was once at rest; in this case, he argues, only soul could have set it in motion (*Leg.* 895a).

This at once gives us a view very different from that of the *Timaeus*; it makes soul prior to all bodily motions. In fact, however, it seems that an even stronger claim is being defended: that soul is prior to body itself (892a, 896a ff.). This can be seen as justified if we see generation as a motion; if soul is prior to all bodily processes, this must include the process that brings bodies into being. (Plato may well be assuming, as he does in the *Timaeus*, that all bodies are generated in some way.) It seems, therefore, that in the world as it is envisaged here, God does not create order out of disorder. It may be that, like the God of traditional theism, he is to be seen as creating the world out of nothing; soul is referred to at a number of points as generated, presumably by God (892c, 896a, 967d), and body in turn is generated by soul.

The Athenian draws two further consequences from the claim that soul is the source of all motion: first, as we have seen, that it is the source of good and evil, and secondly that all the attributes of soul are prior to matter – these turn out to include not only rational attributes, but such things as opinion true and false, joy and grief, hope and fear, love and hate (896d–7a). This seems to go against the position expressed in the *Timaeus*, and also to some extent in the *Phaedo* and *Republic*, that body is a source of evil, and that the disorderly elements in soul arise from the body.

If the independent bodily factor in the world is removed, one might well think that the element of necessity, which limits the creator's power, will also disappear. The *Laws* is not very explicit on this; we are told that the gods "can do anything which is within the power of mortals and immortals" (901d) – that is, if *anyone* can do it, they can – but this need not mean that they are omnipotent. However, earlier in the *Laws* the Athenian said that gods are subject to "divine" mathematical necessities but not to the necessities of ordinary life (818a–b); this could be read as meaning that the only limits on their power are logical and mathematical ones.

Given this new perspective, which seems to eliminate the independent, disorderly material factor, we need to reconsider the origin of evil. Book 10 of the *Laws* does include a consideration of the problem of evil, but in a particular form: the problem of injustice, why the wicked prosper and the innocent suffer (899d ff.). The Athenian claims that God has so ordered the universe that this is rectified in future lives, with good souls ascending to a better situation, bad souls descending to a worse one. This, however, does not explain how wickedness arises in the first place. The Athenian insists, in line with the interpretation of self-motion found in this work, that the cause of good or evil character lies within the soul, although we may sometimes be influenced by other souls (904b–d). But this remains puzzling; if there is no material cause of evil, why should it arise within the soul? Certainly not by a deliberate act of choice; it remains the case in the *Laws* that "no one acts unjustly except against his will" (860d). The causes of wrongdoing are ignorance, anger and pleasure; these are internal to the soul, but it is not clear how they arise there if not by a bodily cause.

Hence, it seems that the position taken in the *Laws* overcomes some of the problems found in the *Timaeus*, in particular that of how the bodily element, as Plato conceives it, can be a source of disorder, but at the same time gives rise to problems of its own. It is interesting, however, as it gives evidence that Plato was rethinking these issues up to the very end of his life.

NINE

Aesthetics

One of the most striking features of Plato's thought is his attitude to the arts, especially poetry, revealed in the severe restrictions he places on them in his account of the ideal state. It is sometimes thought that he banished poetry completely from that state, and indeed some of his own language suggests that,[1] although in fact he allows a place for hymns to the gods and odes in praise of good people (*Resp.* 607a). But it does seem that he condemns almost all of the poetry that existed in his time, and in particular that of Homer and the tragedians,[2] often seen as the supreme achievements of ancient Greek literature. Moreover, while the main focus of his criticism is poetry, he does also propose restrictions on music (398c ff.), and on visual art, including the design of buildings, furniture, clothing and so on (401a ff.). In this chapter, we shall look at Plato's thought about the arts so as to see his reasons for restricting them in this way.

The term "aesthetics" is in some ways anachronistic in the discussion of Plato. For us, it includes both the philosophical consideration of the arts, and that of beauty and related properties and our experience of them. While, as we shall see, Plato did think that beauty can be manifested in the products of art, he would not have seen the topics as particularly closely connected. We shall be focusing here on his account of the arts.

However, even the term "art" is anachronistic in discussing Plato; he has no term that translates as "art", except *technē*, which corresponds to the wider sense of "art" in which it is equivalent to "craft" or "skill". In fact, the idea that painting, poetry, music and so on form a distinctive group, which can be identified as "art" in a more restricted sense, did not develop in its modern form until the eighteenth century. However, Plato does have definite thoughts about many of the activities and products that we would describe as art. He is mostly concerned with poetry, but poetry for him is closely connected with music – the Greek word *mousikē* covers both – as it was often written to be sung or recited publicly. He also draws analogies between painting and poetry.

Poetry and censorship

Discussions of poetry are found in two places in the *Republic*: first in Books 2 and 3, and then in Book 10. The first discussion forms part of Socrates' account of the education of the guardians, the military class, from whom the future rulers of the state will be drawn; the question is what kind of poetic works are suitable for use in their education. In the later discussion, however, Socrates seems to make a more general claim: that poetry should be severely restricted in the ideal state as a whole, not just in education.[3] Moreover, the later discussion seems to propose more radical restrictions on both the form and the content of poetry. Although the earlier discussion proposed fairly severe censorship, it was made clear that some existing poetry, including passages from Homer, would survive (see e.g. *Resp.* 389e). In the later discussion this no longer seems to be the case.

Socrates proposes restrictions on both the content and the form of poetry. His restrictions on form will be discussed in later sections. As far as content goes, he seeks to forbid poetry that promotes views that he finds damaging: for instance, that the gods produce evil as well as good (397e ff.); that they are changeable, and that they can be deceitful (380d ff.); that death is an evil and should be feared (386b ff.); and, by implication, that a just life is an unhappy one (392b–c).[4]

Plato's apparent support of such radical censorship is in itself disturbing. In the context of education, the idea that books should be selected in such a way as to encourage the development of enlightened views is not wholly unreasonable, but even there we might well think that students should be presented with different views and allowed to discuss them and make up their own minds, rather than simply being fed a diet of material that presents views that their teachers approve of. The way in which Socrates restricts the educational diet of his young guardians is particularly striking when we consider that he is here concerned with the education of the most intelligent part of the population, some of whom will go on to become philosophers.

In any case, in Book 10 Socrates goes on to propose restrictions on poetry in the state as a whole, not just in formal education (595a, 607a ff.). However, it is clear there that he is still looking at poetry from an educational point of view; he is concerned that people will look to it for guidance and understanding, and are liable to be deceived by it if it is not grounded on knowledge. This does indeed seem to be how poetry was often seen at the time. Homer was regarded as "the teacher of Greece" (606e), and people looked to him as a source of wisdom. In the light of this Socrates' readiness to censor his work is more understandable.

Nevertheless, it is still disturbing if Plato envisaged the people of his ideal state being taught only the truth as he saw it, and not being presented with alternative positions. Perhaps the explanation of this is, once again, a strong conviction of the power of reason to find the right answer. If we think the truth is uncertain, we will want to consider different possible views and make up our own minds; but if the truth is known, why should we concern ourselves with deceptive views? This does not mean that Plato expects ethical and philosophical truths to be accepted simply on the basis of authority; he believes that philosophers should come to grasp these truths for themselves, by the use of their own reason. But perhaps he sees ethical and philosophical truth as rather like mathematical truth. There, although we should indeed follow proofs for ourselves, we can be confident that if we reason properly we will reach the right answer and agree on it, and therefore it is pointless to consider rival views. For Plato, the same will apply to moral and philosophical truth.

The concept of imitation

In Book 3 of the *Republic*, having set out his proposals for the content of poetry, Socrates turns to its form. His discussion here turns on the concept of *mimesis*, traditionally translated "imitation"; this concept will also be central to his discussion of poetry in Book 10, and has had an important impact on later aesthetic theory, so it deserves to be looked at in some depth. The basic idea expressed by the term is that of copying someone or producing a copy of something. It can be used in contexts as various as mimicking someone's voice, and imitating someone's behaviour when one takes them as a moral example. There is always an implication of likeness; the imitator becomes like the thing imitated or produces something like it. For this reason, "imitation" is a translation that does capture the basic force of the Greek term, although it will not be idiomatic in all the contexts where Socrates uses it. For instance, we do not normally speak of an actor imitating the character he plays, but one can see what would be meant by saying this; he acts, in some respects at least, as that character would act.

In Book 3 the term "imitation" is used to denote a specific kind of poetry (*Resp.* 392d ff.): dramatic poetry, where an actor takes the part of a character, and some parts of epic poetry, the speeches, in which the reciter likewise takes the part of a character and says what that character would say. Both the actor or reciter and the author of such poetry can be spoken of as "imitating". This contrasts with other kinds of poetry, including other parts of epic, which proceed in a straightforwardly narrative way; the reciter or singer simply recounts events and does not speak in the voice of a character. In imitative poetry, the speaker is himself becoming like the character whose part he plays. Socrates seeks to restrict, although not wholly eliminate, poetry that is imitative in this limited sense. In particular, he forbids the imitation of morally bad people, mad people and people of lower classes; he does not here forbid the *description* of such characters, and it is not clear what stories it would be possible to tell without mentioning them.

In Book 10, by contrast, "imitation" is given a wider sense. It is applied to painting (597e), and also to narrative poetry. Socrates speaks of Homer "imitating medical language" (599c), although in the passages he seems to have in mind, Homer is not actually taking the part of a doctor but simply describing what a doctor might do.[5] In these passages, therefore, the point is clearly not that the artist *becomes* like what he depicts, but only that he *produces* something like it. In the case of visual art it is clear enough how he does this; a painting does indeed look, in some ways, like the thing it represents. In poetry the relation is more complex; a poem about a battle, for instance, does not actually look or sound like a battle. But it may bring a battle before the mind, in such a way that the listener will say "a battle is like that".

However, in Book 10 Socrates gives a further twist to the concept of imitation: he uses it specifically for something that reproduces the appearance of a thing rather than the reality – that looks like the thing it represents without being really like it (597e–8c). This is the sense of "imitation" found in expressions such as "imitation marble", or in the warning to beware of cheap imitations. In the case of paintings this applies in a fairly simple way; a painting of a bed looks like a bed, but is not really like a bed – one cannot sleep on it. In the case of poetry, even the similarity of appearance is more abstract, but once again the poem is not really like the thing it represents. This new conception of imitation is particularly emphasized in the first argument of Book 10; there poets are presented as imitating their subject matter in the same sense in which painters do.[6] In the later part of Book 10 Socrates goes back to speaking of poets imitating people,[7] and once again largely has dramatic poetry in mind; the arguments here are more closely linked with those of Book 3.

These two uses of "imitation" fit together rather uncomfortably. It is quite possible that the same work might be imitative in both senses. But they ground different criticisms of poetry that are hard to combine. In Book 3, and the later part of Book 10, the objection to imitation turns largely on the thought that we might actually become like what we imitate. In the first argument of Book 10, however, the central point is that an imitation is *not* genuinely like what it imitates; it reproduces only the appearance and not the reality. There is no direct contradiction, because the objects of imitation discussed in the two passages are different; poetry might produce a false appearance of some *craft* – war, statecraft or education – while actually producing harmful *emotions*, bringing about a genuine likeness to the object of imitation in that sense. Nevertheless the double use of the term "imitation" is confusing.

Before going on to look at Socrates' arguments in more detail, one other point should be noted. Plato has inspired the view, an influential one when the modern concept of art was being developed in the eighteenth century, that imitation is the distinctive feature of art: what all the arts have in common, and perhaps what gives art its purpose. However, Plato's own works contain no such view; indeed, they could not, since Plato has no general term for art. Nor is there any reason to think that he would have seen it as essential to all the activities that *we* describe as art. Although he uses the term in connection with poetry, visual art and music (see *Resp.* 399a–c), he need not have thought that, for instance, architecture was an example of imitation. Indeed, it does not even apply to all poetry; in the sense of "imitation" used in Book 3 it is clear that much poetry is not imitative, whereas in the wider sense used in Book 10 it is less clear, but he does seem to leave room for some that is not.[8] Plato's Socrates is simply identifying imitation as a central feature of some of the activities we call art, and criticizing them on that basis.

Imitation and character

In Book 3 of the *Republic* Socrates raises the question whether the poetry used in the education of the guardians should be imitative, in the sense where this involves the speaker taking a part (*Resp.* 394e). Since the students would themselves have recited the poetry they were learning, not just listened or read silently, this question can also be cast as whether the young guardians themselves should be imitative. One might think that Socrates was going to say the young guardians should not imitate at all, but in fact he allows some imitation of good people: those who are suitable role models for the guardians (385c). However, he rules out imitation of the bad, the mad, those of lower classes and those in damaging emotional states (385d ff.), and he thinks that as a result of this the amount of imitation in the poetry taught to the guardians will be small (386e).

Alexander Nehamas (1988) and others have suggested that what Socrates is really opposing here is poetry which pursues imitation as an end in itself; such poetry would try to imitate as many kinds of person and situations as possible (see also Janaway 1995: 100). Aristotle notes that we take pleasure in imitation, even of things that are in themselves ugly (Ar. *Poet.* 1448b5–12). Plato holds that imitation of this kind is undesirable. The guardians should imitate only the kind of person they aim to become. Imitation is not an end in itself, but something pursued for the sake of development of character.

Socrates' official reason for rejecting indiscriminate imitation is that it conflicts with the principle, central to his ideal state, that each person should perform just one function (*Resp.* 394e). Just as people in actual life should do just one kind of work, the kind they are best at, so in poetic performances they should imitate just one kind of person. One may wonder why this principle applies to imitation as well as to actual life. To start with, Socrates seems simply to be drawing an analogy: as a person cannot be good at doing many kinds of work, so he cannot be good at many kinds of imitation (395a–b). However, he then goes on to make a further point: that imitation, if engaged in repeatedly, actually has an effect on one's character, and one becomes like what one imitates (395d). Here, there is not just an analogy between doing and imitating. What we imitate affects what we do, and if the guardians imitate bad people this will interfere with their ability to do their distinctive function of protecting the state.

It certainly seems possible that imitation should have this effect; taking someone's part can lead us to sympathize with him, and so may lead us to become more like him. It is not clear, though, why this should always be the case. Might we not imitate someone while remaining clear that we are not him, and so avoid corruption? In fact Plato might have accepted this; Socrates says at one point that the guardians may occasionally imitate a bad person "for fun" or "in play" (396e). But the danger of corruption seems always to be present.

Plato returns to this theme in Book 10 of the *Republic*. The first argument against poetry of that book turns on the false appearance of knowledge it produces, and will be considered in the next section. However, there is also a group of arguments that relate to the themes of Books 2 and 3, but develop them further: Socrates argues that poetry appeals to damaging emotions, and can corrupt a good character (605c ff.).

Socrates claims that when we see, presented on the stage, something we would be ashamed of in real life, we nevertheless enjoy it and sympathetically share the feelings of the people we see presented. A part of the soul that we normally restrain – the part that contains these shameful feelings – is strengthened and encouraged by this process, so that we come to have these feelings in our own life. This is developed at greatest length with grief. Great grief, according to Socrates, is not an appropriate reaction to the death of loved ones, but in tragedy we often see people indulging in grief, admire the performance and feel sympathy with them. Something similar happens in comedy; laughable acts that we would normally be ashamed of are accepted and treated with sympathy because they are seen as just a joke. The same effect may result from depictions of other feelings such as anger and sexual passion. In this way, we become like the people we see represented on stage.

This resembles the claim of Book 3 that we become like what we imitate, but goes beyond it in two ways. First, it extends the claim to the audience; we do not have to be acting the parts ourselves to have sympathy with the characters. Secondly, we are told something about how it works; we feel able to sympathize with the characters because we think of them as someone else, not ourselves, and so do not see the emotions we are feeling as damaging to ourselves (606a–b). The point is not that we directly identify with the character, but that, precisely because we are aware of the difference, we allow ourselves to feel what we would not otherwise feel. But, Socrates suggests, this can be damaging; it is dangerous to allow these feelings even in a purely fictional context.

This passage does not simply ignore the difference between enjoying a performance and taking pleasure in the act depicted. Rather, it argues that, despite the difference, one can lead to the other. That it *can* do so seems true; often a powerful performance will lead us to sympathize with the character, even if he is not a person we would normally have sympathy with. We may question whether this happens as widely as Plato seems to think.

Imitation and knowledge

Socrates' principal attack on poetry in Book 10 of the *Republic* turns on the idea that it makes deceptive and dangerous claims to knowledge. Socrates begins by considering visual art. This is done in order to show that there is an activity that reproduces the appearance of a thing, not the reality, and that this activity need not involve any knowledge of the nature of the thing; this activity is then named imitation. Having established this, he goes on to argue that poetry is also an example of imitation in this sense.

Socrates approaches the subject through the theory of Forms (596a ff.). A craftsman, producing, for instance, a bed, works "looking to the Form" (596b). This need not mean, as becomes clear later (601c ff.), that he has knowledge of the Form of bed – his grasp of it may be indirect, and amount only to true belief – but he has some grasp of what a bed is, of its purpose and how it fits together to serve that purpose. A painter, by contrast, painting a bed, need not have any awareness of the Form; he takes the visible bed as his model, and paints on the basis of familiarity with that.

The next step is to claim that if something is copied from visible examples of a kind rather than from the Form, it only reproduces the appearance of the thing, not the reality (598a ff.). A painting of a bed, for instance, reproduces the way it looks from a certain perspective, not how it is in itself. One might try to reproduce something as it is, that is to make a new object of the same kind as it, as, for instance, a maker of reproduction furniture does, but one could not do this simply on the basis of looking at the original object; one would need some grasp of the Form, that is of the purpose of the object and how it worked. However, one can, just by looking at an object, reproduce its appearance.

One should be careful not to over-interpret these claims. They need not be taken to mean that the painter must be copying specific individual beds that he can see; nor do they mean that his aim must be to reproduce the *exact* appearance of the things he is taking as his model. It means only that his work is based on his familiarity with visible things, and aims to look like them. It need not, therefore, be seen as a totally mindless activity. It can involve skill, and this will become important when we come to apply the analogy to poetry. Socrates is not denying that poets are skilful; if they were not, their work would not be so dangerous.

While Socrates is here shown as having a low opinion of visual art, seeing it as trivial, he does not seek to ban it from the ideal state. The discussion of painting is intended to show that it is possible to reproduce the appearance of something without any grasp of the reality. Socrates then goes on to ask if poetry does the same (598d ff.). When painting does this, it is not normally deceptive; most people are able to distinguish between a painting of a bed and a real bed. Socrates does point out that children and stupid people – who have no experience on the basis of which to recognize a work of art – may in fact confuse a painting with what it represents (598c). But such confusion, one may think, is easy to overcome, and in any case will not normally have disastrous consequences. However, if poetry is imitative in the same way, it is much more likely to be deceptive, and this deception will be dangerous.

Clearly, Socrates does not mean that in listening to a poem about a battle or a feast, we may be led to think that a battle or a feast is actually taking place. Rather, his point is that poetry may produce a false impression of knowledge. The poetry of Homer deals with such matters as medicine, war and statecraft. It reproduces the appearance of such things, in that it describes them in ways that remind us of our experience of them, and so it may give us the impression that the poet has knowledge of such matters. This, then, may lead us to see the poet as a source of guidance; and indeed Homer was seen in this way in ancient Greece (598d–e).

However, Socrates argues, Homer does not really have such knowledge. Socrates does not simply rely on the analogy of painting in showing this;[9] rather, he focuses on what was known, or thought to be true, of Homer's life (599b ff.). He argues that we can know that Homer did not have knowledge of central areas such as war, politics and education, since he had no achievements in those fields: he was not a general, a legislator, the founder of a city, an inventor, a practical educator or the founder of a school. In this, Socrates proposes, he is typical of poets more generally.[10] If poets really had knowledge of the matters they write about, he suggests, they would not choose to devote themselves to poetry, rather than to genuinely useful achievements (599a–b); nor would others allow them to do so (600d–e).

Many things can be questioned about this argument. For one thing, it seems to *assume* that the actual achievements of a statesman, a general and so on are more valuable than those of a poet. Moreover, even if we grant that they are, it does not follow that everyone thinks the same; if Homer, or his contemporaries, *believed* that poetry was more valuable, even if they were wrong, this would explain why he devoted himself to poetry. Some people are frustrated by public opinion in carrying out their true vocations; Socrates himself may be an example. Moreover, there *were* some poets who had other notable achievements; for instance the Athenian statesman Solon, who is mentioned in the *Timaeus*, was both a poet and an important legislator who played a significant part in the development of the Athenian constitution.[11]

Nevertheless there seems to be something right in what Socrates says; granted that it is possible to create a plausible appearance of something without an understanding of the reality, it is reasonable to think that poets are often doing so, and that they have no expertise in the matters they write about, and in this case it is indeed dangerous to look to them for guidance.

However, we should notice an ambiguity in the concept of imitation that Socrates is using here. There is an activity that reproduces the appearance of things, not the reality, and this activity *need* not involve any knowledge of, or even true belief about, the reality. It can be based, not on a grasp of what the kind of thing in question is, but just on a familiarity with examples and their appearance. But it does not follow that no one who engages in this activity has any grasp of the reality, nor that a grasp of the reality cannot help them in performing it (as when artists study anatomy in order to help them in drawing human figures). In saying that poetry is imitative, does Socrates mean only that it reproduces appearances of things, not the things themselves, or that it is not based on knowledge of the things themselves?

In his actual discussion of Homer he certainly seems to mean the latter; he seeks to show that Homer lacked real expertise, and concludes on that basis that he was an imitator (*Resp.* 600e). However, if this is right, it seems to leave room for a kind of poetry that is grounded on knowledge. Such poetry would still be imitative in the sense that it reproduced appearances rather than realities; a poem about a city, for instance, is not a city, and it is at least plausible to think that producing such a poem is less valuable than producing an actual city. But it would not be deceptive as the poetry of Homer and others are; it would be guided by a real knowledge of statecraft. While Socrates seems to condemn all existing poets as imitators in a pejorative sense, he may leave open some room for a possible kind of poetry that does not deserve this kind of condemnation. On the other hand one may still ask what the value of this kind of poetry would be. If one has real knowledge of important subjects, would it not be better to make use of it in practical activity or in direct teaching, rather than in the creation of poems? I shall return to this subject later, after discussing another aspect of Plato's view of poetry.

Poetry and inspiration

When we turn from the *Republic* to some other works of Plato, we may be surprised to find a view of poetry that is at first sight very different from that of the *Republic*. According to this view, poetry is the result of divine inspiration, and so can be a vehicle of truth, although not of knowledge. The gods speak through the poets, as they do through prophets, although the poets do not understand what they are saying. This idea appears in some Socratic dialogues, the *Apology* and *Ion*, and is briefly alluded to in the *Meno* (99d), which is generally thought to have both Socratic and Platonic elements, and also appears in the *Phaedrus*, a work normally seen as reflecting Plato's own mature thought.

The idea of divine inspiration of poets was not, of course, new – ancient poets themselves, such as Homer and Hesiod, invoke the muses to inspire them – but Plato emphasizes the irrational nature of the process; rather than speaking *to* the poets the god possesses them, as he does prophets and initiates in some mystery cults, and speaks *through* them. This idea can be seen as having both positive and negative implications. On the one hand, if we emphasize irrationality and the fact that poets do not have knowledge, it seems a negative view of them, opposing their pretensions to wisdom; if we emphasize the connection with the gods, and the way in which this enables the poets to reveal truth, it becomes more positive.

In the Socratic dialogues it is the negative aspect of this view of poetry that is emphasized. In the *Apology* (22a–c), it appears as part of Socrates' unsuccessful search for someone who is really wise; poets claim wisdom, but their claim turns out to be false, since their poetic ability comes from inspiration, not knowledge. The *Ion* is a satirical work, in which Socrates makes fun of Ion, a reciter of epic poetry who claims great wisdom. Socrates tries to convince him that he is not in fact wise, and that his success is due not to expertise, but to inspiration; the god's inspiration of the poet passes itself on to the reciter and through him to the audience (see esp. *Ion* 533c ff.).

However, in the *Phaedrus* the same general account of poetry is used to show it in a more positive light. Socrates is there defending (erotic) love. He has previously condemned it as a kind of madness, but now he argues that, although it is indeed a kind of madness, it is a sort of divinely inspired madness and can therefore be beneficial. To support this, Socrates refers to other examples of divine madness, which are found in prophecy and mystic initiation, but also in poetry, which is here said to recount the acts of heroes for the instruction of future generations (*Phdr.* 245a). It seems that this should be taken seriously, not seen as simply ironic; the praise of love is presumably meant seriously, so the praise of poetry should be likewise.

Of course, Plato certainly thinks that knowledge, gained by reason, is superior to any kind of truth gained by an irrational process; poetry, therefore, continues to be ranked below philosophy. But this does not mean that these irrational ways of gaining access to truth are insignificant. Indeed, the description of love in the *Phaedrus* suggests that it is often through this divinely inspired form of irrationality that we are first moved to do philosophy (252e–3a); the *love* of wisdom must come before wisdom itself, and this is the result of inspiration.

One might ask how poetry can be a vehicle of truth if poets do not agree with one another. An answer to this is suggested by the *Timaeus*, in its account of prophecy: although prophets are inspired, their words need interpretation, which must be done by someone in his right mind (*Ti.* 71d–2b). This may refer to the ecstatic utterances of some prophets, but can also apply to the riddling ways in which prophets often spoke, as the Delphic oracle famously did; their utterances, although they contain truth, are not clear and need interpretation. The same may be true of poetry.

Can this view be reconciled with that found in the *Republic*? In one way they are certainly similar. They both involve the claim that poets do not have knowledge. Indeed, some arguments found in the *Ion* for the view of poetry presented there are very like arguments from the *Republic*: that poets (or, in the *Ion*, reciters) do not have expertise in the subjects they talk about, or people would not allow them to devote themselves to poetry (*Ion* 541b–c); that they produce irrational emotions in their audience (535d–e). But in another way they seem strongly opposed; if poetry is divinely inspired, it should be a source of truth, even if not of knowledge, whereas in the *Republic* it is deceptive.

One might try to reconcile the different approaches by pointing out that the *Republic* deals with an ideal state, in which there are philosopher rulers who can themselves impart truth to the people, and train other philosophers to come after them. In such a state, one may think, poetry would not have even the limited value that Plato sometimes allows it in the actual world. Even if it contains some truth, it is inferior to philosophical teaching, and it is dangerous, because people may look to it as a source of knowledge; only philosophers may be able to interpret it rightly and so avoid damage. Indeed, even in the *Republic* Socrates does allow poetry some value; he permits hymns to the gods and praises of good people to remain, the latter being exactly the function he allows to inspired poets in the *Phaedrus*. (It is often said that works of this kind cannot be inspired, and are an inferior form of poetry; but this is not clearly true. Hymns, such as the works of Charles Wesley, and eulogies, such as Ben Jonson's dedication to Shakespeare, can surely be of high poetic quality.)

Some aspects of the *Republic*, however, are hard to reconcile with the idea of poetry as divinely inspired. One is the claim that imitation, which includes poetry, is merely a game (*Resp.* 602b), although this might perhaps mean only a game in comparison with philosophy. Another is the claim that imitators lack true belief, not just knowledge (602a), although here one might say that they sometimes speak the truth, through inspiration, even without believing it. But the biggest problem may not be in reconciling specific claims made in the different works, but simply in their tone. Would Plato be as hostile to poetry in general as he seems to be in the *Republic* if he thought of it as a divine gift? We should perhaps simply take these as different views of poetry to which Plato was attracted, either at different moments in his career, or even at the same time, being unable to choose decisively between them.

Finally, we could ask whether this idea of inspired speech might help us to understand some parts of Plato's own works. Socrates' speech in the *Phaedrus* may itself be seen as an example of inspired speech. It is said to be the result of inspiration by the muses (*Phdr.*

262d), and to have been largely spoken in play (266c), yet it contains philosophical content that seems to be meant seriously and to resemble, to some extent, positions that Plato favours elsewhere. Might it be seen as a poetic utterance, pointing to truth, but not expounding it with philosophical rigour? Likewise the *Symposium* contains two speeches in praise of love by poets, the comedian Aristophanes and the tragedian Agathon; clearly, neither of these speeches represents the philosophical truth, and both are in fact criticized later by Socrates,[12] yet they seem to contain insights that Plato finds it hard to incorporate within his own thought. Aristophanes presents us with the idea of love for an individual because of the individual he is, not for the sake of the beauty he shares with others (*Symp.* 191d ff.), Agathon with the idea of love as something outgoing, producing peace and harmony, which seeks to benefit others rather than simply to achieve the good for oneself (197d). Both these speeches may be seen as examples of poetic inspiration, pointing indirectly to a truth that is not fully understood.

Art and beauty

As we have seen, Plato has no term corresponding exactly to our "art". Nevertheless, we can ask about the value he ascribes to the kind of activities and products that we would call art: to painting and sculpture, poetry, music and so on. We know that he banishes most poetry from the ideal state, and also severely censors music and design. However, this is not to say that he denies all value in the products of the arts. I would suggest that there are two kinds of value in particular that, within a Platonic way of thinking, can be ascribed to them.

First, works of art may have value simply by being instances of Forms such as beauty, harmony and so on. As such, they can inspire us to philosophy. In the *Phaedrus* (250b ff.), Socrates draws attention to beauty as the only one of the most significant Forms that has visible images; justice, temperance and so on are not visible in the same way. So beauty plays a special role in prompting the soul to recollection of Forms. Not all beauty is visible, for there are beautiful souls and so on. But visible beauty is valuable in itself, as well as prompting people to seek for higher kinds of beauty. Here Socrates is talking about natural beauty, that of people; he is describing the experience of falling in love. But could not what he says be relevant to the arts as well? Could they not produce instances of beauty that are valuable as such? This would not be representational art, or at least it is not as representational that it has this value. A picture of a man – even an idealized man – is an image not of a Form but of a (real or imagined) particular. But a work of art, simply because it is beautiful, may be an image – that is an instance – of beauty itself.

In several places Plato seems to allow works of art this kind of value. In *Republic* Book 3 (399d ff.) Socrates says that young people should be encouraged to develop such qualities as harmony, grace and simplicity in their characters, and should therefore be surrounded by things that have those qualities. Hence craftsmen should produce things that have those qualities. This relates to painting, but also to weaving, embroidery, architecture and furniture design. These arts, Socrates claims, can produce qualities that resemble those desirable in the soul, although clearly works of art possess them a very different way from the soul.

Music is seen by Plato as especially valuable because of the harmonious relationships between musical sounds, which is in some way parallel to the kind of harmony that should exist in the soul. This aspect of music is first emphasized in the *Republic* (531c), but further developed in the *Timaeus*, which includes the passages that give rise to the famous concept of the harmony of the spheres (*Ti.* 35b–d, 38c–d). For Plato this does not mean that the heavenly bodies literally make musical sounds, but that their movements stand in mathematical relations that embody harmonious proportions. Later in the same work he says that musical sounds give pleasure, not only to foolish people but to the wise, "because they imitate the divine harmony in mortal movements" (80b). So music is valuable as an instance of harmonious relationships, which are also manifested in the heavenly movements and, ideally, in the soul.

In the *Philebus*, there is a curious passage in which Socrates discusses beautiful things which produce pure pleasures (*Phlb.* 51c–

d). These include simple, clear, musical notes, but also pure shapes and colours. He emphasizes that by a beautiful shape he does not mean a living thing or a picture (a piece of mimetic art), but just a simple geometrical shape. This would seem to leave room for some abstract visual art, although only of a very simple kind. It appears, then, that the arts can produce some things that are valuable in their own right.

Poetry and philosophy

But can Plato find any distinctive value for representational art, including poetry? We saw earlier that the idea of imitation, as it is explained in Book 10 of the *Republic*, is ambiguous; it can mean either simply work that reproduces the appearance of something, not the reality, or work that is not based on knowledge of the reality. While poetry cannot fail to be imitative in the first sense, it may not always be imitative in the second; there could be a poetry that is based on knowledge. Might poetry of this kind serve the purposes of philosophy?

One may think that we find something of the sort in Plato's own works. Although they are not in verse, they achieve in prose effects similar to those that poets can achieve; indeed, Plato may be thought of as the first writer to do so. The *Republic* can be seen as, among other things, an imitation of an ideal state, intended to create in people's minds an image of what such a state would be like. The dialogues more generally can be seen as imitations of a philosophical life, showing philosophers – primarily Socrates, but others as well – engaged in philosophical enquiry and discussion.

Such imitations still fall short of what they represent. Just as a description of a city is not a city, a description or dramatic reconstruction of a philosophical debate is not a philosophical debate. A real philosophical debate requires live participants, able to think up answers for themselves, and to explain, when questioned, what they mean. No one can actually become wise just by reading Plato's works. But such imitations, if guided by knowledge, can still serve a valuable purpose; they can set before us the ideal of a philosophical life; and they can be a stimulus to philosophical thought.

It is not clear that all of Plato's use of poetic language and methods can be explained in this way. Perhaps he does sometimes speak in a poetic way in an attempt – like the inspired poets he describes – to express something he does not fully understand, and of which he cannot give a philosophical account. This may be the explanation of the various myths that occur in his work, particularly those regarding life after death that appear in the *Gorgias* (524d ff.), the *Phaedo* (108e ff.), the *Phaedrus* (246a ff.) and the *Republic* (614b ff.). This is not to say that no philosophical account of these matters is possible – it is just that it has not yet been achieved – and Plato would have said that a philosophical account was preferable. But when it has not been achieved, a poetic one may have some value. Sometimes, too, Plato may simply be trying to make his work attractive to outsiders; and sometimes his pen may run away with him and lead him to do things that he would find it hard to justify philosophically.

The paradox of Plato

Plato's works have a puzzling feature: they are extremely imitative, not only in the sense found in Book 10 of the *Republic* – that they present the appearance of things – but in that found in Books 2 and 3 – that they are dramatic, with the speaker taking on a part. In fact, both kinds of imitation described in Book 3 are found in the dialogues. Some, such as the *Gorgias* and *Phaedrus*, are actually dramatic in form; others, like the *Symposium*, *Phaedo* and *Republic*, have narrators, but contain many speeches where the narrator repeats someone else's words. Many of the dialogues represent conflict, and therefore involve the presentation of characters whose state of soul is less than desirable. There is imitation of bad characters, like Critias in the *Charmides*, Callicles in the *Gorgias* or Thrasymachus in the *Republic*. There is imitation of figures of fun, like Hippias or Ion in the works called after them. There is imitation of unphilosophical poets, like Agathon and Aristophanes in the *Symposium*. The *Ion* and

Hippias Major can indeed be seen as comedies. And the *Phaedo* is, in a way, a tragedy; it does not actually recommend a tragic view of life, rather telling us not to fear death or mourn for our loved ones, yet it does in fact convey the sorrow that Socrates' companions felt at his death.

This may lead us to ask whether Plato's works would be allowed in the ideal state. One may well think that they would not. They are not hymns to the gods or (only) praises of good people (although of course they do contain the praise of Socrates); they are dramatic and highly imitative works. It is true that in his late work, the *Laws*, he does recommend his own work for use in the state he is there proposing (*Leg.* 811c–12a), but the *Laws* lacks much of the dramatic quality of earlier works.

Plato himself might not have seen this as a problem. He might say that in the ideal state philosophers would be present, could themselves give philosophical guidance and reveal in their own lives what a philosophical life was like. Hence, a literary representation of philosophy would not be needed. But we may well feel that there is in fact something valuable in the works of Plato as we have them – the interplay of characters, the interaction of philosophical and poetic elements – that would be missing in the ideal state. In this case there is something of value in Plato's works that his own principles would exclude, and this is a paradox he may not have been able to overcome.

Notes

1. Introduction

1. The development of Plato's ideas is discussed in Chapter 2.
2. Certainly philosophers can arise by chance outside the ideal state (*Resp.* 520b), but they are not as well educated as those who are brought up within that state.

2. Plato's development and Plato's Socrates

1. A historic defence of the unity of Plato's thought is P. Shorey, *The Unity of Plato's Thought* (Chicago, IL: University of Chicago Press, 1960). The widely accepted developmental view can be found at, for instance, G. Vlastos, *Socrates: Ironist and Moral Philosopher* (Cambridge: Cambridge University Press, 1991), 46–7.
2. The abandonment of the theory is argued for by G. E. L. Owen, "The Place of the *Timaeus* in Plato's Dialogues", *Classical Quarterly* 3 (1953), 79–95. For the view that Plato came to attach less importance to it see for instance I. M. Crombie, *An Examination of Plato's Doctrines*, 2 vols (London: Routledge & Kegan Paul, 1962–3), vol. 2, 356 ff.
3. "No harm comes to a good man either in life or in death" (*Ap.* 41c–d).
4. Plato is not mentioned by name in the second passage, but the parallel with the first shows clearly that he is being discussed.
5. The first position is argued at length in Vlastos, *Socrates*, chs 2–4. For the second see *ibid.*, 117 n.50.
6. See, for instance: "the living thing of which all other living things are parts" (*Ti.* 30c).

PLATO

3. Plato's metaphysics: the "theory of Forms"

1. I capitalize "Form" in order to make it clear when I am discussing the Forms of Plato's theory; but this should not be taken to imply that "Form" in Plato is a technical term; his use of it is continuous with its use in fairly natural ways of speaking, as, for instance, when we speak of different forms of animal.
2. This is argued by G. Vlastos, "Reasons and Causes in the *Phaedo*", *Philosophical Review* 78 (1969), 291–325, reprinted in his *Plato: A Collection of Critical Essays, vol. 1: Metaphysics and Epistemology*, 132–66 (Garden City, NY: Doubleday, 1970).
3. See *Laws* 822a, which seems to affirm that the movements of the heavenly bodies are perfectly regular.
4. This is argued by D. Keyt, "Aristotle on Plato's Receptacle", *American Journal of Philology* 72 (1961), 291–300.
5. See for instance C. Meinwald, "Good-bye to the Third Man", in *The Cambridge Companion to Plato*, R. Kraut (ed.), 365–96 (Cambridge: Cambridge University Press, 1992). The basic distinction was first proposed by Michael Frede, *Prädikation und Existenzaussage* (Göttingen: Vandenhoeck & Ruprecht, 1967).
6. See for instance *Timaeus* 50d, where the Forms are compared to a father and the receptacle to a mother.
7. This analogy seems to have been introduced into the debate by Peter Geach, who says he was inspired to use it by Wittgenstein. See P. Geach, "The Third Man Again", *Philosophical Review* 65 (1956), 72–82, reprinted in R. E. Allen (ed.), *Studies in Plato's Metaphysics*, 265–77 (London: Routledge & Kegan Paul, 1965).

4. Knowledge

1. See *Sophist* 253c, where the Stranger suggests there are some Forms that are responsible for the combination and division of other Forms.
2. Such a view is expressed by Cephalus at *Republic* 331b.

5. The soul

1. *Phaedrus* 248a ff. describes the lower elements being part of the soul even before incarnation. See also *Laws* 896c–d, which seems to imply that all the activities of soul are prior to body.
2. Some of the arguments in this and the following section have previously been published in my "Plato on the Self-moving Soul", *Philosophical Inquiry* 20 (1998), 18–28.
3. The argument starts at *Phaedo* 100c; the crucial passage is 105c ff.
4. The "good horse" in this passage is an image of the spirited part.

5. See for instance *Timaeus* 36c–d, 43a ff., where the rational soul has a circular motion; and 41d–e, where human souls, before incarnation, are set in the stars.
6. It is so presented at *Republic* 442c.
7. See *Republic* 442c–d (the definition of temperance), and 443d–e.

6. Politics

1. The name "*Republic*" represents Greek *Politeia*, whose basic meaning is simply "constitution" or "system of government".
2. The translation "lie" is sometimes condemned as deceptive; the Greek word in question, *pseudos*, can just mean "falsehood", so as to include fiction. But Socrates does say that he hopes the people can be induced to believe the "lie".
3. On this see, for instance, J. Annas, *An Introduction to Plato's Republic* (Oxford: Clarendon Press, 1981), 179–81.
4. For instance at 374b, "We prevented a shoemaker trying to be a farmer …".
5. Some of these points are made by R. Bambrough, "Plato's Political Analogies", in *Philosophy, Politics and Society*, P. Laslett (ed.), 98–115 (Oxford: Blackwell, 1956), reprinted in *Plato: A Collection of Critical Essays, vol. 2: Ethics, Politics and Philosophy of Art and Religion*, G. Vlastos (ed.), 187–205 (Garden City, NY: Doubleday, 1971).

7. Ethics

1. A principle on these lines is stated at *Republic* 435e–6a, although it is not clear how wide its scope is supposed to be; it is not explicitly applied to justice.
2. See *Republic* 441d–e: "when each element in someone performs its own function, he will be just and perform his own function".
3. See *Laws* 630d ff., 705d ff. on virtue as the aim of law.
4. This passage is used as a basis for an interpretation of Plato's ethics by Terence Irwin in *Plato's Ethics* (Oxford: Oxford University Press, 1995), ch. 18.
5. And at *Republic* 364a–b, "they dishonour and look down on those who are weak and poor, even *while agreeing that they are better than others*" (emphasis added).
6. See *Republic* 358a: "which the person who intends to be happy should welcome both for itself and for its consequences".
7. The things listed as examples of things good in themselves at *Republic* 357b–c support this: enjoyment and harmless pleasures are things we value only for their own sake; intelligence, sight and health both for themselves and their consequences. These are beneficial things, things that contribute to our happiness, rather than admirable things.
8. See for instance *Republic* 367d: "praise justice for the way in which it by itself benefits us, and injustice harms us, and leave others to praise rewards and reputation".
9. The description of the tyrannical soul begins at *Republic* 572d.

10. See *Philebus* 21d–e, where it is agreed that no one would accept a life without pleasure.
11. This reading of Plato is in some ways similar to that put forward by R. Kraut, "The Defence of Justice in Plato's *Republic*", in Kraut, *The Cambridge Companion to Plato*, 311–37.
12. On pleasure see *Protagoras* 351c ff.; on knowledge *Meno* 87e ff.

8. God and nature

1. This position can, of course, be challenged. As we saw in Chapter 5, it was challenged by Aristotle, for whom unthinking nature, as well as intelligence, can (of its own accord) act for a purpose.
2. Some of the arguments of this and the following section are taken from my "Plato on Necessity and Chaos", *Philosophical Studies* 127 (2006), 283–98.
3. This structure is explained at *Timaeus* 47e, 68e–9b.
4. This view was proposed by G. Morrow, "Necessity and Persuasion in the *Timaeus*", *Philosophical Review* 59 (1950), 147–64, reprinted in Allen (ed.), *Studies in Plato's Metaphysics*, 421–37.
5. The precosmic state is linked with necessity at *Timaeus* 48b.
6. A rather more explicit statement of this, although in a mythic context, can be found in the *Statesman* 273b ff.; the bodily element of the universe was in great disorder before it came into its present order, and this is the source of the evil that is still present in the world.
7. Called "the overseer" at *Laws* 903b and "our king" at 904a, he is compared to a wise craftsman at 903c.

9. Aesthetics

1. Most explicitly, perhaps, *Republic* 607b: "we were right to banish it [poetry] from the state".
2. See for instance *Republic* 600d: "all poets, starting with Homer, are imitators of images of virtue … and are not in contact with truth". ("Imitator" is, in the context of *Republic* 10, a term of condemnation.)
3. See *Republic* 595a: "Poetry, so far as it is imitative, should not be accepted" [in the state]. And 607a: "hymns to the gods and praises of good people are the only poetry to be accepted into the state".
4. Officially Socrates does not commit himself on this point, since the question whether the just life is advantageous is the topic of the *Republic* as a whole, and has yet not been settled. But it is clear what Socrates thinks, and he claims that if a just life is advantageous, poets are wrong to represent it differently. A more explicit statement of this point is found in the *Laws* 660b ff., where similar proposals for censorship are found.

5. No passages on medical themes are actually quoted in the *Republic*, but see *Ion* 538b–c for the kind of passage Plato probably has in mind.

6. See for instance *Republic* 599b: "If he [Homer] really had understanding about those things which he imitates".

7. For example at *Republic* 603c: "Imitative poetry imitates people acting under compulsion or willingly".

8. This must be so if he bans *all* imitative poetry, and yet accepts hymns to the gods and praises of good people.

9. *Republic* 598d – "after this we must examine tragedy" – makes it clear that only after this is the status of poetry decided. See also 599d. I take Socrates at 597e to be saying only that tragedians are two steps removed from truth *if* they are imitators (as will be decided later), not, as some read it, *since* they are.

10. At 598d Socrates refers to "tragedy and its leader Homer", and at 600e to "all poets beginning from Homer". Although Homer was an epic, not a dramatic poet, he seems to have been widely associated with tragedy.

11. Solon's poems are mentioned at *Timaeus* 21b–d.

12. Agathon is criticized at *Symposium* 199c ff., and Aristophanes at 205d–e.

Plato's works

This list includes all works that are generally agreed to be by Plato, and also some that, while disputed, are widely thought to be his. Dialogues whose authenticity is disputed are marked with an asterisk.

In line with the arguments of Chapter 2, Plato's works are here divided into three groups: Socratic dialogues, reflecting the thought of the historical Socrates; Platonic dialogues, reflecting Plato's thought during the period when he developed his most famous ideas; and later Platonic dialogues, reflecting Plato's thought in the last period of his life. The Socratic dialogues are often believed to have been written early in Plato's career, and to precede the Platonic dialogues, but this cannot be known with certainty.

Socratic dialogues
(In alphabetical order)

*Alcibiades**
Apology
Charmides
Crito
Euthydemus
Euthyphro
Gorgias
*Hippias Major**
Hippias Minor
Ion
Laches
Lysis

Meno
Protagoras

The *Gorgias* and *Meno* are often thought to have both Socratic and Platonic elements.

The *Menexenus* is also often grouped with the Socratic dialogues, though, being a satirical work, it does not directly reflect the thought of either Socrates or Plato.

Platonic dialogues
(In conjectural order of composition)

Cratylus
Phaedo
Symposium
Republic
Phaedrus
Parmenides
Theaetetus

The *Parmenides* and *Theaetetus* are widely thought to be the last of this group, and to have some features in common with the late group.

Later Platonic dialogues
(In conjectural order of composition)

Timaeus
Critias (incomplete)
Sophist
Statesman (also called *Politicus*)
Philebus
Laws
*Epinomis**

The *Seventh Letter*, if genuine, also belongs to the last period of Plato's life.

Further reading

Translations

A comprehensive translation of Plato's works (including doubtful and spurious works) by various translators, is J. M. Cooper, with D. S. Hutchinson (eds), *Plato: Complete Works* (Indianapolis, IN: Hackett, 1997). Many of the individual works of Plato from this edition have also been published separately. For details see below under the various dialogues.

An older comprehensive translation is E. Hamilton and H. Cairns (eds), *The Collected Dialogues of Plato* (New York: Pantheon, 1961), reprinted (Princeton, NJ: Princeton University Press, 1971).

There are many translations of individual works, with introductions and notes. Some important ones are as follows.

Meno
Allen, R. E. (trans.) 1989. *The Dialogues of Plato, vol. 1: Euthyphro, Apology, Crito, Gorgias, Menexenus.* New Haven, CT: Yale University Press.
Beresford, A. (trans.), with intro. by L. Brown. 2005. *Protagoras and Meno.* London: Penguin.
Day, J. M (ed. and trans.) 1994. *Plato's Meno in Focus.* London: Routledge. Includes an introduction and collected essays by various writers.
Grube, G. M. A. (trans.), J. M. Cooper (rev.) 2002. *Five Dialogues.* Indianapolis, IN: Hackett. Also includes *Euthyphro, Apology, Crito* and *Phaedo*.
Waterfield, R. (trans.), with intro. by A. Gregory. 2009. *Meno and Other Dialogues.* Oxford: Oxford University Press. Also includes *Charmides, Laches* and *Lysis*.

Phaedo

Gallop, D. (trans.) 1977. *Phaedo* (with philosophical commentary). Oxford: Clarendon Press.

Gallop, D. (trans.) 2009. *Phaedo*. Oxford: Oxford University Press.

Grube, G. M. A. (trans.), J. M. Cooper (rev.) 2002. *Five Dialogues*. Indianapolis, IN: Hackett. Also includes *Euthyphro, Apology, Crito* and *Meno*.

Tredennick, H. (trans.), H. Tarrant (rev.) 2003. *The Last Days of Socrates*. London: Penguin. Also includes *Euthyphro, Apology* and *Crito*.

Symposium

Allen, R. E. (trans.) 1993. *The Dialogues of Plato, vol. 2: The Symposium*. New Haven, CT: Yale University Press.

Nehamas, A. & P. Woodruff (trans.) 1989. *Symposium*. Indianapolis, IN: Hackett.

Waterfield, R. (trans.) 2008. *Symposium*. Oxford: Oxford University Press.

Republic

Allen, R. E. (trans.) 2006. *Republic*. New Haven, CT: Yale University Press.

Griffith, T. (trans.), with intro. by G. Ferrari (ed.) 2000. *Republic*. Cambridge: Cambridge University Press.

Grube, G. M. A. (trans.), C. D. C. Reeve (rev.) 1992. *Republic*. Indianapolis, IN: Hackett.

Lee, H. D. P. (trans.), with intro. by M. Lane. 1997. *Republic*. Harmondsworth: Penguin.

Reeve, C. D. C. (trans.) 2004. *Republic* (translated from the new standard Greek text). Indianapolis, IN: Hackett.

Waterfield, R. (trans.) 1998. *Republic*. Oxford: Oxford University Press.

Phaedrus

Nehamas, A. & P. Woodruff (trans.) 1995. *Phaedrus*. Indianapolis, IN: Hackett.

Rowe, C. J. (trans.) 2005. *Phaedrus*. London: Penguin.

Waterfield, R. (trans.) 2009. *Phaedrus*. Oxford: Oxford University Press.

Parmenides

Allen, R. E. (trans.) 1997. *The Dialogues of Plato, vol. 4: The Parmenides*. New Haven, CT: Yale University Press.

Gill, M. L. & P. Ryan 1996. *Parmenides*. Indianapolis, IN: Hackett.

Theaetetus

Levett, M. (trans.), M. Burnyeat (rev.), with intro. by B. A. O. Williams (ed.) 1992. *Theaetetus*. Indianapolis, IN: Hackett. The same translation is also published with an extended introduction by M. Burnyeat, in *The Theaetetus of Plato* (Indianapolis, IN: Hackett, 1990).

McDowell, J. (trans.) 1977. *Theaetetus* (with philosophical commentary). Oxford: Clarendon Press.

Waterfield, R. (trans.) 1987. *Theaetetus*. Harmondsworth: Penguin.

Timaeus

Lee, H. D. P. (trans.), T. Johansen (rev.) 2008. *Timaeus and Critias*. London: Penguin.

Waterfield, R. (trans.), with intro by A. Gregory. 2008. *Timaeus and Critias*. Oxford: Oxford University Press.

Zeyl, D. (trans.) 2000. *Timaeus*. Indianapolis, IN: Hackett.

Sophist

White, N. (trans.) 1993. *Sophist*. Indianapolis, IN: Hackett.

Statesman

Rowe, C. J. (trans.) 1999. *Statesman*. Indianapolis, IN: Hackett.

Waterfield, R. (trans.), with intro. by J. Annas (ed.) 1995. *Statesman*. Cambridge: Cambridge University Press.

Philebus

Frede, D. (trans.) 1993. *Philebus*. Indianapolis, IN: Hackett.

Laws

Mayhew, R. 2008. *Laws* 10 (with philosophical commentary). Oxford: Clarendon Press. This book contains most of the religious and cosmological material in the *Laws*.

Saunders, T. J. (trans.) 1970. *Laws*. Harmondsworth: Penguin.

Compilations

Chappell, T. (trans.) 1996. *The Plato Reader*. Edinburgh: Edinburgh University Press.

Murray, P. & T. S. Dorsch (trans.) 2000. *Classical Literary Criticism*. Harmondsworth: Penguin. Includes the *Ion* and extracts from the *Republic*, along with material by Aristotle, Horace and Longinus.

Partenie, C. (trans.) 2009. *Selected Myths*. Oxford: Oxford University Press. Includes extracts from the *Protagoras, Gorgias, Symposium, Phaedo, Republic, Phaedrus, Statesman, Timaeus* and *Critias*.

Reeve, C. D. C. (trans.) 2006 *Plato on Love*. Indianapolis, IN: Hackett. Includes the *Lysis, Symposium, Phaedrus* and *Alcibiades*, with extracts from the *Republic* and *Laws*.)

Books on Plato's work as a whole

There are numerous books on Plato's work as a whole. Short introductory works include:

Annas, J. 2003. *Plato: A Very Short Introduction*. Oxford: Oxford University Press.
Hare, R. M. 1982. *Plato*. Oxford: Oxford University Press.
Kraut, R. 2008. *How to Read Plato*. London: Granta.
Williams, B. 1998. *Plato*. London: Routledge.

Longer works include:

Crombie, I. M. 1964. *Plato: The Midwife's Apprentice*. London: Routledge & Kegan Paul.
Grube, G. M. A. 1935 *Plato's Thought*. London: Methuen.
Guthrie, W. K. C. 1975. *A History of Greek Philosophy, vol. 4: Plato: The Man and his Dialogues: Earlier Period*. Cambridge: Cambridge University Press.
Guthrie, W. K. C. 1978. *A History of Greek Philosophy, vol. 5: The Later Plato and the Academy*. Cambridge: Cambridge University Press.
Melling, D. J. 1987. *Understanding Plato*. Oxford: Oxford University Press.
Rowe, C. J. 1984. *Plato*. Brighton: Harvester.

More advanced and complex works are:

Crombie, I. M. 1962. *An Examination of Plato's Doctrines, vol. 1: Plato on Man and Society*. London: Routledge & Kegan Paul.
Crombie, I. M. 1963. *An Examination of Plato's Doctrines, vol. 2: Plato on Knowledge and Reality*. London: Routledge & Kegan Paul.
Gosling, J. 1973 *Plato*. London: Routledge & Kegan Paul.

Guides and companions

These books consist of new articles, written for the guide in question, aiming to give a survey of major areas of Plato's thought:

Benson, H. (ed.) 2006. *A Companion to Plato*. Oxford: Blackwell.
Fine, G. (ed.) 2008. *The Oxford Handbook of Plato*. Oxford: Oxford University Press.
Kraut, R. (ed.) 1992. *The Cambridge Companion to Plato*. Cambridge: Cambridge University Press.

Collections

These are collections made up of (mostly) existing articles on Plato, aiming to bring together major works in the field.

Allen, R. E. (ed.) 1965. *Studies in Plato's Metaphysics*. London: Routledge & Kegan Paul.

Fine, G. (ed.) 2000. *Plato*. Oxford: Oxford University Press. The paperback edition is published in two volumes: one on metaphysics and epistemology, and one on ethics, politics, religion and the soul.

Smith, N. (ed.) 1998. *Plato: Critical Assessments*, 4 vols. London: Routledge.

Vlastos, G. (ed.) 1970. *Plato: A Collection of Critical Essays, vol. 1: Metaphysics and Epistemology*. Garden City, NY: Doubleday.

Vlastos, G. (ed.) 1971. *Plato: A Collection of Critical Essays, vol. 2: Ethics, Politics and Philosophy of Art and Religion*. Garden City, NY: Doubleday.

Specific areas of Plato's thought

Metaphysics and theory of knowledge
These topics are closely entwined in Plato's thought, and many works deal with both. On metaphysics especially:

Dancy, R. M. 2004. *Plato's Introduction of Forms*. Cambridge: Cambridge University Press.

Fine, G. 1993. *On Ideas: Aristotle's Criticism of Plato's Theory of Forms*. Oxford: Clarendon Press.

Irwin, T. 1977. "Plato's Heracleitianism. *Philosophical Quarterly* 27: 1–13. Reprinted in Smith (ed.), *Plato: Critical Assessments*, vol. 2, 102–15.

Irwin, T. 2000. "The Theory of Forms". In Fine (ed.), *Plato*, 145–72. Adapted from his *Plato's Ethics* (New York: Oxford University Press, 1995), ch. 10.

Malcolm, J. 1991. *Plato on the Self-Predication of Forms: Early and Middle Dialogues*. Oxford: Clarendon Press.

McCabe, M. M. 1994. *Plato's Individuals*. Princeton, NJ: Princeton University Press.

Nehamas, A. 1975. "Plato on the Imperfection of the Sensible World". *American Philosophical Quarterly* 12: 105–17. Reprinted in Smith (ed.), *Plato: Critical Assessments*, vol. 2, 72–92, and in Fine (ed.), *Plato*, 173–93.

Patterson, R. 1985. *Image and Reality in Plato's Metaphysics*. Indianapolis, IN: Hackett.

Silverman, A. 2002. *The Dialectic of Essence: A Study of Plato's Metaphysics*. Princeton, NJ: Princeton University Press.

Vlastos, G. 1965. "Degrees of Reality in Plato". In *New Essays on Plato and Aristotle*, R. Bambrough (ed.), 10–19. London: Routledge & Kegan Paul. Reprinted in his *Platonic Studies*, 58–75 (Princeton, NJ: Princeton University Press, 1973) and in Smith (ed.), *Plato: Critical Assessments*, vol. 2, 219–34.

On knowledge especially:

Gulley. N. 1962. *Plato's Theory of Knowledge*. London: Methuen.

Robinson, R. 1941. *Plato's Earlier Dialectic*. Ithaca, NY: Cornell University Press.

Scott, D. 2003. *Recollection and Experience: Plato's Theory of Learning and its Successors.* Cambridge: Cambridge University Press.

On both equally:

Fine, G. 2003. *Plato on Knowledge and Forms: Selected Essays.* Oxford: Clarendon Press.
White, N. 1976. *Plato on Knowledge and Reality.* Indianapolis, IN: Hackett.

Politics
Bobonich, C. 2002. *Plato's Utopia Recast: his Later Ethics and Politics.* Oxford: Oxford University Press.
Schofield, M. 2006. *Plato.* Oxford: Oxford University Press.
Taylor, C. C. W. 1986. "Plato's Totalitarianism". *Polis* 5: 4–29. Reprinted in Fine (ed.), *Plato*, 762–78.

The most famous attack on Plato's political views is in K. Popper, *The Open Society and its Enemies, vol. 1: The Spell of Plato* (London: Routledge & Kegan Paul, 1945). Issues raised in this book are discussed in R. Bambrough (ed.), *Plato, Popper and Politics: Some Contributions to a Modern Controversy* (Cambridge: Heffers, 1967).

Ethics
Annas, J. 1978. "Plato and Common Morality". *Classical Quarterly* **28**: 437–51. Reprinted in Smith (ed.), *Plato: Critical Assessments*, vol. 3, 206–19.
Cooper, J. 1984. "Plato's Theory of Human Motivation". *History of Philosophy Quarterly* **1**: 3–21. Reprinted in Fine (ed.), *Plato*, 668–88.
Irwin, T. 1995. *Plato's Ethics.* New York: Oxford University Press. This is a recasting of his earlier work, *Plato's Moral Theory* (Oxford: Oxford University Press, 1977).
Sedley, D. 2000. "The Ideal of Godlikeness". In Fine (ed.), *Plato*, 791–810.

Cosmology
Sedley, D. 2007. *Creationism and its Critics in Antiquity.* Berkeley, CA: University of California Press. Esp. chapter 4. (See also further reading on the *Timaeus*, below.)

Aesthetics
Janaway, C. 1995. *Images Of Excellence: Plato's Critique of the Arts.* Oxford: Clarendon Press.
Moravcsik, J. & P. Temko (eds) 1982. *Plato on Beauty, Wisdom and the Arts.* Totowa, NJ; Rowman & Allanheld.
Murdoch, I. 1977. *The Fire and the Sun: Why Plato Banished the Artists.* Oxford: Clarendon Press.
Nehamas, A. 1982. "Plato on Imitation and Poetry in *Republic* 10". In *Plato on Beauty, Wisdom and the Arts*, J. Moravcsik & P. Temko (eds), 47–78 (Totowa,

NJ; Rowman & Allanheld, 1982). Reprinted in Smith (ed.), *Plato: Critical Assessments*, vol. 3, 296–323.

Love

Nussbaum, M. C. 1986. *The Fragility of Goodness: Luck and Ethics in Greek Tragedy and Philosophy*. Cambridge: Cambridge University Press. Esp. chs 6–7.

Price, A. W. 1990. *Love and Friendship in Plato and Aristotle*. Oxford: Clarendon Press. Esp. chs 1–3.

Vlastos, G. 1973. "The Individual as Object of Love in Plato". In his *Platonic Studies*, 1–42 (Princeton, NJ: Princeton University Press, 1973). Reprinted in Fine (ed.), *Plato*, 619–45.

Plato's use of myths

Brisson, L. 1998. *Plato the Myth Maker*, G. Nadaff (trans.). Chicago, IL: University of Chicago Press.

Partenie, C. (ed.) 2009. *Plato's Myths*. Cambridge: Cambridge University Press.

Works on Plato as a writer

Blondell, R. 2002. *The Play of Character in Plato's Dialogues*. Cambridge: Cambridge University Press.

Nussbaum, M. C. 1986. *The Fragility of Goodness: Luck and Ethics in Greek Tragedy and Philosophy*. Cambridge: Cambridge University Press. Esp. Interlude 1.

Rowe, C. J. 2007. *Plato and the Art of Philosophical Writing*. Cambridge: Cambridge University Press.

Szlesak, T. A. 1999. *Reading Plato*, G. Zanker (trans.). London: Routledge.

Works on particular dialogues

Meno
Scott, D. 2006 *Plato's Meno*. Cambridge: Cambridge University Press.

Phaedo
Bostock, D. 1986. *Plato's Phaedo*. Oxford: Clarendon Press.

Bostock, D. 2000. "The Soul and Immortality in Plato's *Phaedo*". In Fine (ed.), *Plato*, 886–906. Adapted from his *Plato's Phaedo* (Oxford: Clarendon Press, 1986), 21–41.

Vlastos, G. 1969. "Reasons and Causes in the *Phaedo*". *Philosophical Review* 78: 291–325. Reprinted in Vlastos, *Platonic Studies*, (Princeton, NJ: Princeton University Press, 1973), 76–110, and in Smith (ed.), *Plato: Critical Assessments*, vol. 2, 16–44.

PLATO

Symposium
Sheffield, F. 2006. *Plato's Symposium: the Ethics of Desire*. Oxford: Oxford University Press.

Republic
Annas, J. 1981. *An Introduction to Plato's Republic*. Oxford: Clarendon Press.
Dahl. N. 1991. "Plato's Defence of Justice". *Philosophy and Phenomenological Research* 51: 809–34. Reprinted in Fine (ed.), *Plato*, 689–716.
Fine, G. 1990. "Knowledge and Belief in *Republic* 5–7". In *Companions to Ancient Thought 1: Epistemology*, S. Everson (ed.), 85–115. Cambridge: Cambridge University Press. Reprinted in Smith (ed.), *Plato: Critical Assessments*, vol. 2, 234–65.
Kraut, R. 2000. "Return to the Cave: *Republic* 519–521". In Fine (ed.), *Plato*, 717–36.
Mitchell, B. & J. Lucas 2003. *An Engagement with Plato's Republic*. Aldershot: Ashgate.
Nussbaum, M. C. 1986. *The Fragility of Goodness: Luck and Ethics in Greek Tragedy and Philosophy*. Cambridge: Cambridge University Press. Esp. ch. 4.
Pappas, N. 1995. *Plato and the Republic*. London: Routledge.
Sachs, D. 1963. "A Fallacy in Plato's Republic". *Philosophical Review* 72: 141–58. Reprinted in G. Vlastos (ed.), *Plato: A Collection of Critical Essays, vol. 2: Ethics, Politics and Philosophy of Art and Religion*, 35–51, and in Smith (ed.), *Plato: Critical Assessments*, vol. 3, 206–19.
Santas, G. (ed.) 2006. *Blackwell Guide to Plato's Republic*.
Smith, N. 1996. "Plato's Divided Line". *Ancient Philosophy* 16: 25–46. Reprinted in Smith (ed.), *Plato: Critical Assessments*, vol. 2, 292–315.
White, N. 1979. *A Companion to Plato's Republic*. Oxford: Blackwell.
White, N. 1986. "The Rulers' Choice". *Archiv für Geschichte der Philosophie* 68: 22–46.
Williams, B. A. O. 1973. "The Analogy of City and Soul in Plato's Republic". In *Exegesis and Argument*, E. Lee, A. Mourelatos & R. Rorty (eds), 196–206. Assen: van Gorcum. Reprinted in Fine (ed.), *Plato*, 737–46.

The *Republic* is also treated at length in Irwin, *Plato's Ethics*.

Phaedrus
Bett, R. 1986. "Immortality and the Nature of the Soul in the *Phaedrus*". *Phronesis* 31: 1–26. Reprinted in Fine (ed.), *Plato*, 907–31.
Griswold, C. L. 1986. *Self-Knowledge in Plato's Phaedrus*. New Haven, CT: Yale University Press.
Ferrari, G. 1987. *Listening to the Cicadas: A Study of Plato's Phaedrus*. Cambridge: Cambridge University Press.

Parmenides
Meinwald, C. 1991. *Plato's Parmenides*. New York: Oxford University Press.

216

Miller, M. H. 1986. *Plato's Parmenides: The Conversion of the Soul.* Princeton, NJ: Princeton University Press.

Vlastos, G. 1954. "The Third Man Argument in the Parmenides". *Philosophical Review* **63**: 319–49. Reprinted in Smith (ed.), *Plato: Critical Assessments*, vol. 4, 3–27.

Theaetetus
Bostock, D. 1988. *Plato's Theaetetus.* Oxford: Clarendon Press.

Chappell, T. 2005. *Reading Plato's Theaetetus.* Indianapolis, IN: Hackett. Also includes a translation.

Sedley, D. 2004. *The Midwife of Platonism: Text and Subtext in Plato's Theaetetus.* Oxford: Clarendon Press.

Timaeus and Critias
Gregory, A. 2000. *Plato's Philosophy of Science.* London: Duckworth.

Johansen, T. K. 2004. *Plato's Natural Philosophy.* Cambridge: Cambridge University Press.

Patterson, R. 1985. "On the Eternality of the Platonic Forms". *Archiv für Geschichte der Philosophie* **67**: 27–46. Reprinted in Smith (ed.), *Plato: Critical Assessments*, vol. 2, 142–60.

Strange, S. 1985. "The Double Explanation in the *Timaeus*". *Ancient Philosophy* 5: 25–39. Reprinted in Fine (ed.), *Plato*, 399–417.

Vlastos, G. 1975. *Plato's Universe.* Oxford: Clarendon Press.

Sophist
Brown, L. 1986. "Being in the *Sophist*; a Syntactical Enquiry". *Oxford Studies in Ancient Philosophy* **4**: 49–70. Reprinted in Fine (ed.), *Plato*, 457–80.

Notomi, N. 1999. *The Unity of Plato's Sophist: Between the Sophist and the Philosopher.* Cambridge: Cambridge University Press.

Statesman
Lane, M. 1998. *Method and Politics in Plato's Statesman.* Cambridge: Cambridge University Press.

Theaetetus, Sophist, Statesman, Philebus
McCabe, M. M. 2000. *Plato and his Predecessors: The Dramatisation of Reason.* Cambridge: Cambridge University Press.

Laws
Stalley, R. F. 1983. *An Introduction to Plato's Laws.* Oxford: Blackwell.

Online resources

The *Stanford Encyclopedia of Philosophy* (http://plato.stanford.edu) includes a number of helpful articles on Plato. On topics covered in this book the following are especially relevant: R. Kraut, "Plato" (a general account of his thought); N. Pappas, "Aesthetics"; D. Frede, "Ethics"; E. Brown, "Ethics and Politics in the *Republic*"; A. Silverman, "Middle Period Metaphysics and Epistemology"; C. Bobonich, "On Utopia"; S. Rickless, "*Parmenides*"; D. Zeyl, "*Timaeus*".

Project Archelogos (www.archelogos.com) has analyses of the arguments of some of Plato's dialogues, with commentaries. At the moment it includes: H. Benson, *Charmides*; T. Chappell, *Theaetetus*; F. G. Herrmann & D. Robinson, *Lysis*; R. Waterfield, *Gorgias*; C. J. Rowe, *Republic V* (forthcoming).

Bibliography

Allen, R. E. (ed.) 1965. *Studies in Plato's Metaphysics*. London: Routledge & Kegan Paul.

Annas, J. 1981. *An Introduction to Plato's Republic*. Oxford: Clarendon Press.

Bambrough, R. 1956. "Plato's Political Analogies". In *Philosophy, Politics and Society*, P. Laslett (ed.), 98–115 (Oxford: Blackwell, 1956). Reprinted in *Plato: A Collection of Critical Essays, vol. 2: Ethics, Politics and Philosophy of Art and Religion*, G. Vlastos (ed.), 187–205 (Garden City, NY: Doubleday, 1971).

Bambrough, R. (ed.) 1965. *New Essays on Plato and Aristotle*. London: Routledge & Kegan Paul.

Bostock, D. 1986. *Plato's Phaedo*. Oxford: Clarendon Press.

Brandwood, L. 1992. "Stylometry and Chronology". See Kraut (1992a): 90–120.

Crombie, I. M. 1962–3. *An Examination of Plato's Doctrines*, 2 vols. London: Routledge & Kegan Paul.

Fine, G. 1993. *On Ideas: Aristotle's Criticism of Plato's Theory of Forms*. Oxford: Clarendon Press.

Frede, M. 1967. *Prädikation und Existenzaussage*. Göttingen: Vandenhoeck & Ruprecht.

Geach, P. 1956. "The Third Man Again". *Philosophical Review* 65: 72–82. Reprinted in Allen (1965): 265–77.

Irwin, T. 1995. *Plato's Ethics*. Oxford: Oxford University Press.

Janaway, C. 1995. *Images of Excellence: Plato's Critique of the Arts*. Oxford: Clarendon Press.

Keyt, D. 1961. "Aristotle on Plato's Receptacle". *American Journal of Philology* 72: 291–300.

Kraut, R. (ed.) 1992a. *The Cambridge Companion to Plato*. Cambridge: Cambridge University Press.

Kraut, R. 1992b. "The Defence of Justice in Plato's *Republic*". See Kraut (1992a): 311–37.

Kripke, S. 1981. *Naming and Necessity*. Oxford: Blackwell.

Laslett, P. (ed.) 1956. *Philosophy, Politics and Society*. Oxford: Blackwell.

Mason, A. S. 1998. "Plato on the Self-moving Soul". *Philosophical Inquiry* **20**: 18–28.

Mason, A. S. 2006. "Plato on Necessity and Chaos". *Philosophical Studies* **127**: 283–98.

Meinwald, C. 1992. "Good-bye to the Third Man". See Kraut (1992a): 365–96.

Morrow, G. 1950. "Necessity and Persuasion in the *Timaeus*". *Philosophical Review* **59**: 147–64. Reprinted in Allen (1965): 421–37.

Nehamas, A. 1988. "Plato and the Mass Media". *The Monist* **71**: 214–34.

Owen, G. E. L. 1953. "The Place of the *Timaeus* in Plato's Dialogues". *Classical Quarterly* **3**: 79–95. Reprinted in Allen (1965): 313–38.

Sachs, D. 1963. "A Fallacy in Plato's Republic". *Philosophical Review* **72**: 141–58.

Scott, D. 1987. "Platonic Anamnesis Revisited". *Classical Quarterly* **37**: 36–66.

Scott, D. 2003. *Recollection and Experience: Plato's Theory of Learning and its Successors*. Cambridge: Cambridge University Press.

Shorey, P. 1960. *The Unity of Plato's Thought*. Chicago, IL: University of Chicago Press.

Vlastos, G. 1965. "Degrees of Reality in Plato". In *New Essays on Plato and Aristotle*, R. Bambrough (ed.), 1–19 (London: Routledge & Kegan Paul, 1965). Reprinted in Vlastos (1981): 58–75.

Vlastos, G. 1969. "Reasons and Causes in the *Phaedo*". *Philosophical Review* **78**: 291–325. Reprinted in his *Plato: A Collection of Critical Essays, vol. 1: Metaphysics and Epistemology*, 132–66 (Garden City, NY: Doubleday, 1970).

Vlastos, G. (ed.) 1970. *Plato: A Collection of Critical Essays, vol. 1: Metaphysics and Epistemology*. Garden City, NY: Doubleday.

Vlastos, G. (ed.) 1971. *Plato: A Collection of Critical Essays, vol. 2: Ethics, Politics and Philosophy of Art and Religion*. Garden City, NY: Doubleday.

Vlastos, G. 1972. "The Unity of the Virtues in the *Protagoras*". *Review of Metaphysics* **25**: 415–58. Reprinted in Vlastos (1981): 221–69.

Vlastos, G. 1973. *Platonic Studies*. Princeton, NJ: Princeton University Press.

Vlastos, G. 1991. *Socrates: Ironist and Moral Philosopher*. Cambridge: Cambridge University Press.

Wittgenstein, L. 1953. *Philosophical Investigations*, G. E. M. Anscombe (trans.). Oxford: Blackwell.

Index